SECURITY
IN NORTHEAST ASIA

Studies in Global Security

Alan Ned Sabrosky, Series Editor

Also in This Series

Alliances in U.S. Foreign Policy: Issues in the Quest for Collective Defense, edited by Alan Ned Sabrosky

SECURITY IN NORTHEAST ASIA

Approaching the Pacific Century

EDITED BY

Stephen P. Gibert

Westview Press / Boulder and London

Studies in Global Security

This Westview softcover edition is printed on acid-free paper and bound in softcovers that carry the highest rating of the National Association of State Textbook Administrators, in consultation with the Association of American Publishers and the Book Manufacturers' Institute.

Published in 1988 in the United States of America by Westview Press, Inc., 5500 Central Avenue, Boulder, Colorado 80301

Library of Congress Cataloging-in-Publication Data
Security in Northeast Asia: approaching the Pacific century/edited
by Stephen P. Gibert.
   p. cm.—(Studies in global security)
 Includes index.
 ISBN 0-8133-7649-1
 1. China—National security. 2. Japan—National security.
3. Korea—National security. 4. Philippines—National security.
5. Soviet Union—National security. 6. United States—National
security. 7. Pacific Area—National security. I. Gibert, Stephen
P. II. Series.
UA830.S365 1988
355'.03305—dc 19

                                                              88-10753
                                                              CIP

Printed and bound in the United States of America

The paper used in this publication meets the requirements of the American National Standard for Permanence of Paper for Printed Library Materials Z39.48-1984.

6   5   4   3   2

Contents

Preface vii

1. The Northeast Asian Arena, *Stephen P. Gibert* 1

Part I

Diplomacy and Power: The Great Powers

2. The Sino-Soviet-U.S. Triangle, *Harold C. Hinton* 7

3. Japan and the Soviet Union, *Thomas W. Robinson* 29

4. The Politics of Japanese Defense, *Michio Umegaki* 53

Part II

Diplomacy and Power: The Lesser Powers

5. Prospects for Korean Security, *Seung-Hwan Kim* 75

6. The Philippines after Marcos, *Larry A. Niksch* 95

7. The Isolation of Island China, *Stephen P. Gibert* 117

Part III

The Military Arena

8. Military Balances in Northeast Asia, *Sarah M. Taylor* 137

9. Chinese Military Modernization, *Martin L. Lasater* 161

Part IV

Toward the Future

10. Approaching the Pacific Century, *Stephen P. Gibert* 181

About the Editor 187

About the Contributors 187

Index 189

Preface

The phenomenal economic growth of most of the countries along the Pacific rim of Asia has led many to speculate that influence in world affairs is shifting away from Europe and that a "Pacific Century" lies ahead. One might dismiss this as hyperbole if the region's importance in the international arena derived solely from its economic prowess. But this is not the case; Northeast Asia and the Western Pacific also impact significantly on world as well as regional security and the countries in the area are increasingly critical to international political stability.

Northeast Asia is the only region where four of the five centers of world power meet and intersect. The fifth, Western Europe, is not present in the region but since the principal threat to European security—the Soviet Union—must always consider its Asian front when formulating policy toward Western Europe, the NATO countries indirectly benefit from Northeast Asian dynamism. Thus, the Northeast Asian-Western Pacific region will play an increasingly important role in international affairs, affecting the security and prosperity of the United States to a degree not imagined a generation ago.

The National Security Studies Program of Georgetown University's Graduate School each year conducts a series of Weekend Seminars for the some two hundred early mid-career defense professionals who constitute its student body. The topic for the series in 1986 was "Northeast Asia in United States Security Policy." Out of this series eight papers were selected for this volume. Each contribution has been updated and revised, with the object of presenting to the reader a comprehensive and integrated discussion of the region and its relationships to United States and world security concerns.

I would like to thank the chapter authors, each of whom is a well-known expert in the field, for their valuable contributions to this book. I also greatly appreciate the editorial assistance of Roger Smith and especially Scott Spoerry, both Ph.D. candidates at Georgetown University. Scott, who was a National Public Information Fellow at Georgetown, also coordinated the mechanical details of preparing the manuscript in the proper format for publication. Finally, I owe a debt of gratitude to Alan Sabrosky, Director of Strategic Studies at the Army War College, and also Editor of the Westview Press series, Studies in Global Security, for his encouragement and helpful criticism. Of course the editor and the contributors assume sole responsibility for the views expressed in this book.

Stephen P. Gibert, Director,
National Security Studies and
Professor of Government
Georgetown University

CHAPTER 1

The Northeast Asian Arena

Stephen P. Gibert

A decade ago it was considered a bit eccentric to remark that political and economic influence and power in world affairs was shifting away from Europe and that a "Pacific Century" lay ahead. Now hardly a day goes by when some public figure does not proclaim the beginning of an Asian-Pacific era and speculates what this portends for America's future security and economic well-being.

In this particular case, the claims of importance for the Pacific Basin nations are not exaggerated; no duo of countries are equal in importance to the American future—and indeed that of the entire world—than China and Japan. China's immense population (three times that of the Soviet Union, four times that of the United States, sixteen times that of Germany and eighteen times that of France) guarantees that it will be among the handful of states which will shape the destiny of the next century. Furthermore, China is currently engaged in a very ambitious modernization effort which, if successful, will lift it from the ranks of the Third World nations to that of an industrial power. With a four-thousand-mile border with the USSR, China also serves to compel the Soviet government not only to maintain large military forces in its Far Eastern military district but always to consider its Asian frontier when formulating policy toward NATO in the West.

Since the exchange of diplomatic relations in 1979 between Washington and Beijing, security cooperation between China, Japan, and the United States has added to Moscow's concerns and, at the same time, improved China's international bargaining power. China has emerged as a key participant in the "Iron Triangle" with the Soviet Union and the United States. Presently, however, China is seeking good relations with the Soviet Union and the United States in order to concentrate on internal economic development. Emphasizing its desire for peace, the PRC has given the lowest priority in its "Four Modernizations" to military defense. Although China claims to be pursuing a policy of "equidistance" between the Soviet Union and the United States, in fact Beijing is clearly "tilting" toward Washington. In addition, America's trade and cultural relations with China are growing and becoming important to both countries, thus adding to stability in the region.

Japan, like China, will be one of the several most important nations of the twenty-first century. Indeed, although Japan's economy is still much smaller than the American economy, in many ways Japan may already be the leading economic power in the world. It is difficult to compare the gross national product of various nations with any degree of confidence—especially between capitalist countries and the statist economy of the USSR. But, to the extent that it can be measured, it is generally thought that Japan may have surpassed the Soviet Union in total productivity. With about half the GNP of the United States, Japan enjoys about equal GNP per capita with America and perhaps about twice that of the Soviet Union.

Whatever the case, Japan is the economic miracle of the era since the Second World War. With a high savings rate, low unemployment, advanced technology and a skilled and educated workforce, Japan is the envy of the rest of the world. While the usual perception of Japan is that of a large producer of heavy industrial goods, Japan is also a leader in the service sector. Seven of the world's eight largest banks, three of the five top insurance companies and the world's largest securities firm are all Japanese. Paradoxically, the only danger looming on the horizon results from Japanese success; that is, the growing resentment among the Europeans, and especially the Americans, of Japan's enormous surplus in trade. While there are many reasons for this situation, undoubtedly the policies of the Japanese government and the cultural propensities of the Japanese people have played a significant role in the hugely favorable trade balance which Tokyo has enjoyed. And, of course, the fact that Japan has not had to devote significant resources to defense has been an important element. Currently, for example, although the United States has only about twice Japan's GNP, the U.S. spends about twenty-one times as much as Japan on defense.

At present it appears that Japan and the United States are on a collision course, both with regard to trade and "fair" security burden-sharing. Given the enormous stakes involved, it must be assumed, however, that Tokyo and Washington will cooperate to solve both the economic and the security problems which divide the two countries. If so, the Japanese-American relationship will powerfully shape world politics in the twenty-first century. Already today the two nations collectively account for one-third of the world's total production, are the two largest sources of investment capital in the world, consume about half of the oil imported by the industrialized nations, have the largest communities of scientists and engineers, and utilize one-third of the world's production of raw materials. With only about eight percent of the world's population, Japan and the U.S. are the largest producers of semiconductors, computers, steel, automobiles, and many other kinds of machinery and heavy industrial products and share leadership in many areas of emerging technology.

But Japan, unfortunately, is in essence a military protectorate of the United States, with insufficient armed forces even to protect Japan itself, to say noth-

ing of a security role in world affairs. While no one—and certainly not the East
Asian countries—desires a return of Japanese militarism, some improvement in
Japanese armed forces would add substantially to deterring Soviet adventurism.
Since it cannot be imagined that the United States will continue indefinitely to
provide Japan with the security Tokyo should provide for itself, probably by the
end of the twentieth century Japan will be forced to become a stronger military
power if it wishes to avoid possible coercion by other states.

The remaining three countries in the area which are associated in one way
or another with the United States—the Republic of South Korea, the Philippines, and Taiwan—are not to be compared with the two giants, China and
Japan. Nevertheless, each is important to the United States, albeit in somewhat
different ways.

The United States, along with the Soviet Union, was responsible for the
division of Korea along the 38th parallel in 1945, thus creating a situation which
led to war in 1950. Undoubtedly failure to deter this conflict resulted from
North Korean doubts that the U.S. would assist South Korea in the event of war.
To remove such uncertainty in the future, in 1954 Korea and the United States
signed a Mutual Defense Treaty and American military forces have remained
in South Korea ever since. While periodically there have been reassessments of
the U.S. commitment to the Republic of Korea, not until 1977 did the American
government decide to remove all U.S. forces from Korea. President Carter,
however, did not follow through on this plan, allegedly because a new intelligence report revealed that North Korean forces were stronger than previously
estimated. More likely, the Carter Administration realized that the issue was not
solely South Korean security; rather Korea was a critical link in Japan's defense
and in containing the Soviet Union in East Asia.

The Korean peninsula is one of the most heavily armed regions of the world,
with large and hostile forces facing each other across the demilitarization zone.
Thus the U.S. security treaty with Korea certainly involves substantial fears that
America will be drawn into another Asian conflict. But Japan, South Korea, and
the Philippines are essential links in U.S. strategy, which contemplates confronting the Soviet Union with war in the East should the USSR attack NATO
in the West. The Reagan Administration especially, through the strengthening
of the U.S. Navy and the adoption of a so-called "Maritime Strategy," and its
corollary, "horizontal escalation," has linked Asian security to the security of
Western Europe. This approach intends to deny the USSR the choice of limiting a NATO-Warsaw Pact war to the European theater and thus, hopefully, contribute to deterring conflict in both Europe and Asia. Not all Asians—and
especially the Japanese—are happy with this strategic concept. Naturally they
would prefer not to be drawn into a NATO-Warsaw Pact conflict. From a
geopolitical point of view, however, it makes sense. It also enhances the
military value of both Korea and Japan to the United States and makes it more
likely the U.S. will continue to bear the risks and burdens involved.

In addition to Korean-American security relations, the economic dimension is becoming increasingly important. The Republic of Korea is one of the very few Third World nations which is joining the ranks of the industrialized states. The "little dragons" of East Asia—South Korea, Taiwan, Hong Kong, and Singapore—are all developing quite rapidly and all have become major trading nations. The United States is Korea's largest export market and Korea now is beginning to compete successfully with Japan in the automobile, shipbuilding, television, and other heavy industries. Unfortunately, however, the growing U.S. trade deficit has begun to adversely affect America's relations with Korea and the other newly-industrializing countries. This situation could certainly jeopardize future cooperation between the two countries.

Finally, the present moves in Korea toward a more democratic society are absolutely necessary if Seoul wishes to continue to enjoy priority in U.S. security concerns; the United States is less and less comfortable with close alliances with military dictatorships. In South Korea itself there appears to be a growing anti-American sentiment, fueled by the belief that the United States has been insufficiently critical of authoritarian rule. But all signs point to the strengthening of democratic forces in Korea which should assist in keeping intact the presently close relations between Seoul and Washington. Very encouraging was President Chun Doo Hwan's willing departure from office in February 1988 in favor of the leadership elected in December 1987.

The Republic of the Philippines has been a key ally of the United States ever since it received independence on the Fourth of July, 1946. The United States has stationed military forces in the Philippines since that date and the Clark Air Force Base and the Subic Bay Naval Base are among the most important U.S. military installations in the world. The immensity of the Pacific Ocean makes it vital for the United States to have forward bases if it is to be a major power in East Asia. The Clark and Subic bases in the Philippines provide this in the southern part of the Western Pacific and the Yokosuka, Sasebo, and Okinawa bases in Japan furnish the forward deployment facilities in the northern sector of the Western Pacific Ocean.

The primary purposes of the Clark and Subic bases in the Philippines are to hold at risk the large Soviet base at Cam Ranh Bay in Vietnam and to guard the sea lines of communication leading from the Persian Gulf area to Japan and Korea. There are no satisfactory substitutes for the bases in the Philippines should Manila decide it no longer wished to retain the present security arrangements. Therefore, good relations between the Philippines and the United States are vital. The U.S. role in removing Marcos from power in the Philippines certainly improved America's image in the eyes not only of the Filipinos, but around the world as well. President Aquino's hold on authority is very shaky, however, and it is clear that many military leaders would like to see her deposed. Even if it risks alienating the military, however, the U.S. should stand firmly behind democracy in the Philippines. The trend throughout East Asia is toward democracy and the U.S. must be a part of this movement if it is to retain

long-term influence in the region. The U.S. should also assist the Philippine
government in its struggle against a growing communist insurgency. Such assistance might help to reconcile the military to the Aquino regime.

The third of the trio of small nations in East Asia in which the U.S. has important interests is the Republic of China on the island of Taiwan. After President Carter's decision in December 1978 to transfer U.S. diplomatic relations
from Taiwan to the People's Republic of China, it looked as if Taiwan would
be almost completely excluded from international affairs. But the Taiwan Relations Act in 1979 placed Washington-Taipei relations on a firm, if less formal,
basis. Accordingly, Taiwan still receives substantial American military equipment and has emerged, as has South Korea, as one of the newly industrializing
nations, with a booming, export-driven economy. As in the case of Korea and
Japan, however, Taiwan's large trade surplus with the United States is an increasing source of tension between the two countries. Unlike Japan, South
Korea and Taiwan have made strong efforts to reduce their favorable balances
of trade,although there remain some problems to be resolved. And also unlike
Japan, Taiwan and Korea contribute their "fair share" to the mutual defense burden. But the trade issue is still very worrisome; Taiwan and Korea, with their
small populations, simply cannot absorb sufficient American imports to offset
their exports to the U.S. market.

Taiwan remains an issue in PRC-American relations. Beijing has always
used U.S. support for Taipei as an excuse to belabor Washington whenever the
PRC wished to place some distance between itself and the United States. Most
analysts do not think it likely that the PRC will force a genuine confrontation
over American policies toward Taiwan. PRC leaders have stated frequently,
however, that China would take military action against Taiwan should Taipei
declare itself an independent state, no longer part of China. Such a development
is very unlikely in the near future, but as native Taiwanese gain more and more
power in Taiwan politics, a decision to establish a Republic of Taiwan might
become a possibility. This, in turn, could lead to a serious crisis in Asia and
would confront the U.S. with very difficult policy choices.

Finally, American-Taiwan relations are likely to remain close providing the
gradual moves toward a more democratic polity in the island country continue.
Very welcome to the U.S. government was the July 1987 decision by Taipei to
lift martial law, which had been effect since 1949. Nevertheless, the transition
from an essentially one-party authoritarian state, dominated by Chinese with
close ties to the mainland, to a more democratic nation, with power fully shared
with native Taiwanese, will be difficult indeed. But distinctions between
"Mainlanders" and Taiwanese are already disappearing as intermarriage occurs
and new generations are born, so friction between the two groups is no longer
significant. Other changes conducive to democracy are now underway; their
continuation should help ensure an acceptable political future for Taiwan
whether or not eventual unification with mainland China occurs.

American stakes in this dynamic region of the world are enormous and growing. This is not to say that the United States, as a global superpower, can turn its back on Europe or terminate its NATO commitments; just as a strong posture in East Asia contributes to deterring a Soviet attack on NATO, so a strong NATO contributes to Chinese and Japanese security. But priorities change; a Euro-centered U.S. stance is no longer either necessary or desirable. America is now challenged to fashion a more global approach to world affairs, thus enhancing both its economic well-being and its national security as the "Pacific Century" begins.

CHAPTER 2

The Sino-Soviet-U.S. Triangle

Harold C. Hinton

By any standard—political, economic, or strategic—the East Asia/Western Pacific region is one of the most important in the world. For well known reasons, to be sure, its indigenous industrial giant, Japan, lacks projectible military power, and partly for that reason it is far from exercising a level of influence on regional or global international politics commensurate with its economic weight. The assets that Japan lacks are possessed, actually or potentially, by three other powers whose interests and policies overlap and interact in the region: the United States, the Soviet Union, and the People's Republic of China. These powers are sometimes referred to collectively as the Iron Triangle.

The Anatomy of the Iron Triangle

Although it is sometimes denied on one ground or another, the two superpowers and China appear to constitute a genuine and meaningful strategic triangle, one in which any significant change in one of three relationships directly affects the other two.

Of these three relationships, the one between the superpowers has been the centerpiece of international politics since World War II. Its essential nature is that of a protracted confrontation arising largely from internal Soviet compulsions—the felt need of the Soviet elite for external triumphs, which cannot be achieved without strenuous effort, to enhance the domestic power and legitimacy of the most authoritarian of the world's major political systems. The United States is the only nation that has, even potentially, the power and determination to contain the Soviet outward thrust on a global scale. At a regional level, in East Asia and the Western Pacific, China also possesses, or at any rate may come to possess, significant capabilities for coping with Soviet expansionism.

Since 1969, when it achieved approximate strategic parity with the United States (in addition to conventional superiority in Eurasia), the Soviet Union has been engaged in one of its recurrent drives for ultimate "hegemony" in the East

Asia/Western Pacific region. Moscow was also stimulated by the American intention (implied in the Nixon Doctrine) to withdraw militarily form the East Asian mainland and was provoked by a clash engineered by Chinese troops on the Sino-Soviet border (on March 2, 1969).

In broad terms, China has tried since 1950 to play the role of balancing or swing power with respect to the superpowers, at least in the East Asian arena; it is clearly too weak to stand alone of its hopes to achieve its leaders ambitious goals for eventual power and influence in that arena. On the other hand, it has also been too weak so far to attain its objectives even by "tilting" toward one superpower or the other. Unlike the superpowers, it possesses no alliance system worthy of the name.

China nevertheless possesses what amounts to a minimum nuclear deterrent against the Soviet Union, even if not necessarily against the United States. It is strong enough to affect the regional balance between the superpowers by either supporting (as it did in the early 1950s) or opposing (as it has since about 1960) Soviet domination of the East Asian mainland. China objects strongly to the post-1969 Soviet drive for ultimate regional "hegemony." As an offshore power, the United States needs at least the passive cooperation of China if it is to fend off such domination. This it has received. China not only is helpful in this connection but also "ties down" large Soviet forces that otherwise could be redeployed against other areas of great strategic importance, notably western Europe and Southwest Asia.

In the 1980s to date, China has tried, by accelerating the modernization of its economy and by shifting its relationships with the superpowers into better balance, to become for the first time what it has wanted to be since 1949: the main beneficiary of the triangle.

The Actors in Early Interaction

The defeat of Japan in World War II left the United States militarily supreme in the Western Pacific for a generation. This position rested on an alliance with and bases in Japan itself, which in turn supported a relatively shortlived occupation of South Korea (1945-1948).

On the East Asian mainland, the Soviet Union was clearly the rising power by virtue of its belated intervention in the war with Japan, its occupation of North Korea, its entry into the "nuclear club" in 1949, and its alliance the following year with the newly victorious Chinese Communists.

The first, and in fact the only, significant consequence of the Sino-Soviet alliance was the Korean War.[1] It resulted from a convergence between Kim Il Sung's eagerness to unite his country and Stalin's interest in disrupting the emerging American peace settlement with Japan and in finding replacements in South Korea, through his North Korean satellites, for the Manchurian ports and railways that he had committed himself (in February 1950) to return to his Chinese allies by the end of 1952.[2] Beijing had prior knowledge of the Korean War but stayed out of it until the northward advance of the United Nations (mainly South Korean and American) forces in October 1950 threatened not only the survival of North Korea but, in Chinese eyes, the security of the Manchurian border region. In mid-October, accordingly, Chinese "volunteers" (actually, regular troops) crossed into North Korea and went into action soon afterward.

As General MacArthur correctly said, Chinese intervention transformed the war. Armistice talks began in mid-1951, after a series of initial Chinese victories followed by major defeats, but were stalemated the following year by the insistence of Beijing and Pyongyang on recovering, after an armistice, all the prisoners they had lost, and by the opposing determination of the United Nations Command that repatriation be voluntary. The newly inaugurated Eisenhower administration broke the deadlock in February 1953 by threatening the PRC with nuclear weapons, whereupon Beijing, left unsupported by the post-Stalin Soviet leadership, saw no alternative but to yield on the prisoner repatriation issue. Accordingly, an armistice was signed on July 27, 1953, on the basis of voluntary repatriation. The United States then reassured the South Koreans by concluding an alliance designed to protect them against another North Korean attack. This alliance was also intended to help restrain South Korea from "marching north" (in President Rhee's phrase) if an opportunity should present itself. This arrangement has worked well to date. With the United States as the strategic equalizer on the peninsula, Pyongyang has not attacked again, and the South Koreans did not try to take advantage of the withdrawal of the remaining Chinese "volunteers" in 1958.

The main result of Sino-Soviet-American interaction in the 1950s, especially in the first half of the decade, was an unstable and dangerous bipolarization of the East Asian international politics, the principal adversaries being the United States and the PRC. The main gainer, among the triangular powers at any rate, was the Soviet Union. Even though its Korean adventure failed, Moscow escaped without serious harm and maintained a rather high level of freedom of action while the United States and the PRC confronted each other tensely at various points along China's eastern periphery, especially the Taiwan Strait.

The Triangle in Changing Shape

The protection of Taiwan by the United States, dating from June 1950 and to a large extent an outgrowth of American domestic politics, was one of the first and largest of the wedges that soon began to split the Sino-Soviet alliance. Denouncing the American role as an "occupation" of Taiwan, which it was not,

Beijing turned in vain for support to Moscow, which was fully aware that at that time it was markedly inferior to the United States in strategic weapons.[3] In effect, although not for the record, the Soviets drew a line through the Taiwan Strait about 1954, the date of the U.S.-Taiwan Mutual Security Treaty. If the United States threatened the mainland of China, Moscow admitted in principle an obligation to come to Beijing's support and defense; if Beijing tried to attack Taiwan, on the other hand, it was on its own. The resulting strain on the Sino-Soviet relationship was unquestionably serious, although at the time largely unpublicized. From Beijing's viewpoint, the Taiwan issue was the centerpiece in an accumulating array of differences with Moscow, most of them deriving from Soviet reluctance either to confront the United States or to render active and effective support to other Communist Parties, ruling or nonruling.

In the fall of 1957 Mao Zedong, smarting both from political setbacks at home (the failure of his Hundred Flowers campaign for free public discussion, which had evoked unexpectedly strong criticisms of his policies) and from Moscow's failure to give him the support he wanted, thought he saw an opportunity to recoup lost ground, first abroad and later in China. Khrushchev had just rid himself of his political opponents, all of whom happened to have been less prone than he to adventurous foreign initiatives, and had orbited the first earth satellite, Sputnik I, with profound psychological effects on the rest of the world, especially the United States. Accordingly, Mao began to advance the absurd yet dramatic slogan, "The East wind has prevailed over the West wind," which purported to mean that the "socialist camp headed by the Soviet Union" (and including China), plus the international communist movement (the nonruling parties as well), plus the "revolutionary people of the world," had acquired an irreversible superiority in the "correlation of forces" (an expressive Soviet phrase) over the "imperialist camp headed by the United States" (the Western-aligned governments and ruling establishments).

Khrushchev did not accept this proposition, because acceptance would have entailed a series of risky confrontations with the United States whose dangers would be borne largely by the Soviet Union, while the beneficiaries, if any, might have conspicuously included the PRC. In the hope of getting Mao off his back, and with the pretense of enabling Beijing to "liberate" Taiwan some day without Soviet help, Khrushchev in the fall of 1957 made a commitment that fortunately is unique to this day. He agreed, naturally in secret, to give Beijing, which had already decided (in the spring of 1956) to acquire a nuclear weapons capability, large scale aid in the production of both nuclear warheads and medium range missiles (MRBMs).[4]

After making this arrangement with the Chinese, Khrushchev continued to avoid acting on the implications of Mao's pronouncements about the East and West winds. Mao then began to try to galvanize him into action, or at least to set him an example of appropriately resolute behavior. This was one of the aims of the famous Great Leap Forward (1958-1960) and of a military action launched by Beijing in the Taiwan Strait in August-October 1958. The negative Soviet reaction to both these initiatives, which was probably a surprise to Mao, further soured the already deteriorating Sino-Soviet relationship and helped push Khrushchev into a detente with the United States, once the formidable Secretary of State John Foster Dulles had resigned and died in April 1959. In June of that year, Khrushchev cancelled his nuclear agreement of 1957 with the PRC, and to Beijing's further outrage he then went to the United States to confer in friendly fashion with Eisenhower. A year later, after the Chinese had begun to express their objections to Khrushchev's policies in public, he terminated the Soviet program of industrial aid to Beijing, at a time when, as he probably realized, China was experiencing a serious agricultural crisis resulting largely from the Great Leap Forward.

Mao's mood, reinforced by the ultraleftist influence of Defense Minister Lin Biao (1959-1971), was so militant by then that he abandoned his previous relatively sensible "united front" strategy. This was based on the principle that, when confronted with two adversaries who were at odds with one another, the Chinese Communists should try to form a tactical and temporary combination with the less dangerous adversary against the more dangerous one. Instead, at the end of the 1950s Mao and Lin adopted a "dual adversary" (or "dual confrontation") strategy of simultaneous confrontation—essentially political but with military overtones and possibilities—with both superpowers at the same time.[5] Beijing persisted in this obviously unviable approach for a decade, the period spanning the equally futile Cultural Revolution, until the geographically closer superpower, the Soviet Union, began to react with massive threats to the Chinese pressures to which it had been subjected. These provocations took the form not only of verbal attacks but also border crossings by Chinese military personnel, beginning about 1960.

The decade of Beijing's commitment to the dual adversary strategy saw the United States involve itself, in spite of profound divisions at home from the beginning, in the struggle over South Vietnam. The purpose—essentially, to prevent the domination of South Vietnam by Hanoi, with a likely "domino" effect on the adjacent parts of Southeast Asia—was not an unimportant or irrational one, but it was based on an exaggerated conception of Hanoi's alignment with Beijing and Moscow and in any case was not sustainable on account of widespread and passionate objections within the United States and elsewhere. Eventually, the United States had to withdraw defeated from the war, leaving the non-Communist governments of South Vietnam, Laos, and Cambodia to inevitable overthrow by Hanoi and its proxies, a process greatly accelerated by a massive competitive escalation of Soviet and Chinese aid to Hanoi once the United States was out of the war. It can be plausibly argued that American intervention bought the rest of Southeast Asia, outside Indochina, a decade of valuable time. Since Beijing refused to cooperate with Moscow in support of Hanoi and insisted on following an independent line, the struggle in Vietnam widened the existing Sino-Soviet rift.

The net effect of the interaction among the triangular powers during this period (roughly 1959-1969) was again favorable to the Soviet Union. It retained reasonable freedom of action and, in part because of the humiliation inflicted on it by the United States in the Cuban missile crisis, built up its strategic forces to a level of approximate parity with the United States and its conventional forces to the point of superiority in Eurasia. The United States, obsessed with Vietnam, hardly noticed the Soviet buildup and in fact in 1965 froze both its landbased and its seabased nuclear missile forces at the levels then prevailing. China, in its ultraradical mood, isolated and discredited itself to a high degree.

China's "Tilt" Toward the United States

The Soviet invasion of Czechoslovakia in August 1968 alarmed both the other parties to the triangle and was the earliest of several forces tending to push them closer to each other. The second such force was the inauguration in January 1969 of the Nixon administration, which hoped by creating some sort of viable relationship with Beijing both to facilitate a settlement of the Vietnam war and to pressure Moscow into an agreement that would tend to cap the growth of its strategic forces; to some extent, although with only temporary effects, both objectives were achieved. The third force was a serious and massive Sino-Soviet border crisis in 1969.

This crisis arose from the military politics of both sides. The Chinese People's Liberation Army had been in reasonably effective control of the provinces since early 1967, as a result of the Cultural Revolution. Although better than the only alternative possible at that time, Red Guard anarchy, this situation was unacceptable to Mao Zedong and Premier Zhou Enlai on several grounds. At Mao's initiative, the army, already politically dangerous, suppressed the Red Guard movement in late 1968 and thereby made itself politically superfluous as well. Zhou then began to move against the army by undercutting, through the media, the legitimacy of its political role. Although not very astute except in military matters, Defense Minister Lin Biao perceived this trend and tried to stem it. He attempted to salvage his and the army's position by organizing a blow, expected of course to be successful, at the generally hated Soviets, whom he mistakenly supposed to be "paper bears." On March 2, 1969, taking advantage of Moscow's presumed preoccupation with a crisis then in progress over West Berlin, Lin orchestrated an ambush of a Soviet patrol on a disputed island in the Ussuri River, which flows between Manchuria and the Soviet Maritime Province.

The outcome was a powerful, and to Lin, presumably, an unexpected Soviet response at a level of massive overkill resulting in a Sino-Soviet border crisis that lasted for several years and still has by no means evaporated. The explanation, apart from the general Soviet dislike and even fear of the Chinese, is evidently to be found in the politics of the Soviet Army at that time. On January 22, 1969, a recently discharged Soviet soldier, later found to be insane, fired a military rifle at a cosmonaut on parade in Red Square whom he apparently mistook for Brezhnev. Under the Stalinist ground rules still more or less in effect, such an event until officially explained otherwise constituted prima facie evidence of an army plot against Brezhnev. The Soviet military therefore responded joyfully to the opportunity, unwittingly offered them by Lin Biao, to prove their patriotism and loyalty by thumping the detested Chinese. The thumping took four main forms: a Soviet-initiated ambush, on a larger scale than the first, of a Chinese unit on the same island, on March 15; a rapid build-up of Soviet conventional and strategic forces in the regions bordering on China, especially during the second and third quarters of 1969; a huge anti-Chinese propaganda campaign, especially in the Soviet military press; and a series of border incidents, pressures, and threats designated to make Beijing negotiate on the crisis, or alternatively to lay the groundwork for an actual attack if it refused to come to the conference table.

The effect was a genuine panic in China, at both the elite and the popular levels. Zhou clearly wanted to negotiate with Kosygin, his opposite number, but he was constrained by countervailing pressures from his radical colleagues, probably including Lin Biao although by this time excluding Mao. A combination of the Soviet pressures just mentioned and representations by North Vietnam, in an influential position because of being the frontline communist state in the Indochina struggle, enabled Zhou to receive Kosygin in Beijing on September 11, 1969. After some further exchanges, the two sides began regular negotiations the following month, but these did not progress very far because the Soviet side rejected Beijing's demand for a cease fire agreement and a "mutual" (actually, Soviet) troop withdrawal from the rather limited areas along the border that are actively in dispute.[7]

In mid-1970, and in order to cope with the Soviet Union, Zhou began to establish covert contact, mainly through Pakistan, with Nixon and Kissinger, despite the continuing opposition of his radical colleagues. In effect, and contrary to the radicals' inclination, Zhou was abandoning the counterproductive dual adversary approach and reviving the earlier Maoist united front strategy, with the Soviet Union in the role of principal adversary and the United States in that of temporary Chinese partner. He was also reciprocating the Nixon administration's interest in an improvement of Sino-American relations. As the two sides stated in the celebrated Shanghai Communique (February 27, 1972), both were opposed to the Soviet Union's effort to acquire "hegemony" in the region (and elsewhere).[8] Zhou began to urge the United States, privately, to take the lead in forming an anti-Soviet united front to include a broad band of nations located near the Soviet Union's southern periphery, from China through Western Europe.[9] Whatever the merits of this idea, it made no headway in practice, partly because lack of enthusiasm on the part of the United States.

This extraordinary, if limited, improvement in Sino-American relations, amounting almost to a reversal of alliances, ushered in a decade-long era (the 1970s) during which the United States was clearly the gainer, although on a modest scale, from the operation of the triangle. Moscow and Beijing absorbed even more of each other's external energies than they had before, to the considerable benefit of international stability in East Asia. As Kissinger intended, the United States enjoyed better relations with both the other parties to the triangle than they had with each other. If the United States did not take advantage of this flexibility to improve significantly its overall capabilities for coping with the Soviet Union, that was to a large extent the result of a strong anti-interventionist and anti-military mood generated by the Vietnam experience. This mood was not especially affected, in either direction, by the more or less expected fall of South Vietnam in 1975, or by the equally predictable surge of Soviet activity in the Third World, especially Africa, that followed it.

The Current Stage: Moscow and Beijing on the Move

A strong case can be made that the two most important trends in East Asia at the present time are the rising military power and, most recently, the growing political activity, of the Soviet Union, and China's intensified effort at modernization. In the 1980s, these two powers have been the main actors in the triangle, both of them trying in different ways to benefit from its operation. The desire is especially acute on Beijing's part, because it has not been a major beneficiary in the past.

In early 1979, the Soviet Union strengthened its forces in the southern Kurile Islands (claimed by Japan) to counter what it exaggeratedly perceived as an emerging U.S.-Japanese-Chinese combination (or triangle) directed against it and signaled by the Sino-Japanese peace treaty (August 1978) and the "normalization" of Sino-American relations (December 1978). Moscow also established a naval base at Cam Ranh Bay (on the coast of South Vietnam) in the spring of 1979, the only one of its kind outside Soviet territory. The invasion of Afghanistan at the end of 1979 strengthened the impression that Moscow's energies in East Asia are no longer absorbed largely by China but have grown to a level at which they can also be directed toward the achievement of Soviet objectives—essentially, influence through intimidation—farther afield as well. The Soviet Union has unquestionably become the strongest regional military power in Northeast Asia and the Western Pacific, as Japan was before World War II and the United States after that. Unlike prewar Japan, fortunately, the Soviet Union is constrained and one hopes deterred by the other parties to the triangle and also by the rising power—economic and, eventually, probably military as well—of Japan itself.

Even though recent Soviet policy in East Asia, as elsewhere, has been strongly military in nature, it has had important political aspects as well. Under Brezhnev, China absorbed most of Moscow's Asian energies in the political as in the military field. Angry at the Chinese over what he regarded as their general stubbornness and their "tilt" toward the United States, Brezhnev tried unsuccessfully in 1973-1974 to get a free hand from Nixon and Kissinger to deal with China as he saw fit.[10] The Soviet leader absorbed with unhappiness Beijing's rejection of his overtures after Mao Zedong's death (in September 1976) for an improvement of relations. Particular Soviet grievances included: Beijing's signing of a peace treaty with Japan (August 1978) including an "anti-hegemony" clause directed against Moscow; its "normalization" of relations with the United States at the end of 1978; its attack on Vietnam in February 1979; its repudiation of the Sino-Soviet alliance in April 1979; its loud calls during that period for an anti-Soviet united front centering on the United States and China; and, finally, its suspension in January 1980 on account of Afghanistan of a series of Sino-Soviet talks that had begun the previous fall. Brezhnev still evidently wanted an improvement of relations with China, but he had little room for maneuver in view of Beijing's attitude and the bitterly anti-Chinese views of his colleague, the influential senior Soviet ideologue Mikhail Suslov.

Suslov died in late January 1982, and a few weeks later Brezhnev initiated a series of overtures to Beijing that led in the fall of that year to the resumption of the talks that the Chinese had suspended in January 1980. Clearly Beijing had become receptive to the idea of an improved relationship with Moscow.[11] The sources and limits of this change in the Chinese attitude are well worth exploring.

During the preceding decade, Beijing had gotten a feeling, somewhat exaggerated, that it was being manipulated by the United States, which was perceived as trying to "play the China card" in order to strengthen its hand within the triangle rather than leading a determined and worldwide struggle against Soviet "hegemonism" as Beijing had been advocating. This feeling, already strong during the Carter years, was reinforced under Reagan for a time by resentment of the new administration's pro-Taiwan attitude, or at least pronouncements. The last straw was a visit by Secretary of State Alexander Haig to Beijing in June 1981, during which his hosts evidently perceived him as trying to buy their acquiescence in deliveries of more modern arms to Taiwan (in particular, the "F-X" fighter) with a possibly spurious promise "in principle" to sell Beijing arms, but not yet the dual use technology that the Chinese wanted most.

Under the combined influence of Moscow's overtures and Washington's perceived refractoriness, Beijing abandoned yet another unviable strategy, its appeal for an anti-Soviet united front, in favor of what it calls an independent policy,[12] which some of its leaders, including Deng Xiaoping, began in late 1985 to describe, in private, as one of "equidistance" between the superpowers. In reality, Beijing is not equidistant between the United States and the Soviet

Union. Even though the Chinese view of the Soviet threat has moderated in recent years, it has not evaporated. If Beijing did not have a viable relationship—not an alliance, which is out of the question—with the United States, it would probably have to accommodate with the Soviet Union more or less on Moscow's terms, which would include a political role for China significantly "less equal" than that of the Soviet Union. In contrast, lack of a relationship with Moscow would not compel Beijing to accommodate with Washington. Furthermore, the United States is much more useful and promising as a source of high and dual use technology for China than is the Soviet Union. In the fall of 1983, the United States more or less simultaneously liberalized its restrictions on the export of dual use technology to China and, with the visit to Beijing of Secretary of Defense Caspar Weinberger, inaugurated a serious program of defense cooperation (as the Pentagon calls it) with China.

If Beijing is not in fact, and cannot really be, equidistant between the superpowers, two questions arise: Why have its leaders used that term? And why have they denied that they have used it? The answer to the first question seems to be that there are elements in the Chinese elite that can be described, somewhat loosely, as pro-American and pro-Soviet; the least total opposition from the two groups combined is generated by using the term equidistant, much as during the Carter administration the term "evenhanded" was applied to American policy toward the Soviet Union and China so as not to arouse unduly either the Sovietwatching or the Chinawatching communities in the foreign affairs bureaucracy. As for the second question, Beijing presumably does not want to alarm the United States or please the Soviet Union excessively by admitting to an abandonment of the previous "tilt," even though that is already implied by the term independent, which it does employ in public.

In the 1980s, Beijing no longer encourages Soviet-American confrontation; it desires instead international stability, including Soviet-American detente and arms control, as the environment most conducive to China's security and modernization. Recent unpublished statements by Chinese leaders indicate that Beijing wants a reasonably good relationship with both the superpowers but does not intend to get very close to either, because to do so would alarm and antagonize the other and would endanger the self-proclaimed Chinese posture of independence. With considerable skill and great persistence, Beijing uses as "control rods," to prevent unwanted closeness, the Taiwan issue in the case of the United States, and the "three obstacles"—the Soviet military presence along the Sino-Soviet border (including Mongolia), in Indochina, and in Afghanistan—in the case of the Soviet Union. Beijing perceives the United States under Reagan as having improved its strategic posture with respect to the Soviet Union, so that the superpowers are now in rough balance in the Chinese view.[13] This of course makes it easier for Beijing to pursue its proclaimed independent policy, or at least to rationalize it.

A number of considerations, including the events at the end of the 1970s already mentioned, coincided with and probably contributed, together with the political re-emergence of Deng Xiaoping at the same time, to a changed Chinese view of the nature and intensity of the Soviet threat. For one thing, China had acquired by then, or even earlier, what it, and apparently also Moscow, viewed as a minimum nuclear deterrent against Soviet attack. China's missile force, although technologically not very advanced, is the world's third largest and is well dispersed, concealed, and hardened in mountainsides. China is no longer an ally of the Soviet Union, and the record bears out the cynical observation that the Soviets only invade their allies. For some time, Beijing has been saying, probably both sincerely and correctly, that Europe, or even more likely Southwest Asia, is the main target of Soviet expansionism. These factors have reduced Beijing's perception both of the Soviet threat to China and of the need to move toward the United States in search of a counterweight to the Soviet Union.

Under Gorbachev, Moscow has broadened its policies toward China into a relatively flexible, although not yet markedly successful, approach to East Asia as a whole. Analysis of current Soviet East Asian policy is greatly aided by a major speech delivered by General Secretary Gorbachev at Vladivostok on July 28, 1986. Although somewhat propagandistic and not entirely original, it deserves more careful consideration than has evidently been given by many who refer to it.

The first half of the speech, approximately, is devoted to the economic shortcomings of the Soviet Far East—to which, as well as to Siberia, "a special place is assigned" in the "plans defined by the Twenty Seventh CPSU Congress," held in early 1986—in the context of Gorbachev's efforts toward an overall "restructuring" of the admittedly ailing Soviet economy. Gorbachev emphasizes the need to increase trade and other "progressive forms of economic links with foreign countries (implicitly and for the most part, the dynamic non-Communist economies of the Western Pacific), including production cooperation and joint enterprises, and the construction of a specialized export base." He also mentions the desirability of promoting foreign as well as domestic tourism in the Soviet Far East—something that would require massive changes in the existing situation, in the direction of "openness"—and of making Vladivostok a "major international center, a seat of trade and culture, a city of festivals, sports meetings, congresses, and scientific symposiums. We should like to see it as our open window to the East," as Leningrad (then St. Petersburg) was intended by Peter the Great to be Russia's window on the West.

The leading priority that Gorbachev indicates in the Vladivostok speech— the need to plug the Soviet Far East into the economic dynamism of the Western Pacific and so invigorate the entire Soviet economy—presumably rules out any serious Soviet desire to launch a war in the region, even though Gorbachev clearly does not want—and politically may be unable—to forgo any advantages, real or imagined, that may accrue from the classic Soviet strategy of deploying massive military power for political effect.

The second half of the Vladivostok speech, more or less, deals with Soviet policy toward the countries of East Asia and the Western Pacific. The centerpiece is the express desire for an accommodation with China, the vast neighbor without whose good will it may be difficult for Moscow to gain that of other Asian countries, even those that dislike or fear China. Gorbachev makes some limited but still potentially significant gestures toward removal of the "three obstacles" to better Sino-Soviet relations on which Beijing continually harps: the Soviet military presence along the common border (including Mongolia), in Afghanistan, and in Indochina (especially support for Vietnamese operations in Cambodia). He states that "the USSR is prepared to discuss with the PRC specific steps aimed at a balanced reduction in the level of land forces." He says that "the question of withdrawing a considerable number of Soviet troops from Mongolia is being examined with the leadership of the Mongolian People's Republic;" in fact, one of the five Soviet divisions has been removed from Mongolia since then. Gorbachev indicates a willingness in principle—communicated privately to Beijing as long ago as 1970—for the common boundary along the Amur Ussuri Rivers to follow the main channel (Thalweg), rather than the Manchurian bank as Moscow had formerly demanded; he does not indicate, however, whether the Soviet side will continue to insist on an exception for Bear Island (Heixiazi to the Chinese), which lies on the Manchurian side of the main channel but also uncomfortably close to the important Soviet Far Eastern city of Khabarovsk. As for Afghanistan, Gorbachev promises—although not exclusively or even primarily as a concession to Beijing—that six regiments will be withdrawn by the end of 1986; they were, but they were promptly replaced at an approximately equivalent level. Gorbachev expresses an interest in an improvement of Sino-Vietnamese relations, but he indicates no intent to press Hanoi in that direction and explicitly refuses to discuss Cambodia, the aspect of the Indochina issue of greatest concern to Beijing (because a Chinese-supported war against Vietnamese domination is in progress there); clearly the Soviets are unwilling to endanger their important air and naval bases in Vietnam.

Gorbachev makes no reference to another issue known to be of concern to Beijing—as well as to South Korea and the United States—and sometimes referred to informally as the "fourth obstacle"—the developing Soviet military relationship with North Korea. It is reasonably clear, however, that this amounts to trading moderate amounts of fairly advanced military hardware, but nothing that is genuinely likely to encourage or facilitate another North Korean attack on the South, for geopolitical assets for the Soviet Union: naval port call privileges and overflight rights for reconnaissance aircraft. Gorbachev's references to North Korea in the Vladivostok speech are pro forma and fall far short of his gestures toward China.

In addition to a routine expression of hope for increased trade and cultural exchange with China—which has occurred but only to a very limited extent—Gorbachev proposes in the Vladivostok speech the completion of a Sino-Soviet rail link through Central Asia—already on the drawing board for three decades—and cooperation with the PRC in space, to include the training of Chinese cosmonauts.

In terms of expressed cordiality, the second most important Asian country mentioned in the Vladivostok speech is India. Clearly Gorbachev has been trying with some success to maintain with Rajiv Gandhi the "special relationship" enjoyed by their predecessors, predicating this relationship on the fact that the Soviet Union—unlike the United States, China, and Pakistan—has for three decades tacitly acknowledged Indian "hegemony" in South Asia.

The Vladivostok speech unavoidably recognizes the importance of Japan and voices a hope for better relations, which indeed Gorbachev has been trying energetically to cultivate since 1985, but also an exaggerated concern over an alleged trend toward Japanese "rearmament." It is worth noting that—as of mid-1987— Gorbachev has not achieved his desire to visit Japan. The Japanese government and public opinion still demand the return of the Northern Territories (the southern islands of the Kuril chain), an issue that Gorbachev has shown a willingness to discuss but not to negotiate.

Not surprisingly, the Vladivostok speech portrays the Soviet Union as a major Asian and Pacific power and in this connection expresses an interest in participating in the supposedly emerging Pacific Basin economic community. Gorbachev also proposes, with minimal chances of success, a "Pacific Ocean conference along the lines of the Helsinki Conference" of 1975, to be held ideally at Hiroshima, a choice obviously intended to foster and exploit anti-American feeling.

Like other aspects of Gorbachev's foreign policy, the Vladivostok speech expresses an ambivalent attitude toward the United States. On the one hand, he concedes that the United States is a genuine Pacific power with legitimate interests in the region. On the other hand, the imperatives of Soviet ideology, politics, and foreign policy, as understood in Moscow, compel him to accuse the United States, although perhaps pro forma, of support for "counterrevolution" and other "imperialist" activities. He expresses support for various possibilities for arms control arrangements covering Asia and the Pacific, including nonproliferation measures, limits on naval movements (especially of nuclear submarines), and "liquidation" of Soviet and American medium range missiles—he specifies SS-20s—in Europe, without redeployment to "any other place" (i.e., Asia).

There is still more in the Vladivostok speech, but enough has been said already to indicate that it is a major, and evidently a credible, statement of Gorbachev's aims and policies with respect to Asia and the Pacific, including Siberia and the Soviet Far East. The keynote, to repeat, is the regeneration of the Soviet economy, in large part through the development of Soviet Asia and the latter's integration, to some significant extent, into the dynamic economic life of the Western Pacific. Both the logic of this position and the tenor of Gorbachev's comments on particular issues and countries indicate that he wants peace and a reasonable level of stability in that region—and presumably else-where as well—but evidently without abandoning the traditional Soviet effort to use military power to gain political advantage. Whether he can have both these things at once remains to be seen. Clearly the interests of the United States and China in Asia and the Pacific, as well as those of other countries, will be considerably affected by the way in which the Soviet Union implements the ideas expressed by Gorbachev at Vladivostok.

To date (mid-1987), the Soviets have urged Mongolia and Vietnam, whose relations with China have been acutely bad for some time, to improve them, but so far with little visible effect. The Mongols are apparently too afraid of China to be capable of responding. As regards Vietnam, it is Beijing more than Hanoi that has shown some interest in detente.

The relationship of the third small Asian Communist country, North Korea, to the Soviet Union and China is more complex. Beijing does not want Pyong-yang to move either militarily against Seoul or politically toward Moscow. The North Koreans do not care much for this ambivalent attitude, nor for the infor-mal relations (trade, cultural contacts, etc.) that have developed between China and South Korea since the beginning of the 1980s. Since about the time of the shooting down of the South Korean airliner (KAL 007) by a Soviet pilot (Sep-tember 1, 1983), therefore, North Korea has "tilted" toward the Soviet Union, which has been happy to reciprocate. Moscow is in a particularly favorable position because Beijing has been careful not to let its relations with Pyongyang deteriorate openly, as its relations with Ulan Bator and Hanoi have done, and the Soviets therefore have no need to urge Pyongyang to cultivate Beijing as part of the new, more conciliatory, Soviet approach to China.

On the contrary, the Soviets have continued to seek unilateral advantages in North Korea. In early 1985, in exchange for MiG-23s, Moscow acquired over-flight rights across North Korea for its reconnaissance aircraft, which now fly more or less daily missions over the Yellow Sea. The Soviet Union has gotten naval port call privileges and may be seeking actual facilities (bases) on both coasts of North Korea, which if acquired would reduce somewhat its reliance on the major base at Vladivostok, which lies behind "chokepoints;" to date, Pyongyang is not known to have promised any such facilities. Beijing has claimed that it welcomed the recent improvement of Soviet-North Korean rela-tions; the aptest comment on that is one made to the writer by a high American official: Anyone who believes that will believe anything. Beijing has been trying to compete with the Soviet effort in Pyongyang by urging the United States to accept a North Korean proposal for three-party talks (the United States and the two Koreas) on unification and by supporting, even though it privately opposes, North Korea's insistence that the United States withdraw its troops from South Korea.

Probably the most important of Gorbachev's Asian initiatives has been directed toward Japan. Since 1978, the year of the Sino-Japanese peace treaty and Sino-U.S. normalization, Moscow has claimed to be concerned over a

developing anti-Soviet U.S.-Chinese-Japanese combination.   Until 1985,
nevertheless, Soviet behavior toward Japan was almost unbelievably crude and
self-defeating. It was presumably grounded in a profound hatred; insofar as it
had a rational basis, it must be assumed to reflect a calculation that Japan could
eventually be intimidated into breaking its ties with the United States and Fin-
landizing itself.   In mid-1985, the Soviet approach changed sharply.   The
timing was propitious.   Japanese opinion was worried over the threat of
American protectionism, and the summer brought a series of fortieth anniver-
saries of events relating to the defeat of Japan by the United States. Among the
signs of Moscow's new approach were a major Soviet cultural exhibition in
Tokyo and a reported promise that if the Japanese government would make a
formal commitment of some kind to its "three non-nuclear principles," Moscow
would agree formally not to use nuclear weapons against Japan. The Japanese
public did not fail to notice, however, that Moscow was showing no inclination
to return the Northern Territories, which are strategically important to the
Soviet Union, or to reduce its force of about 170 SS-20 missiles in the Far East
(unless the United States agreed to remove a comparable number of its missiles
from the region). In January 1986, Foreign Minister Shevardnadze visited
Tokyo and impressed his hosts by his willingness to discuss the Northern Territories issue and the matter of a peace treaty, which had been stalled for thirty
years largely by the territorial question. It appeared that Shevardnadze's main
purpose was to talk the Japanese government out of participating in the
Strategic Defense Initiative (SDI, or "Star Wars"); if so, he was evidently un-
successful.[14]

Beijing's position on SDI is worth noting. It is opposed, for the usual
reasons given in the United States and Europe: SDI is said to be bad for detente
and arms control, largely because the Soviet Union objects to it. There are two
additional considerations specifically relevant to China: Beijing fears that SDI
will widen the already vast technological gulf separating it from the United
States and will provoke the Soviet Union into a comparable effort that will tend
to nullify the Chinese nuclear deterrent against Soviet attack.[15]

The other truly significant development in East Asia beside the growing
power and assertiveness of the Soviet Union, as already indicated, is the enhanced seriousness with which Beijing, since shortly after Mao Zedong's death,
has been tackling the task of modernization.[16]

In 1979, shortly after Deng Xiaoping's return to the leadership, agriculture
was virtually decollectivized under something called the "responsibility system," under which peasant households contract with the authorities to deliver
specified amounts of produce and can then dispose as they see fit of anything
they raise above those amounts. This system has had a very beneficial effect
on agricultural production and overall rural living standards, but it has also
reintroduced income inequalities and distressed the remaining Maoists, including some of the senior military. The industrial sector, by contrast, remained essentially overcentralized and unreformed for five years longer. In the late

1970s, the "open" policy was adopted toward trade and technological contact with the outside world, especially the advanced non-communist countries and above all Japan and the United States. By 1984, Beijing had grasped the fact that its large offshore oil development program, for which it had contracted a few years earlier with foreign (including American) firms, and on which it had apparently been counting heavily as a foreign exchange earner, was not going to have a large or quick payoff, especially given the declining price of oil. It was in this context that the Communist Party Central Committee adopted an important decision on economic reform on October 20, 1984. The scope of central planning was to be reduced, plant managers were to get greater autonomy, the price system was to be overhauled and liberalized, and consumer subsidies (for food and other necessities) were to be cut.

The reform was implemented with a rush, and over-enthusiastically as it turned out. Instead of a combination of the best features of socialism and capitalism as the regime hoped, the result resembled more a random mixture of some of the worst aspects of both. There was a surge of official corruption and inflation, although the economy grew at a nominal 15 percent in 1985. Plant managers used their expanded authority to order new equipment and consumer durables, usually from Japan, so that foreign exchange reserves soon dropped by several billion dollars. Millions of peasants, sensing a more permissive atmosphere, got out of grain into other less laborious and more profitable lines of work, with the result that the grain harvest was about 50 million tons less in 1985 than the year before.

These trends inevitably evoked criticism and opposition not only from the remaining Maoist radicals but also from believers in centralized Soviet-styled economic planning and administration; chief among the latter was Chen Yun, a very senior specialist in economic affairs and party discipline. The objections surfaced around the time of an important party conference in September 1985, and Deng Xiaoping thought it wise to accommodate them to a degree; for example, the projected growth rate was to be held to 7 percent, a rate that was officially expected to yield a fully modernized China by the middle of the twenty-first century, and there was a renewed emphasis on grain production. On the other hand, Deng succeeded in retiring a large number of senior and presumably superfluous party and military officials.

During 1986, Deng's protege, General Secretary Hu Yaobang, developed serious differences with more conservative members of the party leadership by spearheading a movement for political reform (including greater freedom of expression), over and above the existing movement for economic reform. At the end of the year, large numbers of students, dissatisfied with Hu's half measures, began to demonstrate. This precipitated a crisis within the leadership; Deng supported the conservatives against Hu, who was ousted in mid-January 1987. Political reform was indefinitely postponed, except for very limited programs to make personnel changes and improve administrative performance within the ruling Communist Party. It appeared for a time that economic reform might suffer the fate of political reform, but in the spring of 1987 it began to emerge from a temporary limbo and give the impression of being again "on track."

Both the future composition of the party leadership and the status of economic and political reform are scheduled to be clarified, to some extent at any rate, at the Thirteenth Party Congress in October 1987.

In spite of problems and setbacks, the Chinese economy does appear to be on the move under rules that are significantly more flexible and nurturing than those in effect in most other Communist countries, including the Soviet Union at least until very recently. This trend, or apparent trend, has begun to create uneasiness in countries already suspicious of China for one reason or another, such as the Soviet Union and some Asian states, notably Indonesia. There is a plausible basis for this feeling, given China's potential power and its important—and sometimes expansionist—traditional role in Asia. There is no reason to doubt that, although the military aspect of modernization is not at the top of Beijing's list of priorities, its overall industrial development program will generate sooner or later a significant increment of projectible military power. Under those conditions, it cannot simply be assumed that China will continue indefinitely to maintain its present fairly low profile in Asia, although neither can that possibility be excluded.

The United States has not tried to match the recent Soviet military buildup in Northeast Asian and the Western Pacific in a quantitative sense, but it has been improving the qualitative capabilities of its forces in the region, of which the most powerful component is the Seventh Fleet. It has also tried to get Japan to increase its level of defensive readiness and assume responsibility for the security of its air and sealanes for one thousand miles out from Tokyo. Japan's budget deficits, although small by American standards, and popular reluctance have slowed Tokyo's fulfillment of these goals. The Self Defense Forces, however, are cooperating more closely with their American counterparts than formerly, and Japan is beginning to make some of its technology with military applications available to the United States. American military cooperation with the South Korean armed forces, in potential anti-Soviet as well as anti-North Korean missions, has also increased. But despite these improvements, the level of tripartite cooperative mine laying capability that would be needed dependably to interdict passage of the three crucial straits—Soya or La Perouse (between Hokkaido and Sakhalin), Tsugaru (between Japan and Korea) and Tsushima (between Japan and Korea)—by the Soviet Pacific Fleet in time of war is not yet at hand.

Even after World War II, the United States has never been strong enough to be able to accomplish all its goals in East Asia and the Western Pacific without the cooperation of some regional partner or ally. Apart from a brief spell of attempted collaboration with the Soviet Union at the end of World War II, the United States has generally tried to work with Japan or China, in alternation. It has never been very successful in this, because the objectives of China and Japan have always differed significantly—although not necessarily totally—

from those of the United States. To go back only a few years: Nixon and Kissinger tried to work with China, Ford and Kissinger with Japan and Carter and
Brzezinski with China, Reagan and Haig also with China (in spite of the
salience of the Taiwan issue at that time) and Reagan and Shultz initially with
Japan. In the second half of 1983, two important steps already mentioned were
taken toward China—the liberalization of control on exports of dual use technology and the initiation of defense cooperating at a significant level—with the
result that for the first time China and Japan have roughly equal status as
American regional partners, with the difference of course that Japan is an ally
of the United States whereas China is not. On the Chinese side, the American
steps of late 1983 struck an especially responsive chord because Beijing had
concluded that Reagan was likely to be re-elected in 1984. All this has tended
to lend at least a little reality to Moscow's charges of anti-Soviet collusion
among the three powers, or at any rate it would if it were not for the fact that
the Chinese elite is currently in a strongly anti-Japanese mood.

Some Triangular Scenarios

   The Korean peninsula has been the most sensitive focus of triangular interaction in Northeast Asia since World War II. If North Korea should launch
another attack on the South, as it is clearly trying to achieve the capability to
do, the United States would presumably fight, China would probably do what
it could to restrain the North Koreans or at least to limit the damage to Sino-
American relations, and the Soviets would very likely try to exploit the crisis
without getting directly involved. A U.S.-Japanese-Chinese combination and
Japanese rearmament, both of which Moscow appears to fear, might be given
a major impetus. The effect on the triangle, although difficult to forecast,
would almost certainly be significant.
   Japan is unlikely to respond to Soviet pressures, which as we have seen have
recently been supplemented with blandishments, by weakening or cutting its
ties with the United States. If it did, however, the strategic position of the
United States in the Western Pacific would be unhinged, with potentially
catastrophic effects on the regional balance. The United States would probably have to move closer to Beijing on essentially Chinese terms, which would
include an American abandonment of Taiwan.
   If the United States should lose its bases in the Philippines, on account of a
hypothetical eventual Communist takeover or for some other reason, another
although less drastic shift in the regional balance would probably take place. It
would be even more serious if the Soviet Union should replace the United
States, as it has at Danang and Cam Ranh Bay; to be sure, Moscow's prompt
endorsement of Marcos's fraudulent "re-election" has harmed Soviet standing
in the Philippines and made such an outcome less likely. If it did eventuate

nonetheless, Beijing might feel compelled to try to accommodate further with the Soviet Union if it believed that a trend toward Soviet regional "hegemony" had gotten under way, or with the United States if it did not.

A true Sino-Soviet accommodation, including a significant level of cooperation with respect to third countries, is unlikely under current and foreseeable conditions. If one occurred, however, it would seriously chill the relations of both the United States and Japan, drive the latter two powers closer together, alarm the rest of Asia, and—unless the combination became overwhelmingly strong and threatening—foreclose many political and diplomatic opportunities that might otherwise be available to Moscow and Beijing separately.

The opposite, and also seemingly improbable possibility, a Sino-Soviet war, would be seriously destabilizing not only for both belligerents but for the rest of Asia, or at least Northeast Asia. The effect on the peace of the world, and not merely that of the region, might also be highly adverse. The United States did what it could, short of an alliance with China, to deter such a war when it seemed most likely, from 1969 to about 1973. The problem has diminished in apparent intensity since then, although it has not evaporated. If the Soviet Union should attack, China would presumably be devastated and seriously weakened, as an actor in the triangle and in all other respects. The United States would be faced with a decision of the utmost seriousness; there can be no certainty how it would react, and this uncertainty appears to date to have exerted a powerful restraining influence on Moscow.

Regardless of its point of origin, a U.S.-Soviet war would presumably involve more than East Asia and the Western Pacific. In that region, there would probably be an emphasis by both sides on the sea of Okhotsk, and on Japan and its sealanes. The Soviet leadership appears to feel some fear that in the event of such a war the Chinese might try to move against Siberia; accordingly, one of the earliest Soviet moves might be some sort of pre-emptive strike against China, unless Beijing promptly declared its neutrality.

Fortunately, none of these "hypothetical horribles" seems very likely at the present time. A major reason for this low order of probability is the existence of the "Iron Triangle," which objectively acts as a mechanism for buffering the actions of the three parties and thus helping to promote regional stability.

At a somewhat less dramatic level, it is worth considering the possibility of a full scale accommodation between Japan, a nation of great importance to all parties to the triangle in spite of Tokyo's relative military weakness and current political ineffectiveness, and China. Under present conditions, this is not very likely, but it could happen in the mid-term future. The effect on and reaction of the United States would probably depend on whether it had good relations with both parties; if it did, the U.S.-Japanese-Chinese triangle that Moscow has worried and complained about since 1979 might materialize; otherwise, both superpowers might find their influence and activities in the region significantly curtailed. Barring a major, and improbable, improvement in the Soviet Union's relations with both China and Japan, Moscow's reaction to a Sino-

Japanese accommodation would be strongly negative. China's weight in the "Iron Triangle" would in all likelihood be significantly enhanced.

Some Triangular Observations and Conclusions

The analysis present here suggests that the concept of a U.S.-Soviet-Chinese strategic triangle is a valid and useful one. Until about 1970, its existence and functioning served mainly the interests of the Soviet Union, the world's chief troublemaker, and were therefore adverse, on the whole, to East Asian stability and security. This situation changed greatly in the 1970s, when the main beneficiary from the triangle was the United States, the party most strongly committed to regional stability and security. In the 1980s, the situation is more obscure; the Soviet Union and China are each trying vigorously to use the triangle for its own purposes, the former by essentially military means—although increasingly also by political methods—and the latter by primarily economic means. The United States, while not a true Asian power, is able to play the role of regional balancer to a degree largely because it is buttressed by its security relationship with Japan, although emerging U.S. defense cooperation with China is also helpful. Barring major, and currently unforeseen, developments, the triangle is not likely to change its shape and functioning very much. If it does not, it will continue to be helpful to the maintenance of regional stability and security.

NOTES

1. The best general book on the Korean War is David Rees, *Korea: The Limited War*, New York: St. Martins Press, 1964. On the Chinese role, see Allen S. Whiting, *China Crosses the Yalu*, (New York: Macmillan, 1960).

2. In an agreement attached to the Sino-Soviet alliance of February 14, 1950.

3. The classic study of the early phases of the Sino-Soviet dispute is Donald S. Zagoria, *The Sino-Soviet Conflict, 1956-1961*, (Princeton University Press, 1962).

4. Evidence of the Sino-Soviet nuclear relationship was picked up by American intelligence at the end of the 1950s; the first public reference to it was by Beijing in a statement of August 15, 1963 (text in Harold C. Hinton ed., *The People's Republic of China, 1949-1979: A Documentary Survey*, 5 vols., (Wilmington: Scholarly Resources, 1980), vol. 2, p. 1143.

5. The classic statement of the dual adversary strategy is Lin Biao, *Long Live the Victory of People's War!* (September 3, 1985) in Hinton, Vol. 2, pp. 1222-1239.

6. Cf. Gene T. Hsiao ed., *The Role of External Powers in the Indochina Crisis*, (Edwardsville, Illinois: Southern Illinois University Press, 1973).

7. Harold C. Hinton, *The Bear at the Gate: Chinese Policymaking under Soviet Pressure*, (Stanford, California: Hoover Institution, 1971).

8. John W. Garver, *China's Decision for Rapprochement with the United States, 1986-1971*, (Boulder, Colorado: Westview Press, 1982); Henry Kissinger, *White House Years*, (Boston: Little, Brown, 1979), Chs. 6, 19, 24.

9. Henry Kissinger, *Years of Upheaval*, (Boston: Little, Brown, 1982), p. 55.

10. Kissinger, *Years of Upheaval*, pp. 233, 294-295, 1173.

11. Donald S. Zagoria, "The Moscow-Beijing Detente," *Foreign Affairs*, vol. 61, no. 4 (Spring 1983), pp. 853-873.

12. Cf. Zheng Weizhi, "Independence is the Basic Canon," *Beijing Review*, no. 1 (January 7, 1985), pp. 16-19, 38.

13. Cf. Shi Wuqing, "Superpowers Reach Military Balance," *Beijing Review*, no. 3 (January 21, 1985), pp. 14-15; and no. 4 (January 28, 1985), pp. 25-27.

14. Richard Nations, "The Russian Revolution," *Far Eastern Economic Review*, (January 30, 1986), pp. 26-29; Richard Nations, "Star Wars Dilemma," *Far Eastern Economic Review*, (February 13, 1986), pp. 32-34.

15. Cf. Zhuang Qubing, "United States Prepares for Star Wars," *Beijing Review*, no. 45 (November 5, 1984), pp. 16-19. Also based on private discussions with Chinese strategic analysts.

16. See *China's Economy Looks Toward the Year 2000*, 2 vols., (Washington: Government Printing Office for Joint Economic Committee of Congress, 1986). Recent developments in Chinese economic policy have been well covered by John Burns in a series of articles in *The New York Times* (for August 4, 1985; December 23, 1985 and January 1, 1986).

CHAPTER 3

Japan and the Soviet Union

Thomas W. Robinson

Devoting an entire article to Soviet-Japanese security relations might at first seem to be a luxury. In the context of overall Northeast Asian security developments, to say nothing of the larger world, Moscow-Tokyo relations have been a relative constant. Japanese-Soviet relations, despite the regional and global importance of the two states since the 1950s, has not normally contained elements of dynamism or drama. Nor are their current actions toward each other at the top of the list in terms of regional importance.[1]

Nonetheless, good reasons exist for addressing this topic. The general situation in Northeast Asia is changing, and a new dynamism is appearing in the security (and other) policies of Japan and the Soviet Union. The Kremlin is making a concerted effort to involve itself in the region, backed by substantially increased military power, and a firm geographic base in Siberia and the Soviet Far East. Japanese policy itself can no longer be regarded as primarily dependent on American leadership; Tokyo has an agenda of its own and is progressively more willing to act on it. Further, there are a growing number of national security policy issues involving Tokyo and Moscow that are already on the docket for consideration—by the United States and the other regional states, as well as the two states in questions—or shortly will push themselves to the fore. These "over the horizon" issues possess the capacity for introducing a new dynamism into Japanese foreign policy. Finally, Soviet-Japanese "national security" relations illustrate the extent to which that term has expanded in meaning to where no topic in international relations—political, diplomatic, economic, or security—is not relevant to consideration.

A useful way to proceed is to first sketch out the setting of Soviet-Japanese security relations, in historical, domestic, and international dimensions; then to examine the resulting policy issues that currently comprise the nub of attitudes and policies in Moscow and Tokyo; and finally to essay on topics more strictly in the national security realm. That moves the discussion from the general to the specific, gradually building up a base, in fact and policy, for more sophisticated consideration of policy issues, thus providing us with the capability for making accurate policy judgement.

Historical Background

Historically, the situation is clear. Japan has become, in the course of somewhat more than a century, a thoroughly modern state in every regard. In the 1980s, Japan has become a Western nation in terms of internationalization of its society and foreign policy. Japan did, of course, take an unfortunate and expensive detour during the 1930s and 1940s, electing to use its new power for territorial expansion into all of Asia. But since 1945, Tokyo has been forced to give up all thought of the use of force for offensive purposes and has strongly internalized that change. Just as strongly, the Japanese system has substituted the economic instrument as the central means by which to complete its modernization program and move into a position of world leadership. The result is that Japan has become, once again, Asia's dominant regional power.[2]

The Soviet Union is, in some ways, not entirely different from Japan. The Soviets have also attempted to modernize rapidly. As did the Japanese fifty years ago, the Soviet Union today expresses its new found power mostly in military terms. As was the case during the 1930s with Japan, so today the principal policy issue in Asia is how to deter Russian military aggression. But there the parallel stops. Moscow has not been, until quite recently, an Asian power *per se*, having subordinated its approach in Asia to the more important demands for security and development, respectively, in Europe and in European Russia. Moscow's involvement in Asia thus has evinced a cyclical character, advancing at the turn of the century, the early 1920s, at the close of World War II and more recently with the enormous growth of Russian military power and the melioration of the Sino-Soviet dispute. Conversely, Moscow has been forced out of Asia by defeat at the hands of Japan in 1905, the rise of the Nazi German threat in the middle 1930s, and the Sino-Soviet dispute and the split of the international communist movement in the 1960s. Today, although Moscow once again pursues an aggressive foreign policy in Asia, there is an important difference: strong Russian military units of all four service arms threaten Asia as no external power has ever done before, while the domestic base in Soviet Asia for such power projection is solid and growing.[3]

Domestically, the two societies are vastly different. Japan is politically, socially, and racially stable; still growing rapidly in its economy; crowded but not growing in population; and a world leader in the arts, science, and culture. Because of the searing effect of World War II and the universal acceptance of Article Nine of the Constitution (the "no war" provision), Tokyo evinces no propensity to interfere in the internal affairs of other states, even in economic segments of life where Japanese influence is often a very strong element. Rather, Japan is content to continue life as it is, which for that country is good and getting better. No major issues threaten the country internally.[4]

In contrast, consider the Soviet Union. The country is politically stable, but only because of the imposition of totalitarian measures over a severely repressed population. Although the country appears socially at peace, Soviet society contains many fault lines—linguistic, national/ethnic, economic, historical, and political. The Soviet Union is actually a vast internal empire, governed by a small and self- perpetuating oligarchy with an idealogy either rejected or looked upon with indifference by most of the populace. Soviet expansionist tendencies tend to follow from the very nature of Soviet society— paranoid, xenophobic, and interventionalist, and from a basic reality of modern international life, that a state with an excess of military resources will find reasons to use them and then justify the resulting conquests in terms of the allegedly superior ideology.[5]

The international setting for the Soviet-Japanese relationship is a function of the political, economic, and security environments in which each finds itself. These environments are quite different in each case. The Japanese political environment is filtered through the lens of the Security Treaty with the United States, which provides basic direction, as well as setting severe limits on how far Tokyo can move on its own. Because Tokyo has elected to link itself so completely with Washington (and this choice has long since become voluntary, resulting from the many benefits of letting Washington carry the burden of Japanese defense), what happens in Washington, and in areas (Europe, the Middle East, etc.) where the United States carries a global security burden, is directly relevant and of instantaneous concern to Tokyo. The problem is that Japan can do little, in any given instance, to follow a strictly independent policy line. With no military projection capability, little usable cultural influence, and an economic instrument that is essentially unusable in any specific instance (witness Japanese kow-towing to OPEC in the two oils shocks of the 1970s), Tokyo is especially vulnerable to the violent and treacherous forces that comprise American-Soviet relations. So long as Tokyo remains within the confines of the Security Treaty with the United States, prospects for succumbing to threats, blandishments, and blackmail from Moscow are minimized. Nevertheless, the potential, and temptation, are ever-present and supply at least the possibility, in a Soviet-American crisis or conflict, for drastic change in Japanese-Soviet relations in favor of Moscow.[6]

The Soviet international political environment, in relation to Asia, is similarly difficult. So long as the Kremlin pursues as policy of expansion in influence, projection of power, and outright seizure of territory, Asian states must be on their guard. The new element of Asian international security relations is that the Kremlin has become a major threat to most regional states, thus configuring international orientations in the area into those supporting and those opposing the Russian forward movement. Moscow has managed to divide most of Asia (with the exceptions of Burma and perhaps Sri Lanka) into pro-and anti-Soviet camps. Even India has drawn back from Moscow's embrace since Afghanistan. The anti-Soviet "camp," however loose a conglomerate of alliances, alignments, and informal arrangements, still comprises by far the preponderance of power, territory, and other assets in Asia. This arrangement will probably continue for the foreseeable future, thus severely limiting Kremlin maneuverability in Asia. Nevertheless, the Soviet Union has succeeded in becoming an important element in every region of Asia, reaffirming Soviet superpower status. For Japan, at the center of the American-administered series of anti-Soviet arrangements, the ups and downs of Soviet influence anywhere in Asia, immediately affect Tokyo and its relations with Moscow.[7]

The international economic environment is as central for Japan as is the political. Since Japan prospers as a result of the open structure (free trade, convertible currency, ease of investment flows, etc.) in the international economic system, Tokyo has an enormous interest in assuring the maintenance and expansion of this system. Conversely, Japan must fear long-term trade imbalances in its own favor because such imbalances will inevitably result in anti-Japanese protectionism and other measures designed to close off or limit markets and supply sources. This has not happened to any significant degree, but remains Tokyo's most important concern. Meanwhile, Japan is one of the leaders in constructing a world economy of rapidly increasing interdependence and the beginnings of trans-Pacific economic community.

Moscow is incapable of participating in this economic system because of the nature of the closed Soviet economic system, which stresses autarky, currency inconvertibility, and refusal to engage in reciprocally beneficial trade practices. Since the Asian economy is dominated by free market economies and processes—with even China moving cautiously into the broader, interdependent system—Moscow has only a small degree of economic maneuver in the region. The Soviets simply cannot appeal to the region on the basis of their comparatively inferior technology, non-participation in regional development institutions like the Asian Development Bank, unwillingness to open Soviet industry to at least partial foreign ownership, largely non-existent agricultural surpluses, and their poorly developed consumer goods sector. The Kremlin is thus forced to reduce the Soviet economic appeal to the three areas where it performs reasonably well: arms production, raw materials, and the lower end of the producer goods sector. Of these, the latter two are not appealing because of the Soviet economic system—in the face of inherent limitation Moscow must attempt to work out barter deals—and because of superior competition from Western and even Third World economies. That leaves only the military sector, at which the Russians excel.[8]

Thus, Soviet-Japanese economic relations are poorly developed and will probably remain so. Two-way trade has never gone above $5 billion per year. Japan is hardly likely to purchase Soviet military equipment, consumer goods, low technology, or three-generations-old producer goods. And so long as Japan remains closely allied with the United States, Washington can, and does, set severe limits on the one area where there might be room for comparatively large growth in Japanese-Soviet trade: Japanese investment in Siberian oil, timber, and mineral development in exchange for the export of a healthy percentage of these items in Tokyo. On the other hand, any lasting melioration in American-

Soviet conflictual relations, however unlikely that seems at present, could lead to a disproportionate response in this component of Russian-Japanese trade.[9]

The international security environment severely constrains Tokyo's ties with Moscow. So long as Tokyo places its security in Washington's hands, and so long as American policy makers find reason to remain adamantly opposed to Soviet policies and pretension, Japan has comparatively little maneuverability vis-a-vis Moscow. The Kremlin constantly finds the road to Tokyo blocked by its own perfidity and by American-manufactured obstacles. The global and the Asian security environments are dominated not only by the Washington-Moscow standoff, but further, by the very nature of modern weapons. The three post-World War II military revolutions—infinite destructive power, instantaneous delivery, and near total accuracy from great distances—configure the form of modern military systems and shape the time-span, the geographic extent, and the level of destructiveness of contemporary conflict. One reason the Kremlin so severely threatens Tokyo, and why Japan must depend so greatly on American protection, is the very nature of such systems, the conflicts they induce, and the strategies they engender. Domination of offensive operations, the essential nature of strategic warning systems, the credibility of a deterrence strategy dependent on enormous numbers of widely dispersed nuclear weapons, a large and diverse military research and development system, none of which Tokyo possesses, all force Japan to line up behind the United States merely out of fright at Soviet capabilities to destroy all of Japan within a very short time.[10]

Two policy conclusions follow directly from the international strategic environment. First, Japan's security interests and its security policy are contradictory. Tokyo must act as if it will back the Americans in any and all confrontations with Moscow, come what may. And Japan must go at least some distance toward implementing such a policy: allowing American use of Japanese soil and ports for the anti-Soviet nuclear deterrent and supporting American foreign, military, and arms control policies in every forum and situation. Japan's security interest, on the other hand, is not to go the wall with the Soviet Union every time a Soviet-American crisis arises, not to place its economic policy toward Moscow so completely in American hands, and certainly not to allow the United States to involve itself in open conflict with Russia. This contradiction flows from the very nature of strategic nuclear deterrence and is therefore not unique to Japan. The Japanese case is more severe, however, and it is that severity that places tensions on Japanese-American security relations. Tokyo might even be tempted, in an American-Soviet showdown, to back away from Washington just when the Soviet threat was at its height and when unanimity most important.

The second policy conclusion is a reflection of the first. In a nuclear crisis with the United States, originating outside of Asia, Moscow would feel constrained to do its utmost to assure Tokyo's neutrality in the ensuing conflict; indeed to do whatever possible to make sure Washington could not use Japanese facilities to launch an attack on the Far Eastern and Siberian portions of the

Soviet Union. The only way to do that would be to threaten use of nuclear weapons against Japan. And yet, that threat would not necessarily be credible, for what would the Kremlin gain by destroying Japanese cities? Additionally, this might risk driving Japan even further into the American embrace and thus precipitate the outcome such a policy of nuclear blackmail would be intended to avert. Therefore, for the Russians, as well as for the Japanese, the strategic situation drives decision makers into corners they do not wish to occupy. The most that can be said is that such stability as presently exists is precarious, and could evaporate in time of crisis. So despite great military power, the Soviet Union is not much better off, in such a situation, than would be Japan.

Current Japanese-Soviet Relations

Current Japanese-Soviet policy issues tend to flow from the historical and domestic situations of the two countries, and from the international political, economic, and security environment, as noted above. Only three issues are out-standing, of which two have been before the governments for many years. In all three instances, the static nature of Moscow-Tokyo concerns virtually guarantees little or no change in the years to come. Presuming no major change in the domestic and international settings, were new crisis to arise, Japanese-Soviet security relations need not be considered an important element in the overall Northeast Asia equation. Although such stability is likely, it is not in-evitable, as we will note in Section III.

The first current policy question is the Northern Islands issues. This issue has remained perhaps the most significant stumbling block between Tokyo and Moscow since 1945, when the Russians occupied the four islands of Kunashiri, Etorofu, Shikotan, and Habomai, off northeast Hokkaido. Although the legal situation is somewhat clouded, one might accurately assert that Moscow il-legally took these territories and should return them (as indeed the Soviets near-ly did, judging from negotiations in the early 1950s). Moscow only lightly defended these islands until the late 1970s, when, as part of a major Far Eastern buildup, tanks, helicopters, combat aircraft, and a full division of troops were introduced into the area. Forces have been augmented since, permanent fort-ifications built, and supply and logistic bases constructed. Obviously, the Rus-sians intend to remain there, the apparent purpose being to threaten Japan directly and to assure that the Kurile Islands defense chain (which transforms the Sea of Okhotsk into a kind of Russian lake) remains intact in time of war.[11]

Japan never recognized the legitimacy of the Soviet occupation, and conse-quently has not signed a peace treaty with Moscow. Lacking a peace treaty, a treaty of friendship and commerce cannot be initialed, thus severely limiting trade relations. The issue is emotional in Japanese politics, something the Liberal-Democratic Party has not been reticent in exploiting. The Nakasone government in particular has used this issue to stir up anti-Soviet feelings and to propel higher defense budgets (albeit still exceedingly low in relative terms) through the Diet. The Kremlin dares not return the islands, lest it admit that they were taken illegally in the first place, thus opening the Pandora's box of all Russian territorial seizures during and after World War II. Although there have been hints from time to time (the latest put forward by Soviet Foreign Minister Shevardnadze in January 1986) that talks might again be opened on the question, essentially the matter is frozen and will probably remain so in the future.

The Northern Islands question in recent years has also been linked with the second policy issue: How should the Japanese respond to the Soviet military buildup in Northeast Asia? The Soviet Union does not really need over 50 divisions, 1200 missiles, 2500 aircraft (including Backfire bombers), thousands of nuclear warheads, and more than 400 ships, merely to defend its Asian boundaries. The Kremlin's forces are configured for offensive operations and train at invading other countries. Japan, as well as most other Asian states, cannot be blamed for being concerned about Russian military potential, particularly since no single Asian military force could resist a determined Russian onslaught. The only hope is in organizing a common resistance, which is why the United States, Japan, and China are at least discussing the problem, and in the case of American-Japanese military cooperation, are beginning to act in response to the threat.[12]

What can, in fact, be done? The first task is to assess the threat accurately. In this regard, one should note that the actual projection force available to Moscow is relatively small, once forces configured for other duties are subtracted from Soviet totals. Thus, most of the ground force, and a high percentage of missiles, warheads, and aircraft are intended for use against China. These should moreover, be put into the column of deterrence, since the Soviet Union has no intention to attack China except at the end of a successful Third World War against the United States. Further, the some 30 nuclear ballistic missile submarines and their support ships, together with at least 120 SS-18 ICBMs located East of Lake Aikal, must also be subtracted from the total, since these are global strategic forces, under central Moscow control, directed against the United States. Finally, adjustment must be made for the unfavorable geography of the Western Pacific; a geography that forces the Soviet Far East Fleet to pass through narrow straits around Japan and Korea and to plow through (or not be able to pass at all) thick ice much of the year around Vladivostok and farther north. As a result, much of the Russian air arm, naval air, and navy in the region is in fact devoted to coastal defense and rarely ventures over broader Pacific expanses. This residual, relatively small, is much reduced from the oft-quoted massive totals for the Soviet Asian force.[13]

Such an accurate appraisal of Soviet forces must nevertheless conclude that this residual is a potent offensive force. It is also true that America, China, and Japan must plan and deploy their own forces to deter or deal with the entire Russian Asia force, not just a portion. But this raises the question: under what circumstances would the Soviet force be used? This is the second approximation to considering what Japan's role might be in countering the Soviet military threat. Four possibilities come to mind. First, the Russians might attack Japan directly. Japan could hardly hold out for long, and would have to appeal to the United States under the Security Treaty. Legally, America would have to respond, and would surely do so, as it is central to Washington's interests to keep Japan out of Russian hands. An attack on Japan is thus an attack on America, which would precipitate World War III. But Moscow would hardly risk all, merely to gain Japan. Such risk is particularly high for the sometimes mentioned "Hokkaido scenario," wherein the Kremlin would seize that portion of the Japan and then try to negotiate. If the first possibility is vanishingly small, the second, a Russian offensive against China, is also highly unlikely. Any such move would surely invite Chinese retaliation, including the use of nuclear weapons aimed at dozens of Russian cities. Moscow would not likely sacrifice a goodly portion of its population in exchange for the death of some hundred million Chinese, possibly a portion of Chinese territory, and a tight anti-Soviet global alliance involving all nations of consequence, led by America, lasting perhaps a century. A large-scale Sino-Soviet conflict is thus unthinkable, and both the Russians and Chinese understand this reality.[14]

A third possibility would be the spread to Asia of a Soviet-American conflict begun elsewhere, perhaps on the Central Front or in the Middle East. Such a conflict would in all probability be nuclear and involve an exchange of massive nuclear strikes at each other's homelands. Indeed, part of the American deterrent strategy against the Soviet Union is to station nuclear capable forces in the Far East ready to attack Asian portions of the Soviet Union. As we discuss below, some of these forces are in Japan and would thus serve to guarantee some sort of Japanese involvement.[15]

The last possibility involves escalation out of a Korean conflict. Given the potential Soviet role in supporting a Northern attack, Moscow would become more deeply involved. Since Japan would again serve as the staging base and rear area for American forces assisting the South, and since the prospects for nuclearization of the conflict at an early stage are not low, the probability of some kind of Soviet attack on American facilities in Japan cannot be ruled out. But as in the first case, an attack against Japan would bring into play the Security Treaty and, hence, World War III. Moreover, Moscow's direct involvement in a future Korean conflict is far from guaranteed; indeed, Russian representatives have often stated that the Soviet Union would seek to stay out. So even in this instance, the prospect for conflict involving Japan and the Soviet Union is quite low. In sum, if the prospect of Soviet military involvement in Asia is very small, against Japan the probability of Soviet attack is even less.

The third policy issue, if it can be called that, between Tokyo and Moscow is the recent Soviet diplomatic initiative in Asia and the "proper" Japanese response. Another way to pose this question is to ask: what is Japan's place in Russia's Asian *Weltanschauung*? Kremlin motives concerning Asia are a mixture of military defense centering on China, power projection throughout the region, care not to be drawn into conflicts (such as in Korea) not of its own choosing, advancing the cause of Soviet-oriented and (hopefully) Marxist-Leninist controlled revolutions, and doing whatever possible to usher the United States out of the region. Many particular tactics are possible in carrying out such a diverse strategy, and one should always keep in mind the best method to analyze the Russian military mentality is the chess analogy. The Soviet communist has a single long-term goal in mind, tends to think several moves ahead, considers the likely countermoves of his opponent along with his own, and makes each tactical foray an element in support of the broader strategy.

Thus, Russian purposes must be considered carefully when examining events such as the Soviet Foreign Minister's visit to Tokyo. Moscow cannot compete in this economic arena. The one element of change in Japanese foreign policy concerns China. Here the potential for further Japanese gains, in terms of markets and influence, is high. Some repair work is clearly in order, on the manner in which representatives of the two Asian giants approach each other on a personal level. But that work has already begun, and the march to the common drummer of rapid Chinese economic growth, and a large Japanese role therein, will continue. This trend can only spell further trouble for Moscow in Asia: a strong Japan closely associated with a strong China, and even more closely linked to a strong America—all highly anti-Soviet—means that the Kremlin is likely to remain frozen out of Northeast Asia. The only way the Soviets could break into the region is by force—very unlikely as we have seen—or by a thorough going alteration of the basics of the Soviet system—just as improbable, even under the comparatively forward-looking leadership of Mikhail Gorbachev.

Major Policy Issues of Concern

These three policy issues, all unresolvable, comprise what there is of current Japanese-Soviet relations. Were there no other matters of relevance, the topic could be closed off quickly and cleanly. Additional interesting issues do lurk just over the horizon, however, and these could alter the picture. Interestingly, all of them are in the national security area, in the restricted sense of the term. When inspected as a group, they have the potential for imparting a dynamism to the relationship that has, pleasantly, been absent for nearly four decades. We consider each briefly and then attempt to essay on what they might imply as a set.

1. *How to Deal with the SS-20s?* The Asian locations of Russian SS-20s pose a new and severe threat to all of Asia, including Japan. As of late 1985, some 207 of these mobile, three-warhead missiles were deployed east of the Urals at nearly 20 sites. In event of World War III or a major Sino-Soviet conflict, their

use could tip the conflict in favor of the Soviet Union. Moreover, their very presence in Asia has already led America and China to search for a response, which for the United States, could well involve Japan. The SS-20s have thus become a catalyst to the arms race in Asia. The most important consequences of their deployment and the Sino-American counters are three. First, by deployment, the Russians have managed to draw Asians even further together against Moscow. Already there have been joint Japanese-Chinese and Japanese-Indian declarations on the subject of how Asia fits into the military equation elsewhere, and warnings that Asian interests must be taken into consideration at the several American-Soviet arms talks. Second, the deployment has the effect of bringing the regional Asian balance of power into the European and global balances, for the first time in history. Henceforth, none of the concerned states at either end of the Eurasian land mass can conduct a military policy independent of how such policy affects the equation throughout the Northern Hemisphere. Third, the American response directly affects Japan and its security relations with the Soviet Union. The United States, wisely, eschewed the temptation to counter the SS-20s by deploying the American near-equivalent, the Pershing II, in South Korea. Rather, the response has been to trade on the American comparative advantage on the sea and in technology. Thus, the United States is deploying Tomahawk cruise missiles on ships in Asia and their air-launched equivalent on F-16s based in Japan and Korea. These deployments concern Japan since, in an American-Soviet conflict, American attacks against Vladivostok and other Soviet Pacific targets could be launched from Japanese territory or from American ships home-ported or outfitted in Japanese ports. Alternatively, American bases throughout Japan could be struck, in a pre-emptive attack, by Soviet Far East forces.[16]

2. *The Several Uses of Misawa.* The United States is in the process of deploying two squadrons of F-16 combat aircraft to a base at Misawa, in Northern Honshu. Their stated purpose is to help protect Japan from the very large increase in Russian offensive aircraft deployed to the Soviet Far East in the last decade. They will do that, but will also have two other missions. One is to be ready to fly to Korea in event of a North Korean invasion of the South. Their purpose would be to help turn back the invasion by first seeking air superiority, and then attacking North Korean ground targets. As mentioned above, the Soviet Union would try to stay out of a direct involvement in the conflict, even though Moscow would surely support the North with equipment and supplies, and might even give the green light for a Pyongyang invasion. If Moscow did become involved directly, there would be a temptation to try and blackmail Japan into prohibiting use of Misawa by American aircraft supporting the South. If American F-16s were transferred to Korea, and thus a gaping hole opened in Japanese air defenses, the Kremlin might demonstrate Japanese weakness by staging massive flights over the country or even shooting down a few Japanese fighters. The risks for all sides from such escalation would, of course, be high. Thus, the very presence of American aircraft in Misawa could,

in an escalating Korean scenario, act as a catalyst for (unwanted) Japanese involvement in direct conflict with the Soviet Union.

The third mission of the F-16s is to attack, directly and perhaps without warning, military targets along the Soviet Primoraskaya and ships in the Seas of Japan and Okhotsk. Such attacks could be in conjunction with a Soviet-American conflict elsewhere in the globe or as part of the escalation to World War III. Although in violation of the Japanese-American Security Treaty, the United States could always claim that a Soviet attack was imminent and that strikes were "defensive." Moscow could also make such claims, of course, and launch similar strikes at Misawa. One should note that the United States has placed F-16s at Misawa, among other purposes, as a potential offensive force against the Soviet Union in circumstances out of Japanese control, but nearly guaranteeing Japanese involvement in any major American-Soviet conflict. This further mission of the F-16s is not widely known either in America or Japan. Once this knowledge becomes generally known, a major fissure could open in defense ties between the two countries.

3. *The Changing American-Soviet Naval Balance in Asia.* What kind, and how many, ships should the United States deploy to counter the large increase in the Russian Far East fleet, and how should the Japanese Maritime Self-Defense Force (MSDF) be integrated into joint American-Japanese strategy vis-a-vis Moscow? If present trends on both the American and Russian sides continue, this balance, presently about equal if one includes the entire American Seventh Fleet (i.e., ships normally stationed in the Eastern Pacific and along the American West Coast), will turn increasingly in favor of the Soviet Union. While many elements enter into a net assessment of the balance, trends indicate that Moscow will eventually achieve overall preponderance in the Western Pacific. This is likely to be so even after the United States deploys an additional carrier task force to the regions, thus redressing the shortfall created by the absence, most of the time, of one of the two such forces normally assigned to the Western Pacific (that task force is more often in Southeast Asian waters or even farther distant, in the Indian Ocean). Perceiving that trend, Washington has been pressuring Tokyo to build up the MSDF faster and, of equal importance, to integrate Japanese activities with those of the Seventh Fleet into a joint anti-Soviet force using American war-fighting strategy. In practical terms, this means depending increasingly on the 40-60 Japanese destroyers, 15-plus submarines, and c.220 combat aircraft of the MSDF to patrol an area extending approximately 1000 miles out from Yokohama Bay. Given the near-instantaneous nature of modern warfare and the critical need to assure the security of forces at sea by keeping enemy ships, planes, and missiles at maximum distance, the probability of Japanese involvement in American or Soviet launched combat operations against the other is increasingly high. Such involvement would also be beyond the terms of the Security Treaty, to say nothing of the MSDF charter and the Japanese Constitution. In a crisis, Washington would likely find itself highly dependent on Japanese naval cooperation against Moscow. That could,

once again, open a major fissure between the two allies were Tokyo, as would seem likely, seek to disengage SDF forces. So at the least, the Soviet naval build-up, together with lack of a sufficiently adequate American response, tends to draw Japan more closely into the changing naval balance of power in the Western Pacific, where an American-Soviet maritime crisis might well precipitate an American-Japanese diplomatic explosion.[17]

Similar conclusions emerge when one adds the Chinese naval component into the overall picture. China now possesses the third largest navy in the world, one that has increasing blue water capability, that is growing in size, capability, and experience, and that is a spearhead of the emerging Chinese drive not merely to defend territory from the Russians but also to project Beijing's influence throughout Asia and more distant regions. Since the Soviet Union is the principal threat to China, Japan, and the United States, and given the Russian maritime buildup, there is pressure to draw the Chinese into the common American-Japanese effort. Although matters are still at a preliminary stage, staff talks have already begun between Washington and Beijing and exchanges of naval delegations (suitably disguised by the Japanese, who have sent retired naval officers) have occurred between Tokyo and Beijing. Washington thus acts as a linchpin in an emerging (although indirect) anti-Soviet Asian security system, which includes Japan as an indispensible component. Although this development is not well known in Japan, once it comes plainly into view, great domestic controversy will ensue, as will further difficulties in American-Japanese defense cooperation.[18]

4. *Mining the Straits.* As American naval superiority over the Soviet Union declines in Northeast Asia, the United States must depend increasingly on non-hardware factors. Among other possibilities, that means utilizing those geographic features of the region unfavorable to Moscow, especially the necessity suffered by Soviet ships of traversing the four straits around the Japanese islands. American naval strategy in Northeast Asia depends squarely on the capacity to close those straits by mines. However, the United States does not possess this capacity, to the extent necessary to do the job quickly at the beginning of an American-Soviet conflict, i.e., before the Soviet fleet breaks out into the open waters of the Pacific. The United States thus leans more and more heavily on the MSDF to perform this mining. However, the MSDF is not presently configured for that task nor would it automatically do so in event of an American-Soviet conflict.

Thus, for the foreseeable future, the Soviet navy can escape from the four straits-bottlenecks. However, Washington is pressing Tokyo to develop the necessary mine-laying capacity—both airborne and ship deployed. If the United States succeeds in that endeavor, military dependence on Japan will increase, as will American pressure for Japan to cooperate materially against the Soviet Union in an American-Soviet conflict. All this comes at a time of tension and contradiction in American-Japanese security relations. On one hand, Washington tries to pressure Tokyo into a posture of greater military activism.

On the other hand, Tokyo tries to make itself a bit more independent from the United States by resisting that pressure even as force levels are increased. Practical questions like mining the straits tend to exacerbate, and perhaps accelerate, differences.[19]

5. *The Self-Defense Force Buildup: Composition, Pace, Direction, and Magnitude.* As the United States becomes increasingly dependent on Japanese military power, correspondingly the characteristics of the Japanese Self-Defense Force (SDF) will be of greater consequence to regional security. As is well known, the rate of growth is reasonably rapid (c. 5-6 percent per year during the 1986-1991 Five Year Plan), but the numerical base for most weapons systems is quite low. The budget is only around $16.5 billion (Fiscal 1986 amount) and only 1 percent of gross national product. Weapon quality is, of course, very high, with the latest domestic or American (often domestically produced) equipment. These include tanks, PGMs, F-15s, P3Cs, destroyers and frigates, and an assortment of helicopters. In terms of budgets, the SDF is already the world's eighth largest military. Eventually, it should be capable of defending Japan and the surrounding waters out to a considerable distance—perhaps not to a thousand miles, however—against some kinds of Soviet attack. However, the SDF will never by capability or design, be able to defend Japan against the most determined Soviet attack, which would surely be nuclear.[20]

The SDF eventually will become of specific concern to the Russians, and will correspondingly become an ever more important element in overall American anti-Soviet strategy. As that trend continues, Tokyo will have greater leverage in Washington to obtain policy objectives from the United States. In short, Japan is slowly but clearly providing itself with a new instrument with which to bargain with America over economic policy issues. Once the Japanese force becomes reasonably strong, the tendency in both capitals will be to accelerate the linkage of economic and security issues, a wicked and potentially disastrous combination.

6. *Japan in a Broader Trans-Pacific Security Network.* In any formal sense, prospects are not high for construction of a trans-Pacific mutual security treaty or for a north-south arrangement combining the Association of Southeast Asian Nations (ASEAN), Japan, South Korea, Australia and New Zealand, and the United States. Nevertheless, an informal tendency exists in this direction, if only because of the threatening nature of the Soviet build-up. As this trend continues, the United States must intensify its hunt for regional military forces to help deter Soviet aggression. The trend will also accelerate to link, through the medium of augmented Soviet military power, security developments in Northeast and Southeast Asia. Washington will remain the center of any new security framework, formal or informal, since all lines of communication for these purposes must pass through the American capital.

Japan's task will be, first and foremost, to decide how deep a role should be played in Asian security questions, aside from self-defense, and independent of the United States. Currently there is no pressure to make such a decision. But with the growth of the SDF, the certain increase in American pressure to participate in anti-Soviet military plans and deployments, and perhaps even some rise in domestic support for the SDF, Japan could become a kind of leader in establishing an Asian-centered defense system. Certainly Tokyo would be a vital link between Northeast and Southeast Asia and, once China begins to use its burgeoning power, the Japanese will become an important participant in the inevitable recasting of the entire Asian security framework. Already Japan is the most important foreign economic power in Southeast Asia, thanks to healthy trade and aid policies. A strong political-diplomatic component, now absent but the product of progressive policy independence from Washington, could well contribute to a major restructuring of the Southeast Asian balance of power, even though Tokyo might deliberately elect not to depart significantly or publicly from American policy directions. Such a development could only add to Japanese-Soviet tensions.[21]

In the more immediate future, the probability of more-than-tacit Japanese cooperation with the United States (and perhaps China) in specific security-related circumstances is relatively high. But when those circumstances, as described in items 2-5 above, are summed, the multilateral security situation must be described in terms significantly different from the American and Soviet-centered system in place today. For example, consider the possibility of Japanese cooperation with the United States and South Korea to control the air and sea space over, on, and under the Sea of Japan. For reasons of culture, history, and nationalism, there is little prospect for establishment of a Japanese-Korean jointly-manned air defense system or an arrangement to monitor Soviet warships and submarines in that area. But prospects improve if the United States is included as a third party, standing between Tokyo and Seoul, and leading the way, diplomatically and materially, to construction of a unified communications and control net. Moscow would not approve, of course, and would complain to Tokyo. The upshot would be the emplacement of a further impediment to improvement of ties between the two countries.

7. *Other Linkages Between Japanese-Soviet Relations and Developments Elsewhere in Asia.* Situations and trends elsewhere in Asia will also affect the cast of Japanese-Soviet relations, as Tokyo and Moscow increase the degree of their respective involvements in the region. Four examples come to mind: the Philippines, Kampuchea, Camn Rahn Bay, and Afghanistan. In the Philippines, loss of the American bases at Subic Bay and Clark Field—a possibility after 1991—would represent a disaster for the American military position in Asia and possibly precipitate major shifts in the regional security equation. At a minimum Japan would have to brace itself for vastly increased American pressure to accept then-dispersed sea and air forces and to strengthen the SDF. Needless to say, Japanese-Soviet security relations would vary accordingly. Tokyo would have no capability to affect this situation, since the course of events in the Philippines, and the American role therein, are far outside Japan's influence.

In Indo-China, continued (and augmented) Soviet military presence in, and military assistance to, Vietnam enables that state to maintain its domination of Kampuchea and to threaten Thailand. As Japan becomes a more important player in non-Indo-Chinese Southeast Asia, and as Tokyo takes a more important security role in deterring the Soviet forward thrust, another obstacle to repairing Tokyo-Moscow relations emerges. Since the Kremlin is hardly likely to abandon a communist ally in that part of Asia, the only hope for avoiding difficulties over this question is to await a change for the worse in Hanoi-Moscow ties or improvement in Washington-Hanoi relations. Neither is impossible, but Tokyo policy makers would be ill-advised to hold their breaths in anticipation. The Soviet use of Camn Rahn Bay, to the extent that Soviet aircraft and ships pose a threat to American facilities in the Philippines (as they do), also worsens prospects for improvement in Tokyo-Moscow relations. The reason, obviously, is Japanese dependence on the United States for defense against Kremlin military initiatives. Since Japan is defended in part by American forces located in the Philippines, declination of American capabilities could only raise pressure on Tokyo to see more clearly to Japanese defense.

Although Afghanistan is far away from Japan, the seamless web of Asian security means that a change in the Southwest Asian balance of military power impacts directly on the equation elsewhere in the region. Thus, after 1979, not only did Japan put on hold further investment in Siberia (at American insistence), but also turned more receptive to Washington's campaign to construct a general anti-Soviet security net in Asia. Japanese-Soviet relations deteriorated accordingly. It should be noted that Tokyo's ties with New Delhi, previously almost invincible, have progressively emerged into view since the Soviet invasion, as India seeks to distance itself gradually from Moscow and cast its eye around Asia for sources of diplomatic support and economic assistance. Once again, Japanese-Soviet bonds have suffered a blow.[22]

8. *Japan and the Soviet Union in a New Korean War.* For several reasons, massive and lightning invasion of the South by North Korean forces is increasingly likely. One reason, unfortunately, is the recent Soviet propensity to seek improved ties with Pyongyang through transfer of more up-to-date military equipment to the North. In the Soviet case, aside from acting as a catalyst to North Korean invasion by supplying some of the requisite means, it is not impossible to reason that the Kremlin could well give the green light to Pyongyang, were a crisis with the United States elsewhere in the globe to heat up. Soviet leaders might reason that a new Korean War could divide American strength and thus lessen American pressure on Moscow. The Soviet Union would not have to participate directly in the conflict, instead, might simply remain on the side-lines and only resupply the North with replacements for destroyed equipment. The United States, however, could call the Kremlin's bluff and carry out strikes directly against Soviet supply bases.

Obviously a new Korean conflict would put a halt to any thought of improving Japanese-Soviet relations. Japan's role in the conflict would, at minimum,

repeat the performance of the 1950s: again acting as the rear area for Allied forces and as the *place d'arms* from which the United States would launch air and
sea sorties onto the Peninsula. However, Japan could be drawn more directly
into the battle, even if against its will. This would occur were either the United
States or the Soviet Union to escalate to a more direct confrontation—in which
case some of the scenarios discussed previously would come into play—or
were Japan to be enlisted by the United States to assist in sea and air control in
the Sea of Japan and farther out into the Pacific. The prospect of direct
Japanese-Soviet military clashes could not be ruled out in such circumstances.

Conclusion

Let us sum up the argument of this article. The situation, at least in terms of
analysis, is reasonably clear. Severe historic, domestic, and international constraints on Japanese—Soviet security relations for four decades have ruled out
any melioration of the relatively cold situation that emerged from World War
II. Those constraints are likely to persist and even grow in the years ahead. In
terms of current issues—the Northern Islands question, what to do about the
Soviet military build-up in Northeast Asia, and the proper response to Soviet
diplomatic initiatives—prospects are also poor for lessening the national
security standoff between Tokyo-Washington and Moscow. If the future were
limited to simply playing out of these issues, one might reasonably conclude
that the static and frozen situation of the present would continue.

But when specific over-the-horizon national security issues are considered,
trends immediately become dynamic. In each instance, more than marginal
change could occur. In some cases, major restructuring of the state of Asian and
Japanese-Soviet security affairs could result. The reasons are three: growing
Soviet military power; loosening American-Japanese ties; and emerging
fluidity in the Asian political, economic, and diplomatic arena. In such a
dynamic situation, past and current trends will not serve as guides to the national security policies Japan and the Soviet Union choose to pursue toward each
other. In particular, such a situation would only increase prospects that Japan
and the Soviet Union will stand more directly opposed to each other in military
matters. This potential dynamism could place the two states on opposite sides
of a shooting war. At least in Japan's case, Tokyo would bear little responsibility for the causes of the conflict, which would tend to stem from American
and Soviet initiatives. Upcoming national security issues could thus impart considerable change, and not a little danger, to Japanese-Soviet security relations.[23]

NOTES

1. For some previous literature on this subject, see Roger Swearingen, *The Soviet Union and Postwar Japan* (Stanford: Hoover Institution, 1978), Chapter 14; Donald S. Zagoria (ed.), *Soviet Policy in East Asia* (New Haven: Yale University Press, 1982), Chapter 10; Douglas T. Stuart and William T. Tow (eds.), *China, the Soviet Union, and the West* (Boulder: Westview Press, 1982), Part Two; Thomas W. Robinson, "Soviet Policy in Asia," in William E. Griffith (ed.), *The Soviet Empire: Expansion and Detente* (Lexington: D.C. Heath, 1976), pp. 285-337; Gerald Segal (ed.), *The Soviet Union in East Asia* (Boulder: Westview Press, 1983), Ch. 5; and Robert A. Scalpino (ed.), *The Foreign Policy of Modern Japan* (Berkeley: University of California Press, 1977), pp. 321-364.

2. See, *inter alia*, Richard Storry, *A History of Modern Japan* (Baltimore: Penguin Books, 1963); William G. Beasley, *The Modern History of Japan* (New York: Praeger, 1975); Edwin O. Reischauer, *Japan, The Story of a Nation* (New York: Knopf, 1970); Hugh Borton, *Japan's Modern Century* (New York: Penguin Books, 1970); and James B. Crowley (ed.), *Modern East Asia* (New York: Harcourt, Brace, and World, 1970).

3. Bhahani Sen Gupta, *Soviet-Asian Relations in the 1970s and Beyond (New York: Praeger, 1976; Harriet L. Moore, Soviet Far Eastern Policy, 1931*-1945 (Princeton: Princeton University Press, 1945); Ye. M. Zhukov et al. (eds.), *Mezhdunarodniye Otnosheniye na Dal 'nem Vostoke, 1945-1978* (Moscow: Nuisel, 1973); Adam Ulam, *Expansion and Coexistence* (New York: Praeger, 1974); Allen S. Whiting, *Siberian Development and East Asia* (Stanford: Stanford University Press, 1981); Herbert J. Ellison (ed.), *The Sino-Soviet Conflict* (Seattle: University of Washington Press, 1982): Donald S. Zagoria, *The Sino-Soviet Conflict, 1956-1961* (Princeton: Princeton University Press, 1962): C.G. Jacobsen, *Sino-Soviet Relations Since Mao* (New York: Praeger, 1981); O.B. Borisov and B.T. Koloskov (eds.), *Soviet-Chinese Relations*, 1945-1970 (Bloomington: Indiana University Press, 1975).

4. Edwin O. Reischauer, *The Japanese* (Cambridge, Mass.: Harvard University Press, 1978); Chie Nakane, *Japanese Society* (Berkeley, University of California Press, 1970); Nathaniel B. Thayer, *How the Conservatives Rule Japan* (Princeton: Princeton University Press, 1969); Gerald L. Curtis, *Election Campaigning, Japanese Style* (New York: Columbia University Press, 1971); Hugh Patrick and Henry Rosovsky (eds.), *Asia's New Giant: How the Japanese Economy Works* (Washington: The Brooking Institution, 1976).

5. Erik P. Hoffmann and Robbin F. Laird (eds.), *The Soviet Policy in the Modern World* (New York: Aldine, 1984); Robert F. Byrnes (ed.), *After Brezhnev* (Bloomington: Indiana University Press, 1983); David K. Shipler, *Russia* (New York: Penguin Books, 1984); Sewern Bialer, *Stalin's Successors*

(Cambridge: Cambridge University Press, 1980); Jerry F. Hough and Merle Fainsod, *How the Soviet Union is Governed* (Cambridge: Harvard University Press, 1979); Archie Brown and Michael Kaser (eds.), *Soviet Policy for the 1980s* (Bloomington: Indiana University Press, 1982); Stephen F. Cohen et al. (eds.), *The Soviet Union Since Stalin* (Bloomington: Indiana University Press, 1971); Erik P. Hoffmann (ed.), *The Soviet Union in the 1980s* (New York: The Academy of Political Science, 1984).

6. On Japanese foreign relations, in addition to the Scalapino volume see Lawrence Olson, *Japan in Postwar Asia* (New York: Praeger, 1970); Frank Langdon, *Japan's Foreign Policy* (Vancouver: University of British Columbia Press, 1973); John K. Emmerson, Arms, Yen, and *Power: The Japanese Dilemma* (New York: Dunellen, 1971); Morinosuke Kajima, *Modern Japan's Foreign Policy* (Tokyo: Tuttle, 1969), Donald C. Hellman, *Japan and East Asia: The New International Order* (New York: Praeger, 1972); and Takuya Kubo, "Security in Northeast Asia," in Richard Solomon (ed.), *Asian Security in the 1980s* (Cambridge, Mass.: Oelgeschlager, Gunn, and Hain, 1980), pp. 93-108.

7. Aside from the sources noted in (3) above, see William Hyland, "The Sino-Soviet Conflict: A Search for New Security Strategies," in Solomon (ed.), *Asian Security in the 1980s*, pp. 39-53; "The Soviet Union and East Asia," yearly articles in the January *Asia Survey* by T. W. Robinson, T. P. Thornton, and D.S. Zagoria, (1980-1986); Ivan Kovalenko, *Soviet Policy for Asian Peace and Security* (Moscow: Progress, 1980); Hiroshi Kimura, "Soviet Policies in the Asian Pacific Region: A Japanese Assessment," *Asian Affairs*, (Winter, 1985), pp. 21-38; Lawrence Zirling, "Soviet Policy on the Rim of Asia: Scenarios and Projections," *Asian Affairs*, (January-February 1982), pp. 135-146; John Michael Newman, Jr., "Soviet Strategies in Asia, (1977-1979)" *Asian Affairs*, (May-June 1980), pp. 305-311; W. Scott Thompson, "Regional Instability in Northeast Asia: Soviet Policy and the World Power Balance," *Conflict* (November 1979), pp. 327-240; Michael B. Goetz, "Soviet-Japanese Relations in Northeast Asia: A Century of Conflict and Tension," Maxwell Air Force Base, Alabama, Air War College Research Report No. 347, (April, 1978); Joseph G. Wehlen, *The Soviet Union in the Third World, 1980-1985: An Imperial Burden or Political Asset?* (Washington, D.C.: House Committee on Foreign Affairs, 1985); Paul Dibb, "Soviet Capabilities, Interests, and Strategies in East Asia in the 1980s," *Survival*, (July-August 1982), pp. 155-162; Rajan Menon, "The Soviet Union in East Asia" *Current History* (October 1983), pp. 313-317ff; Norman D. Palmer, "Soviet Perspectives on Peace and Security in Asia," *Asian Affairs*, (September-October 1981), pp. 1-19.

8. Edward F. Denison and William K. Chung, *How Japan's Economy Grew So Fast* (Washington, D.C.: The Brookings Institution, 1976); Chalmers Johnson, *MITI and the Japanese Miracle* (Palo Alto: Stanford University Press, 1982); James C. Abegglen, *The Strategy of Japanese Business* (Cambridge,

Mass.: Ballinger, 1984); Alec Nove, *The Soviet Economic System* (London: Allen and Unwin, 1978); Alex Nove, *An Economic History of the USSR* (New York: Penguin Books, 1976); Marshall Goldman, *The USSR in Crisis: The Future of an Economic System* (New York: W.W. Northon, 1983); Peter Wile, *Communist International Economics* (New York: Harcourt Brace Jovanovich, 1970); Robert Scalapino (ed.), *The Foreign Policy of Modern Japan, op. cit.*, pp. 2-5-318; Kazuo Ogawa, "Japanese- Soviet Economic Relations: Present Status and Future Prospects," *Journal of Northeast Asian Studies*, (March 1983), pp. 3-16; Japan, Ministry of International Trade and Industry, White Paper on International Trade (Tokyo; annually); *Far Eastern Economic Review*, Asian Handbook (Hong Kong, annually). The last two sources list trade statistics.

9. Swearingen, *The Soviet Union and Postwar Japan, op. cit.*, Part 9; Gerald L. Curtis, "The Tyumen Old Development Project and Japanese Foreign Policy Decision-Making," in Scalapino, *The Foreign Policy of Modern Japan, op. cit*, pp. 147-174.

10. *Adelphi Papers* 133-134, 144-145, 150, and 187- 188, respectively; "Precision Guided Munitions", by James Digby; "The Diffusion of Power; New Conventional Weapons and East-West Security; Soviet Perspectives on Security," by William Hyland and Helmut Sonnenfeldt; and Soviet Tactical Nuclear Forces, by Stephen M. Myer; Albert Legault and George Lindsey, *The Dynamics of the Nuclear Balance* (Ithaca: Cornell University Press, 1976); Seymour J. Deitchman, *New Technology and Military Power* (Boulder: Westview Press, 1979); Franklin D. Margiotta and Ralph Sanders, *Technology, Strategy, and National Security* (Washington: NDU Press, 1985); Ilena Kass and Michael J. Deane, "The Role of Nuclear Weapons in the Modern Theater Battlefield: The Current Soviet View," *Comparative Strategy*, No. 3, (1984), pp. 193-213; Philip A. Petersen and John G. Hines, "The Conventional Offensive in Soviet Theater Strategy," *Orbis*, (Fall 1983), pp. 695-739; Richard K. Betts, "Conventional Deterrence: Predictive Uncertainty and Policy Confidence," *World Politics*, (January, 1985), pp. 153-179; S. Neil MacFarlane, "The Soviet Conception of Regional Security," *World Politics*, (April, 1985), pp. 295-343; Michael M. May, "The United States-Soviet Approach to Nuclear Weapons," *International Security*, (Spring 1985), pp. 140-152.

11. Tetsuya Kataoka, "Japan's Northern Threat," *Problems of Communism*, (March-April 1984), pp. 1-16; K. Andreyev and K. Chervko, "Fact and Fiction About the Northern Territories," *International Affairs* (Moscow, April 1983), pp. 108-114; Pierre Fistie, "Le Probleme Territorial des Kouriles du Sed dans les Relations Nippo-Sovietieqes." *Etudes Internationales*, (March 1982), p. 23-52; Swearingen, *The Soviet Union and Postwar Japan, op cit.*, Chapter 13; John J. Stephen, *The Kurile Islands: Russo-Japanese Frontiers in the Pacific* (Oxford: Clarendon Press, 1979); John J. Stephen, "The Kurile Islands: Japan and Russia," *Pacific Community*, (April 1976); John A. Harrison, *Japan's Northern Frontier: A Preliminary Study in Colonization and Expansion with Special*

Reference to the Relations of Japan and Russia (Gainsville; University of Florida Press, 1953); Japan, Ministry of Foreign Affairs, *The Northern Territory Issue: Japan's Position on Unsettled Questions* (Tokyo: Public Information Bureau, 1968) et. seq.; Fuji Kamiya, "The Northern Territories: 130 Years of Japanese Talks with Czarist Russian and the Soviet Union," in Zagoria (ed.), *Soviet Policy in East Asia*, ops. cit., pp. 121-152; n.a., *A Border Yet Unresolved: Japan's Northern Territories* (Tokyo: Northern Territories Issue Association, 1981).

12. The two best listings of Soviet military strength in Asia are *The Military Balance* (London: International Institute for Strategic Studies, annually) and *Asian Security* (Tokyo: Research Institute for Peace and Security, annually).

13. *Defense of Japan* (Tokyo: The Japan Times, 1977- , annually); Dennis Warner, "Japanese Perceptions of the Soviet Threat," *Atlantic Community Quarterly*, (Spring, 1980), pp. 80-84; Colin S. Gray, *The Geopolitics of the Nuclear Era: Heartland, Rimlands, and the Technological Revolution* (New York: Crane, Russak, 1977); Franklin B. Weinstein (ed.), *U.S.-Japan Relations and the Security of East Asia* (Boulder: Westview, 1978), Chapters by James W. Morley and Makato Momoi, pp. 49-92; Norman Polmar, *Soviet Naval Power: Challenge for the 1970s* (New York: Crane, Russak, 1974); *Understanding Soviet Naval Developments* (Washington, D.C.: Office of the Chief of Naval Operations, 1978); Michael McGwire and John McDonald (eds.), *Soviet Naval Influence* (New York: Praeger, 1977); Robert W. Herrick, *Soviet Naval Strategy: Fifty Years of Theory and Practice* (Annapolis, MD: U.S. Naval Institute, 1968); Sergei G. Gorshkov, *Sea of Power of the State* (Moscow: Military Publishing House, 1976).

14. Lilita I. Dzirkals, *"Lightning War" in Manchuria: Soviet Military Analysis of the 1945 Far Eastern Campaign* (Santa Monica, Calif.: The Rand Corporation, 1976).

15. After some years of classified-only discussion, the so-called "Maritime Strategy" was mentioned officially in public print in early 1986. Its outlines have been known for some time, however, as per this discussion. See Admiral James D. Watkins, *The Maritime Strategy* (Annapolis, MD.: U.S. Naval Institute, January 1986); Robert W. Komer, "Maritime Strategy vs. Coalition Defense," *Foreign Affairs*, (Summer 1982), pp. 1124-1144; Colin S. Gray, "Maritime Strategy," *U.S. Naval Institute Proceedings,* (February, 1986), pp. 34-42; Charles E. Morrison (ed.), *Threats to Security in the Pacific Basin* (Lexington: Heath, 1984); Martin Weinstein (ed.), *Northeast Asian Security After Vietnam* (Urbana: University of Illinois Press, 1982); Marian Leighton, "Soviet Strategy Toward Northern Europe and Japan," *Survey,* (Autumn-Winter 1983), pp. 112-151; U. Alexis Johnson et al, *The Common Security Interests of Japan, the United States, and NATO* (New York: Ballanger, 1981); Michael Howard, "On Fighting a Nuclear War," *International Security,* (Spring 1981), pp. 3-15; Thomas Powers, "Choosing a Strategy for World War III," *Atlantic,* (Novem-

ber 1982), pp. 82-110; Colin S. Gray, "War-Fighting for Deterrence," *Journal of Strategic Studies,* (March 1984), pp. 5-281; William T. Tow, "NATO's Out-of Region Challenges and Extended Containment," *Orbis,* (Winter 1985), pp. 829-856.

16. *Defense of Japan, op cit.,* for 1982, 1983 and 1984; *Report of the Secretary of Defense, op cit.,* for 1983; and *Strategic Survey* (London: International Institute of Strategic Studies, 1982); Dennis M. Gormley, "A New Dimension to Soviet Theater Strategy," *Orbis,* (Fall 1985), pp. 537-565; Jennie A. Stevens and Harry S. Marsh, "Surprise and Deception in Soviet Military Thought," *Military Review,* (June 1982), pp 2-11 and (July, 1982), pp. 24-35; William F. Scott, *Soviet Sources of Military Doctrine and Strategy* (New York: Crane, Russak, 1975).

17. Harry Train, "The Growing Soviet Naval Menace," *Atlantic Community Quarterly,* (Spring, 1981), pp. 50-62; Allen S. Whiting, "Major Power Threats to Security in Asia," (draft, March, 1984), 39 pages; Anthony H. Cordesman, "The Western Naval Threat to Soviet Military Dominance: A Soviet Assessment," *Armed Forces Journal,* (April 1983), pp. 45; James M. Garrett, "Conventional Force Deterrence in the Presence of Theater Nuclear Weapons, *Armed Forces and Society,* (Fall 1984), pp. 59-83; Desmond Ball, "Nuclear War at Sea," *International Security,* (Winter 1985-1986), pp. 3-31.

18. Bruce Swanson, *Eighth Voyage of the Dragon: A History of China's Quest for Seapower* (Annapolis, MD: Naval Institute Press, 1982), which provides an extensive bibliography.

19. The Japanese Maritime Self-Defense Force is configured largely for anti-submarine warfare. But the same ships, aircraft, and helicopters can also carry out mine laying. The American Navy does not have the requisite capability in Western Asian waters, and the American drive has been to push the Japanese into acquiring the mines in sufficient quantity and then practice with American forces in perfecting techniques.

20. John Endicott, *Japan's Nuclear Option* (New York: Praeger, 1975); James Buck, "Japan's Defense Policy," *Armed Forces and Society,* (Fall 1981); Osamu Kaihara, "Japan's Defense Structure and Capability," *Asia Pacific Community,* (Spring 1981); Taketsugu Tsurutani, "Japan's Security, Defense Responsibilities, and Capabilities," *Orbis,* (Spring 1981), pp. 89-106; Mike M. Mochizuki, "Japan's Search for Stragey," and Masashi Nishihara, "Expanding Japan's Credible Defense Role," *International Security,* (Winter 1983-1984), pp. 152-205; S. Modenov, "Remilitarization of Japan," *International Affairs* (Moscow), (February 1982), pp. 134-155; Kamija Fugi, "Japan's Postwar Security and Defense Policy," *Asian Forum,* (Spring-Summer 1979), pp. 1-8; Yukio Satoh, *The Evolution of Japanese Security Policy* (London: International Institute of Strategic Studies, Adelphi Paper 178, 1982); Larry A. Niksch, "Japan's Defense Policy: Suzuki's Shrinking Options," *Journal of Northeast*

Asian Studies, (June, 1982), pp. 79-95; Martin E. Weinstein, "Japan's Defense Policy and the May 1981 Summit," *Journal of Northeast Asian Studies,* (March 1982), pp. 23-34; Hisahiko Okasaki, "Japan's Security Policy: A Time for Strategy," *International Security,* (Fall 1982), pp. 188-196.

21. J.W.M. Chapman et al., *Japan's Quest for Comprehensive Security* (New York: St. Martin's 1983); Taketsugu Tsurutani, *Japanese Policy and East Asian Security* (New York: Praeger, 1981); Yukio Satoh, "Le Japan et sa Defense," *Politique Entrangere,* (December 1981), pp. 823-836; Wolf Mendl, "The Security Debate in Japan," *International Affairs* (London), (Autumn 1980), pp. 607-621; Francis J. West, Jr., "U.S. Japanese Defense Cooperation and United States Policy," (statement to U.S. Congress, House Sub-Committee on Asian and Pacific Affairs, March 1, 1982); Yatsuhiro Nakagawa, "The WEPTO Option: Japan's New Role in East Asian/Pacific Collective Security," *Asian Survey,* (August 1984), pp. 828-839; William M. Carpenter and Stephen P. Gibert, "Japanese Views on Defense Burden-Sharing," *Comparative Strategy,* (Fall 1982), pp. 36-51.

22. Robert W. Barnett, *Beyond War: Japan's Concept of Comprehensive National Security* (New York: Pergamon, 1984); Tetsuya Kataoka, Waiting for a 'Pearl Harbor': Japan Debates Defense (Stanford, CA: Hoover Institution, 1981); S. Modenov, "USSR-Japan: Looking Ahead," *International Affairs* (Moscow), (March 1985), pp. 80-83; V. Ryzhov, "The USSR and Japan," *International Affairs* (Moscow), (August 1982), pp. 28-36; V. Dalnev, "Impediments to Soviet-Japanese Relations," *International Affairs* (Moscow), (February 1981), pp. 49-53; Yukio Satoh, "Western Security: A Japanese Point of View," *Naval War College Review,* (September-October 1983); Ellen Frost, *U.S.-Japanese Security Relations in the 1980s and Beyond,* U.S.-Japan Advisory Commission, (September, 1984), 40 pages; Taketsugu Tsurutani, "Old Habits, New Times: Challenges to Japanese-American Security Relations," *International Security,* (Fall 1982), pp. 175-187; Hiroshi Kitamura, Ryohei Murata, and Hisanhiko Okasaki, *Between Friends: Japanese Diplomats Look at Japanese-U.S. Relations* (New York: Weatherhill, 1985); Stephen Gibert, "Northeast Asian in American Security Policy," in William T. Tow and William R. Feeney (eds.), *U.S. Foreign Policy and Asian-Pacific Security: A Transregional Approach* (Boulder: Westview, 1982).

23. Susan L. Clark, "The Soviets and Japan's Defense Efforts," Soviet Union, forthcoming 1986, is a goldmine of Soviet sources. For further reading, the writings of Hiroshi Kimura are indispensible. See his "The Soviet Proposal on Confidence-Building Measures and the Japanese Response," *Journal of International Affairs,* (Summer 1983), pp. 81-104; "Recent Japanese-Soviet Relations: From Clouded to 'Somewhat Crystal'," *Journal of Northeast Asian Studies,* (March 1982), pp. 3-22; *Soviet Policy Toward Japan,* (Brown University Center for Foreign Policy Development, 1983), 51 pages; "Japanese-Soviet Relations: Framework, Developments, Prospects," *Asian Survey,* (July, 1980),

pp. 707-725; "The Love-Hate Relationship with the Polar Bear: Japanese Feelings Toward the Soviet Union," *Japan Quarterly*, (January-March 1981), pp. 39-44; "Soviet Policy Toward Asia Under Chernenko and Gorbachev: A Japanese Perspective," *Journal of Northeast Asian Studies*, (Winter 1985), pp. 45-66; and "The Soviet Military Buildup: Its Impact on Japan and Its Aims," in Richard H. Solomon and Masataka Kosaka (eds.), *The Soviet Far East Military Buildup: Nuclear Dilemmas and Asian Security* (Dover: Auburn House, 1986).

CHAPTER 4

The Politics of Japanese Defense

Michio Umegaki

The Japanese have continuously debated their defense policy since they regained their independence in 1952. In fact, defense policy has never left the center of the political vortex, drawing defense specialist and non-specialists alike in perhaps the most divisive of all partisan debates in postwar Japan. However, a sense of incongruity has emerged among many Japan-watchers as they observe the intense political debate on defense co-existing with the appearance of no significant change in defense posture. The improving economy has only aggravated this incongruity as expectations have risen for a Japan more willing to project its political presence. But observers are met by a continuing Japan's reluctance to increase the role of military in defense of its own, and this presents an intriguing puzzle for political scientists, historians, and strategists of all persuasions. Is Japan merely a "cipher in international affairs?" Is Japan still deep in a "slumber" since the defeat in World War II? Where does Japan's "politophobia" come from? How could a nation with an economy surpassed only by the United States and the Soviet Union remain so oblivious to the concerns of *realpolitik*?[1]

What is often missing in these characterizations of Japan, however, is attention to the manner by which the ruling Conservatives (merged into the Liberal-Democrats in 1955) have faced and reconciled themselves to this incongruity. After all, it is the Conservatives who have neutralized the pressures to correct this apparent incongruity. The Conservative-led governments, enjoying a staying power unmatched by any other ruling party in the industrial democracies, have perpetuated this situation without allowing it to cause any serious strain in the political system. Thus, a search for the sources of this resilient incongruity, or for its change, would have to be made into the Conservatives and their management of policy.

This analysis[2] offers a deceptively simple proposition: the incongruity originates in the Conservatives' monopoly of power during the crucial decade from the late 1940s to the 1950s. The Conservatives' efforts to remain in power since then have led to an aggressive economic growth policy combined with conspicuously passive defense posture. The efforts have involved the cumbersome tasks of creating the coalition of factions within so as to stabilize the party-government relationship, and of defusing the particularly divisive issue of defense confronting Japan at the closing years of the Allied Occupation. The efforts have resulted in moderating the impact of changes in the international and domestic environments before they could generate corresponding changes in defense policy. Consequently, the subsequent decades of the 1960s, the 1970s, and even the 1980s have witnessed a Japan slow to react to some of the changes in the international environment, and reluctant to translate its economic power into a corresponding political presence. But the reluctance is, in fact, nothing but a testimony to the successful efforts by the ruling conserva-tives to stay in power.

The Postwar Origins of Defense Issue

That the Conservatives were in power at the recovery of Japan's sovereign status is of utmost significance to Japan's subsequent defense policy. The Con-servatives have not been able to dislodge the issue of Japan's national security from the unique political chemistry of that time. This chemistry was the crea-tion of complex interplay among three key factors: The particular political climate of Japan at the end of the Allied occupation; the Constitution of 1947 with its famous non-war clause; and the original U.S.-Japanese Security Pact of 1951.

The political climate of Japan of the late 1940s and the early 1950s emerged from the intense national engagement in cleansing Japan of its recent, militarist past. The purge of military, business, and political leaders, the denunciation of emperor's divinity, and the trials of the "war criminals" amounted to staging a show in which not only the militarist Japan of the 1930s and 1940s but also much of the preceding decades of rapid modernization were condemned. A result was a peculiar void in the identity of the nation. For the Japanese, their own past was not allowed to recede; rather, it became the point of departure, the distance from which would indicate to them how successful their efforts of remaking Japan were. The Constitution of 1947, with the articles highlighting the popular sovereignty and denouncing the possession of "war potentials," was a particularly significant document. It confirmed the national pledge to renounce anything remotely resembling the earlier militarist Japan.[3]

The two other political documents, signed by Yoshida Shigeru-led Conser-vatives in 1951, rendered this climate ripe for political polarization. The first was the Peace Treaty, with some 40 allies of the United States, that restored Japan's sovereignty. The Second, with the United States alone, was the U.S.-Japanese Security Pact, an opportune arrangement for both, given that the Korean War was raging less than a few hundred miles away. Yet, the Peace Treaty did not fully correct Japan's anomalous status from the preceding five years of the Allied occupation. After all, Japan was still in the state of war with the Soviet Union, denied its membership in the key international organizations, and allowed to retain only residual sovereignty over Okinawa. The Security Pact, too, contained serious problems. In fact, the suspicion ran deep among the Japanese that the Pact might do serious damage to the sovereign status the Peace Treaty had just restored, because of a clause allowing the United States to interfere with Japan's domestic unrest when deemed necessary.[4]

Thus, the Conservatives were met with reactions far from uniformly positive, instead of enjoying the credit for regaining the sovereign status for Japan. At issue was the consistency between these two documents and the Constitution of 1947. Already critical of the Peace Treaty, which did not include the People's Republic of China and the Soviet Union, the critics feared that the two agreements drew Japan into the vortex of the Cold War, diminishing the possibility for Japan to remain neutral and to promote its pacifist stance as projected in the 1947 Constitution. The Pact was suspected of evading the provisions of the Constitution that stressed non-violent and multilateral conflict resolution. The Progressives, especially the Socialists, were vehement in protesting that the Security Pact was the violation of the Article 9 of the Constitution, as the Pact allowed the presence of fighting forces on Japanese soil whose use in Japan and elsewhere in East Asia was strictly under U.S. control. The Progressive's argument might appear contrived,[5] but it voiced the fear of many Japanese of being drawn into an international conflict over which they had little control.

The Progressives' challenge to the constitutionality of these two political documents had a profound influence on the management of Japan's postwar defense policy. A strong Conservative backing of the agreements purely on the basis of Japan's security needs would have made them vulnerable to the Progressives' far more potent and broader attack on the Conservatives' dubious commitment to the emerging national concern with making a clear break from the past, militarist Japan. Thus an important precedent was set: the defense issue was to engage the Conservatives in the efforts to defend their commitment to the promotion of the Constitution.

At the same time, these two political documents and the Progressives' reactions also offered political opportunities to be exploited by the Conservatives. They allowed the Conservatives to sustain what has later come to be known as the "Yoshida doctrine," a political framework for a pacifist-commercialist Japan, shrewdly designed by premier Yoshida and his lieutenants to take advantage of the United States' interest in protecting a newly independent Japan.

Prior to the signing of the two documents, various policy pronouncements from Washington had indicated that the United States' interest in protecting Japan as its ally might take precedence over its interest in a pacifist Japan. Furthermore, already committed to the economic recovery of Western Europe with the Marshall Plan in 1948, the United States appeared to be willing more to insure a stable industrial Japan than to create an active military alliance partner, if such were the only two choices to choose from.[6] The culmination of these indications was the enunciation in January of 1950 of the short-lived Asian

Defense Perimeter, by which the United States defined the line of U.S.'s Asian interest to be drawn from the Aleutians, through the Japanese archipelago, to the Philippines, excluding Korea and Taiwan.

These indications were of the utmost significance to the Conservatives in the late 1940s, who were preoccupied with the prompt recovery of Japan's independent status which was deemed urgent to the recovery of the faltering economy. To the Yoshida-led Conservatives, the emerging Cold War, and not the successful completion of postwar transformation of Japan, was the key factor in prompting the United States to end the Occupation. At the same time, the emerging Cold War in Asia, with the establishment of the People's Republic of China in 1949, cast a cloud of uncertainty over the timing of an early peace treaty. The United States might argue, it was feared, that an independent Japan without military forces would be certain to fall victim of the expanding communist forces.[7] Thus, the course of action for the Conservatives would have to lead Japan to regain the sovereign status promptly, without allowing the United States to use Japan's inability to defend itself as the pretext for delaying a peace treaty. Thus prepared was the "secret message" of Yoshida, a key document behind the Security Pact, communicated to the United States by Ikeda Hayato in April of 1950:

> The Government of Japan hopes to conclude a peace treaty, at the earliest possible opportunity. With such a peace treaty it would be still necessary to station the U.S. armed forces in Japan in order to insure the security of Japan and Asia. If the United States found it difficult to request [the stationing of its forces in Japan itself, the Government of Japan would be prepared to examine the ways in which Japan could initiate the request. We have been examining the opinions of the specialists of the Constitution on this matter. Their arguments indicate that the inclusion of a clause in a peace treaty requesting the stationing of the U.S. armed forces would be less problematic constitutionally, and that an independent and separate request for the stationing of the U.S. armed forces would still not be against the Constitution.[8]

In Yoshida's calculation, the signing of the two documents of 1951 would create the conditions necessary to promote his most urgent goal of economic improvement, with a minimum of financial and political strain in defending Japan. The Conservatives were to take advantage both of the United States' unwavering commitment to protect Japan *regardless* of Japan's readiness to arm itself, and of the Progressives' pressure to protect the Constitution as leverage to defuse U.S. pressure to remilitarize Japan. Ironically, the Cold War strengthened Yoshida's position, for the Cold War intensified the Progressives' constitutional argument for Japan's disengagement from the emerging bipolar division in East Asia, on the one hand, and deepened the need for a stable and friendly Japan for the United States, on the other.

Thus began the broad framework for Japan's postwar security policy, whereby the ruling Conservatives have balanced domestic pressures for minimum defense with U.S. pressure for a more positive defense and a fuller participation of Japan as an ally in the bipolar international political system. However, as will be shown below, the "Yoshida doctrine" never fully established itself as the uncontested policy orthodoxy among the Conservatives. The doctrine owes its survival as much to its own merits as it does to the internal conditions of the Conservative policy orthodoxy. If anything, the survival of the doctrine has taken place in a peculiar void in which the Conservatives have consciously avoided, due to its factional divisions, the refinement, reexamination, and review of the doctrine against the changing political and economic conditions within and without Japan.

The Conservatives and the First Liberal-Democratic Government

The Conservatives in the late 1940s and the early 1950s were in disarray, constantly challenged by the Progressives from the outside and threatened by the unstable relationship among themselves from within. Slapped with the purge orders from the Occupation authorities, the conservative parties of prewar origins such as the Jiyuto and the Shimpoto were without their leading parliamentarians for some time. The Shimpoto lost nearly 95 percent of their members to the purge in January of 1946.[9] The Jiyuto lost Hatoyama Ichiro, the key figure in its postwar resurrection, just when Hatoyama was about to form his government on the strength of the party's election victory in the spring of 1946. Hatoyama's makeshift replacement was Yoshida Shigeru, chosen in part due to his wartime criticism of General Tojo and his pro-Anglo-American leaning prior to the Pacific War. Yoshida's government was to be a caretaker government in the interim of Hatoyama's absence, and Yoshida was expected to rely on the party strength which Hatoyama claimed the credit for.[10]

However, Yoshida quickly proved that he was far more skillful than was expected of a former diplomat. He demonstrated an infighter's instinct in steering his political survival through a maze created by the rising Progressive political forces (such as the labor-backed Socialists), the reform-weary business leaders, and the Occupation authorities who appeared divided between the reform-minded New Dealers and McArthur's loyal followers.[11] Yoshida's astuteness was also evident in his successful recruitment to the Jiyuto of a score of able government bureaucrats including Ikeda Hayato and Sato Eisaku.[12] Yoshida's recruitment compensated for the weak basis of his own power within the Jiyuto, even at the cost of increasing suspicion among Hatoyama's followers that Yoshida was there to stay.

Given this background, the two documents of 1951 had a profound impact upon the internal relationship among the Conservatives. They gave Yoshida and his followers all the credit for ending the Occupation, just when Hatoyama was expected to return to public life and end Yoshida's interim government. Thus the two documents placed Yoshida in a precarious position within the Conservative camp, allowing him, on the one hand, to enjoy the successful ending of the Occupation, while forcing him, on the other, to face the challenge of the legitimate leader of the Conservatives, Hatoyama Ichiro.

In addition, both documents were not without certain problematic implications for Japan's new sovereign status. In fact, some among the Conservative ranks even joined the Progressives in voicing the suspicion that the two documents might extend the *de facto* occupation by the United States. This Conservative challenge to the Yoshida doctrine was further intensified when it was joined by the Hatoyama followers who were eager to justify Hatoyama's return to his rightful place within the Conservative camp by distancing him from Yoshida's achievements.[13] What was apparent at the signing of the two documents was the likelihood that the Yoshida doctrine could become the catalyst for partisan division within the ranks of the Conservatives, rather than becoming a source for unity.

The end of the Occupation did little to moderate the internal divisions among the Conservatives. The next few years were punctuated with incessant alignments and realignments among different factions of the Conservatives. The divisions deepened with the return of scores of prewar political leaders to public life. In addition to Hatoyama and his followers, Kishi Nobusuke, among others, also began his postwar political career with a certain distance both from Hatoyama and Yoshida. Consequently, it took a challenge as formidable as the merger of the Left and Right Socialists in 1955 for the Conservatives to form the unified Liberal-Democratic Party.

Such a fluidity cast the Yoshida doctrine into the political vortex in which the major issue revolved around who would claim the legitimate Conservative leadership for post-Occupation Japan. Having just completed the successful campaign to end the Occupation, Yoshida was hardly willing to step down. If anything, he was even more committed to insuring Japan's domestic improvement and to settling some of the issues which the Peace Treaty had left unresolved. Rallying around him were some of the younger Conservatives, including future premiers Ikeda Hayato and Sato Eisaku, united in defense of the Yoshida doctrine and committed to completing the tasks of domestic improvement which now appeared far more feasible than before. The Conservatives critical of Yoshida leadership found a rallying point in Hatoyama Ichiro. Some of them, only recently depurged, felt that the governing powers had unduly eluded Hatoyama since the spring of 1946, and thus sought the source of their unity in challenging the Yoshida group of former bureaucrats. Others, including Kishi, infused into the challenge to Yoshida-led Conservatives their own policy preference at odds with Yoshida's pacifist-commercialist Japan. Hatoyama himself, exploiting the increasing anti-Yoshida sentiment within the ranks of the Conservatives, marked his return to public life by announcing his preference in 1952 for rearmament of Japan, the revision of the Constitution and the correction of the unilateral reliance on the United States.[14] Eventually, Yoshida, amidst the dwindling popularity, lost the contest for premiership in 1954 to Hatoyama. He subsequently left his group to the collective leadership of a handful of loyal lieutenants and saw the establishment of the Liberal-Democratic Party in 1955 under Hatoyama's leadership.

The significance of the Yoshida-Hatoyama contest in the crucial years between 1951 and 1955 goes beyond the ousting of the very architect of the basic political framework for post-Occupation Japan. It lies, also, in the obscuring of distinctions in the power struggle between two issues, the Yoshida doctrine of pacifist-commercialism and the power politics for the Conservative hegemony. Any attempt to forge a winning, anti-Yoshida coalition within the Conservatives had to challenge the Yoshida doctrine; and any attempt to tamper with the Yoshida doctrine easily opened up a partisan division within the Conservatives, as such an attempt helped to solidify the Yoshida loyalists. Thus, the Yoshida doctrine emerged as the focal point during the crucial years of Japan's postwar political development because the doctrine was deeply entrenched in the Liberal-Democrats' internal politics and not because it was the Conservatives' accepted political orthodoxy.

The merging of all these groups of the Conservatives into one party in 1955 therefore promised to produce an unpredictable political dynamics. The Convention for the Preparation of the New Party in October of 1955 was the testimony to the difficulty in instilling the unity among the Conservatives. The Yoshida supporters demanded the election of the new party president, and the Hatoyama supporters assumed that Hatoyama, the premier, was slated to become the president of the new Party as well. The stalemate resulted in an arrangement at odds with the principle of the party government: Hatoyama remained as premier even though the party basis for his government now changed drastically. Consequently, the new Party was run by several acting chairman (including Hatoyama himself), without its own party president for the time being. A strong assumption was allowed to float that, in due time, Hatoyama would have to hold the party convention to select its first party president.[15]

Thus, the internal conditions of the new party deprived its first premier of the political leverage to create the support with which to stabilize the relationship between the party and its first government. More significantly, such conditions made it virtually impossible for Hatoyama to extricate the policy issues from the power politics of the party chieftains. Regardless of Hatoyama's efforts to project his preference of revising the Constitution, rearming Japan, and projecting more autonomy from the United States,[16] he could not avoid the charge that he was the challenge to Yoshida and his followers, and thus to the Yoshida doctrine. In turn, Hatoyama's policy management itself was deeply entangled with the power politics of the party.

The list of policy achievements by the first Liberal-Democratic government was conspicuously short. Of them, perhaps the most significant was the normalization of the relationship with the Soviet Union, which also meant the removal of the obstacle to Japan's participation in the United Nations. However, even this achievement was severely damaged by the fact that the negotiation for the normalization made no progress in the recovery of the disputed Northern Islands.[17] By contrast, the list of the unachieved included most of the policy goals which would have set the course of the post-Occupation development in line with Hatoyama's ideal for a more autonomous, Asia-oriented, and nationalistic Japan. The list included the correction of Japan's unilateral dependence on the United States, the improvement of the relationship with the People's Republic of China, the recovery of some of the lost territories, rearmament corresponding to the improving economy, and the revision of the Constitution.

This list of the unachieved belies where the real significance of the policy management by the first Liberal-Democratic government lay: power politics within the party determined the policy outcomes. For the Yoshida followers, Hatoyama's preference was a direct challenge to the Yoshida doctrine. The emphasis upon the autonomy would damage the doctrine carefully designed to take advantage of the United States' Asian policy, where a stable and pro-U.S. Japan was given a specially protected place; tampering with the Constitution with an eye toward rearmament was inconsistent both with the doctrine and with the ultimate goal of domestic improvement for which the doctrine had been constructed: and the Asian orientation that neglected the U.S.-Taiwan axis would turn the clock back to the pre-1951. The most effective defense of the Yoshida doctrine in the face of Hatoyama's attempts at modification was to undermine the Hatoyama government itself. Accordingly, the challenge by the Yoshida supporters was directed against both the Hatoyama government as a whole and any specific policy remotely impinging upon the Yoshida doctrine. Partisan divisions within the Liberal-Democratic Party thus paralyzed Hatoyama's policy management. Sufficient party support even for normalization with the Soviet Union did not materialize without Hatoyama's pledge to step down afterwards.[18]

The internal challenge was muted only by fear of the Progressives' taking advantage of the absolute division within the LDP. The other LDP members had begun to grow weary of exposing their first government to the same sort of protests from the Progressives that Yoshida faced in 1951. This sense of weariness became stronger since the 27th Lower House General Election in February of 1955 assured the Progressives a number of seats (one third) large enough to block any Conservative initiatives to revise the Constitution. Given this, Hatoyama's unwavering projection for the constitutional revision inevitably deepened a fear among the Conservatives that their struggle with the Progressives might not be contained within the parliamentary battle and would have to spill into the election fields.

Moreover, there were Socialists and their supporters who had viewed the merging of the Conservatives itself as a first step toward the revision of the

Constitution and reversing the process of a pacifist Japan. Their view towards Hatoyama was undoubtedly suspicious, and even the normalization with the Soviet Union did not help in alleviating that suspicion. The counter-offensive by the Yoshida followers came to have a much broader, receptive base.

When the party divisions were thus obscured, an unexpected irony emerged: the Yoshida group became one with the Progressives in their defense of the Constitution and the pacifist Japan. Still another, far more consequential irony is that the challenge to Hatoyama obscured the basic commonality in policy preference running through the rival LDP factions. Yoshida himself several years later published a book in which he presented his political framework as flexible enough to accommodate some of Hatoyama's policy preferences, especially a gradual rearmament commensurate with the improving economy,[19] a policy proposition which was lost with the end of the Hatoyama government in 1957.

The first Liberal-Democratic government thus exhibited what has proven to be an archetypal relationship between the party and the government. The factional strife within the party more often than not determines what the government, led usually by an LDP faction leader, could accomplish. This party-government relationship was to repeat time and again in the subsequent decades of Conservative rule. The factional alignments shifted to the point of rendering the original Yoshida-Hatoyama division virtually obsolete. Yet, the key lesson has remained: any divisive policy issue could easily be exploited for the manipulation of factional dynamics.

Defense as Politics: The Legacies of the First Liberal-Democratic Government

Of the legacies of the Hatoyama government, or of the Conservatives as a whole at their creation of their own party, two have weathered the passing of time and played a significant role in Japans' defense policy. One is the intermeshing of the defense and constitutional issues; and the other is the particular style of policy management that emerged at the end of the Hatoyama government.

Hatoyama's challenge to the Yoshida doctrine brought about the joining of the two otherwise incompatible forces, the Yoshida-led Conservatives and the Progressives. The Yoshida supporters criticized Hatoyama for tampering with what they believed was a sound and resilient political framework for the post-Occupation political development. By contrast, the Progressives challenged Hatoyama for initiating a further deterioration of Japan's postwar development toward a pacifist Japan which, to them, had already been damaged by the Yoshida doctrine's heavy reliance on the U.S. military presence. The Progressives raised the issue of the constitutionality of every defense effort by the Conservatives, and questioned the latter's position on the broader issue of Japan's new identity, which the Progressives argued was unmistakably expressed in the Constitution. The unlikely joining of the Progressives with the Yoshida forces, then, reinforced the intermeshing of the defense and constitutional issues.

Born from this first legacy was the general weariness among the Conservatives of the entanglement of any defense issue with the broad and perhaps self-perpetuating debate on postwar Japan's national identity. The developments involving Japan's defense efforts since the end of the Occupation, such as the creation of the Self-Defense Forces in 1953, the revision of the Security Pact of 1960, and its renewal in 1970, have served as the catalysts for the Progressives to continuously challenge the Conservative's stance on a new identity for Japan. Every defense effort by the Conservative government has been countered by the Progressives' questioning of its constitutionality and the argument that such an effort was an irretrievable first step backward toward the militarist Japan. The Progressives have compelled the Conservatives to defend their commitment to a new Japan, expressed in the Constitution, whose identity lay in increasing the distance from its militarist past.

This exchange between the Conservatives and Progressives gave birth to and has helped perpetuate Japan's unique, if latent, conception that an external threat cannot be defined solely in terms of the physical preparation it requires Japan to amass. What matters is the magnitude and the direction of change that external threat requires Japan's postwar political structure to absorb in order for Japan to survive the threat. External threat is destabilizing because the response to it might also lead to a Japan at odds with a commercialist-pacifist stance. Regional or international disruption could be threatening to the extent that it might compel Japan to suspend the efforts to create and protect the new basic identity of its postwar political life. In other words, Japan's defense policy does not exist apart from an unusual, self-regulating equilibrium at work between the cost to society of the failure to meet the threat and another of the cost to society of successfully defusing the threat.[20]

The second legacy is the emergence of the particular style of policy management at the end of the Hatoyama government. It was the result of the joining of two distinct factors. One is the presence of a number of policy issues crucial for Japan's efforts to recover its normal status following the end of the Occupation. These included, among others, the improvement of the problematic 1951 Security Pact; the recovery of some of the lost territories; the ending of the state of war with Japan's formidable neighbors, the People's Republic of China and the Soviet Union, or with a hostile ally, the Republic of Korea; the acquisition of membership in the key international political and economic organization; and the full recovery of the economy. By calling these issues the *sengo i shori mondai, the postwar settlement issues, the Japanese expressed the sentiment that the Peace Treaty did not end the anomalous status inflicted upon Japan due to the defeat in the war, and that Japan would not be without the suffix sengo*—Japan is always the postwar Japan— until these *sengo* issues have been solved. As such, the presence of these issues figured prominently in Japanese foreign policy management, and no Conservative government could last without addressing at least one of them.

The other factor is the internally fragmented Liberal-Democratic Party itself. As witnessed amply by the short-lived first Liberal-Democratic government, the internal conditions of the LDP were the obstacles to creating a stable government of its own. In light of this, Hatoyama's resignation following the normalization with Soviet Union proved to be a significant precedent for the management, both of the key foreign policy issues and the stable party-government relationship. An LDP premier was to draw on the party's full support for his administration in exchange for the promise to leave the premiership to his contenders once he solved some of these critical issues. Thus emerged was a unique practice of linking an LDP administration with one or more of the key *sengo issues as the method of stabilizing the party-government relationship.*

This one-administration-*sengo*-issue linkage began to benefit the Liberal-Democrats quickly. The linkage helped moderate the internal challenge during a given Conservative administration and minimize the disruptive transition from one administration to another. The Liberal-Democrats, fragmented into a handful of factions, have always needed to create a coalition of the factions strong enough to support a Liberal-Democratic government. The coalition-building could always be a protracted and grueling process of negotiations among the factions leaders. The issues typically involve who will benefit directly (i.e., the post of the party president *cum* premier for a faction leader) and indirectly (i.e., the cabinet and party posts for the remaining faction leaders and followers) from the resulting coalition.[21] All the bargaining, however, would still leave an ultimate compromise to be worked out by the faction leaders: the remaining faction leaders' own chances in the future to assume the premiership. The one-administration-*sengo*-issue linkage provided the final missing piece for a successful coalition- building: the certainty that an LDP government ends itself with a solution to one *sengo* issue, thereby assuring the contending faction leaders that their turn would come.

A quick scan of the post-Hatoyama Conservative administrations readily produces a consistent pattern whereby the individual administration is associated with one or more of the *sengo* issues: Kishi's (1958-1960), with the replication of the new Security Pact with the United States; Ikeda's (1958-1964), with the replication of the West German economic "miracle;" Sato's (1964-1971), with normalization with Republic of Korea and the reversion of Okinawa; and Tanaka's (1972-1976), with the ending of the state of war with the People's Republic of China.

The impact of this second legacy on defense is considerable. First and foremost, the Conservative premiers have directed attention to these issues crucial to Japan's postwar development, thereby giving them the credit as well as the appearance that they are the legitimate managers of Japan's postwar political development, while often casting the Progressives and the internal dissidents in the role of obstructionists. For the party as a whole, too, it is easier to generate popular support for the party by way of its association with particular *sengo* issues than with particular Conservative administrations. Thus, as long as the *sengo* issues exist, there is little incentive to bring up the issue of defense at the risk of exposing themselves to the predictable repercussions from the Progressives and the unpredictable reactions from the voters.

The second legacy, however, was laden with the seeds for its undoing from the very beginning. Obviously, there have been fewer *sengo* issues with the passing of each Conservative adminstration. With the diminishing of these issues, the faction leaders began to see each coalition-building as actually reducing the remaining faction leaders' opportunities to form their governments. By the mid-1970s, the *sengo* issues were all but gone, with the possible exception of the Northern territorial issue. Yet this is virtually a non-issue since the Soviet Union refuses to recognize its existence. In other words, there has been an increasing tendency since the mid-1970s among the contending faction leaders to see every transition from one administration to another as perhaps their final opportunity to come to power.

Consequently, the average tenure of the LDP premier in the 1970s became much shorter. The transition from one premier to another began to appear more the result of the failure to build a stable coalition of the factions supporting an LDP government. The infamous *two-year tenure agreement* between Fukuda Takeo and Ohira Masayoshi in 1977 prior to the formation of Fukuda administration was an example of a new method by which to promote the factional compromise. The two contending faction leaders found no ground for compromise, leaving them only the alternative that whoever took the first turn would step down after two years in the office for the other, regardless of his administration's performance.[22] As such, the agreement is a significant indication that at least one of the two key legacies of the first Liberal-Democratic government may be coming to an end.

The increasing factional paralysis has also resulted in the changes of direct consequence to Japan's defense policy. The signs are still limited but evident in the increasing willingness among at least some of the LDP members, as well as some political commentators, to question the Yoshida doctrine, and thus Japan's defense policy. With all the anomalies of the Occupation era seemingly corrected, there appear to be two distinct manifestations of this willingness. One is to consider the 1947 Constitution itself as a *sengo* issue.[23] Since the Hatoyama administration, the issue of the constitutional revision had been something of a taboo. However, this taboo has been gradually eroding due to the convergence of several factors. First, the decline in the popular votes for the LDP in the 1970s prompted some of the LDP leaders to consider a change in the electoral system, which as been carefully protected by the 1974 Constitution. Second, the Oil Crisis of 1973 helped instill among many Japanese a sense that their prosperity was a fleeting phenomenon precariously bordering on unforeseen disaster, prompting many Japanese to wander into the unfamiliar realm of crisis management. Third, the decline in popularity since the mid-1960s of the Socialist Party, the most committed of all the pro-1947 Constitution forces, helped create a political climate conducive to debating Japan's defense far more openly than it ever was in the preceding two decades.[24]

Recently there has also been a re-reading of the Yoshida doctrine that it did not preclude the gradual rearmament of Japan commensurate with the improving economy. According to this approach, the completion of the Yoshida doctrine is itself a *sengo* issue, since the conception of the doctrine was strictly dictated by the strictures of time. At the Lower House Budget Committee hearing on February 21, 1985, Shiina Motoo, an LDP theoretician, argued that the commercialist-pacifist Japan with unilateral reliance on the U.S. for defense was by no means what Yoshida had presumed as Japan's permanent state, and that the completion of the real doctrine was to entail a fuller participation in the Western bloc by diminishing the unilateral dependence on the United States. Premier Nakasone duly concurred and, citing his own meeting with Yoshida, went even so far to suggest that the architect of the doctrine was not averse even to revising the 1947 Constitution.[25] The merit of this approach is that it does not discredit the achievements of Yoshida and thus allows its proponents to avoid the friction with the Yoshida loyalists. It also promotes the party consensus among the Yoshida supporters and the pro-defense LDP members who had often been suspected, like Hatoyama and his supporters earlier, of tampering with one conservative orthodoxy.

The change would probably come about only as a compromise between these new trends some of the LDP members are now entertaining, and the resilient legacies of the first Liberal-Democratic government. As such, the change would be slow in coming. One should also note the strong resignation that constitution revision is an issue just as dead as the Northern Island issue.[26]

Defense as Policy

Nonetheless, Japan does have a defense policy. It is a culmination of a series of several multi-year build-up plans since 1958. Cast in a broad evolutionary framework, the two basic foundations of the Yoshida doctrine have retained their original places. Both the U.S.-Japanese Security Pact and the Constitution (Article 9) figure prominently throughout all phases of the evolution of defense policy. The reliance on the United States and the observation of the Constitutional requirements have given birth to and perpetuated a broad division of labor in defense: Japan's role was to defend only Japan proper and the U.S.'s role was a more diversified, including the extension of nuclear deterrence over Japan, the maintenance of regional stability, and its eventual military involvement in the breakdown of Japan's self-defense.

The evolution of Japan's defense policy has defined this division of labor in increasingly clearer terms. The earlier Japanese efforts in the mid-1950s were tailored to meet several requirements at once: the declining U.S. military presence within Japan, the capital-resource shortage for the improving and expanding economy, and the creation of what could become the core for future expansion of the Self-Defense Forces, biased in favor of air and maritime.[27] Through the subsequent developments, Japan's defense policy has become more specifically defined. On the one hand, the contingencies that Japan may have to face might arise from the drastic change in any one or more of the following fronts: 1) the U.S.-USSR stalemate in the nuclear balance; 2) the Soviet Union's preoccupation with the European front; 3) the Sino-Soviet rift; 4) the Sino-U.S. detente; and 5) the stability in Korea.[28] On the other hand, Japan's defense efforts are even more clearly defined in relation to the ultimate invocation of the U.S.-Japanese Security Pact. Japan is to create a defense capability aimed at projecting Japan's rejective power (*kyohiryoku*) to dissuade an aggressor; failing to dissuade, hold off the conventional aggression of a scale smaller than regional war; and presume U.S. intervention beyond that point.[29]

This division of labor was by no means an accepted proposition about Japan's defense from the very beginning, as far as defense policy-makers were concerned. Earlier in the mid-1950s, even with the U.S.-Japanese Security Pact, Japan's role was ambiguous in the eyes of defense policy-makers. Thus, it is believed to be a fairly common practice to suppose a scenario of some bizarre international disruption in order to arrive at a level of preparedness exceeding the imagination of many Japanese at that time. For example, prior to the first (1958-1962) of the multi-year defense build-up plans, the policy-makers even contemplated the coming of a Third World War by around 1960, for which they presumed the scale of Japan's self-defense forces would need to be three to ten times larger than even the current level.[30] Another practice also emerged in which the defense policy-makers saw Japan's defense efforts to be only as a requirement of an overall U.S.-Japanese security cooperation. Without a clear definition of the type of contingency in which Japan's cooperation was to be called upon, however, Japan's defense efforts could become much too elastic to the U.S. responses to the contingency.[31]

Inherent in either of these practices was the tendency toward more active Self-Defense Forces, restricted perhaps by the budgetary constraints but verging on neglect of the broad, if ambiguous, requirements of the Constitution. Such a concern with an ambiguous upper ceiling for Japan's defense efforts gave birth to the idea that Japan's defense efforts are a sort of premium to secure the insurance coverage—the U.S. military involvement in defense of Japan. The need to remove the final ambiguity—when the U.S. invokes the Security Pact—is met by defining the most serious disruption Japan's Self-Defense Forces alone could manage.[32] Thus, the concept emerged of a division of labor in defense, by which Japan's efforts are geared toward a defense capability not too potent nor too vulnerable: too potent a defense capability could only result in a prolonged destruction by the aggressor before U.S. involvement, and too vulnerable a defense capability might not give the U.S. the opportunities and time to invoke the Security Pact. Thus, the division of labor allows Japan in a peculiar way to stay within the requirements of the Constitution and satisfy the minimum requirement of the Security Pact with the United States.

A closer look at Japan's defense policy also reveals the marks of having had the Liberal-Democratic Party as the governing party. Of them, the impact of the factional politics figures prominently in many aspects of Japan's defense policy. That the ministerial appointments are entangled with the maintenance of equilibrium among the factions has resulted in a constant re-shuffling of cabinet ministers, including director-general of Defense Agency. There are forty-seven directors-general, as opposed to twelve premiers, since the end of the Allied Occupation in 1952. Such a constant reshuffling took place often in the middle of the preparation for a multi-year build-up plan, thereby making the drawing of the plan inconsistent and leaving the final product to be determined by such extrinsic factors as precedent—let us not at least go below the level of the previous plan.[33]

The appointment of director-general as a part of the management of the factional politics also creates a situation where premier and the director-general may belong to two opposing factions, or are of two different persuasions on the matter of defense, thereby neutralizing one another's political view. The case in point is the appointment of Nakasone Yasuhiro in 1970 in the Sato government toward the end of the preparation for the Fourth Build-up Plan (1972-1976). Nakasone had been known for this strong leaning toward a more autonomous defense policy, which once brought him closer to Hatoyama and to Kishi in the 1950s. Thus, as expected, Nakasone did make his presence felt within the community of the defense policy-makers and specialists.[34] Nakasone pushed the publication of the first Defense White Paper. In the past, the publication has been suspended for fear that it would have an explicit reference to the sources of external threat, and that the Progressives would exploit such a reference as the sign of deviation from the gist of the Constitution. Nakasone also made public the Agency's draft plan, while reversing the previous practice whereby both the office of National Defense Council and the relevant ministries had reviewed the draft plan prior to its announcement. These and other actions were part of a larger goal of popularizing Japan's defense efforts, which in turn was to serve another purpose of creating a more autonomous defense policy. In point of substance, however, Nakasone's ideal for Japan as a non-nuclear, medium grade nation was hardly reflected in the Fourth Build-up Plan. This failure was partly due to Nakasone's attempts to make the Defense Agency the key decision-making body, which created friction within the government, and partly due to his projection of the increase in defense spending for the duration of the Plan to be 18.8 percent per annum, a drastic jump from the increase during the previous plan.[35] But, the most significant deterrence to Nakasone came from within the LDP. The conservative wing led by Kishi suspected that

Nakasone was attempting to build his own factional strength and was less committed to making Japan more autonomous; and the mainstream, led by Sato, a Yoshida protege, saw Nakasone's efforts as the emergence of a new defense policy and as inherently destabilizing for the Conservatives as a whole who had protected the Yoshida doctrine.[36]

The one-administration-one-*sengo*-issue approach to stabilize the government-party relationship also played a significant role in Japan's defense policy. As mentioned earlier, when the *sengo* issues were abundant, an LDP premier preferred to address one or more of these issues which tended to gain popular support more easily. In addition, each and all of the *sengo* issues involved difficult diplomatic negotiations with the parties involved and with the fragmented LDP itself. The tackling of the *sengo* issues was thus a consuming venture for any LDP premier. The obvious result was the demotion of defense to a secondary status in the pecking order. Or else, the issue was considered as a matter of non-decision. Cast in this implicit framework of policy management, defense policy has hinged not so much upon the changes in the surrounding environment as it does upon what went before it. Margins of changes in the policy are determined by the perceived difference from the preceding phase of the policy. Nothing is more telling of this "non-decision" than the discussion of the level of defense spending. The discussion that could evoke a wide range of repercussions both from the right (too little) and left (too much) has been conspicuously absent since the figure was settled in the neighborhood of 1 percent of GNP in the early 1960s. Yet, with the GNPs annual growth consistently nearing 10 to 11 percent for the 1960s and part of the 1970s, the defense spending was assured of a 10 percent or more annual increase.

Finally, the legacy of the more political nature of the Hatoyama- Yoshida rivalry also has its own mark in Japan's defense policy, particularly in the attempt by one of Yoshida's followers, Ohira Masayoshi, who came to power late in the 1970s. Ohira's presidency promised to be a difficult one. For one, the growth-first policy of the previous decade had left many problems, such as heavy industrial concentration, over-urbanization, and pollution. As a result of the Progressives' exploitation of these problems, the LDP was suffering from some severe election set-backs throughout the 1970s. For another, by the mid-1970s, the *sengo* issues had been mostly removed, leaving the Party without a method of dissolving the internal factional paralysis. Furthermore, the pressures from the outside were mounting for Japan to take a substantial lead in pulling the world economy out of recession and for its fuller participation in the Western bloc, in the face of consistent Soviet military buildup in East Asia and elsewhere. Japan, for the majority of the LDP members including Ohira himself, appeared to be at the crossroads of leaving the basic tenets of the Yoshida doctrine.

Ohira's answer to this confrontation with this turning point proved to be far more consistent with the past. Ohira was acutely aware that Japan's vulnerability to international and regional disruptions was the result of complex factors, such as the heavy urban concentration and the population density, Japan's maritime position, the near-total reliance on the import for industrial raw material and energy resources, and even the need to constantly upgrade its industrial structure. Like Yoshida earlier, Ohira saw that the significance of these primarily economic factors diffused, if not outweighed, the salience of military factor in Japan's conception of its national security.[37] Thus born was the idea of the Comprehensive Security, a product of a score of scholars and political analysts commissioned by Ohira himself in 1979. It had a look of a new policy as it freely used the term "national security," and even a explicit suggestion for breaking the 1 percent-of-GNP-ceiling on defense spending. Both were the signs which the Progressives had used to loath as signalling the Conservatives' move to evade the Constitutional requirements. Yet, the idea was also true to the form of the Yoshida doctrine. It placed the highest value on the U.S.-Japanese security cooperation, and derived the role of Japan's military only residually, after considerations were made for economic security, energy security, food security, and the like. Ohira's Comprehensive Security thus was in and of itself not a novel effort, and was more a testimony to the resilience of the Yoshida doctrine, or of how deeply the Yoshida doctrine has become locked in place. The resilience, in turn, serves to moderate the move of the LDP in either direction of a more or even of a less positive defense policy.

What, then, is a possibility of the LDP's departure from Japan's defense policy from the past? A speculation on such a question may in fact help confirm the foregoing points about the relationship between the LDP and Japan's defense as policy. One possibility in which the LDP might depart from its previous, cautious defense policy may arise from the decline of the LDP as a whole to the point of losing the majority seats in the Diet. An LDP on the verge of losing the governing power would need a drastic policy projection, such as an initiative toward the revision of the Constitution. Yet, at the same time, a declining LDP would most likely have to coopt one or more of the opposition parties of centrist-orientation, which in turn would require the LDP to moderate its stance toward the revision of the Constitution. The other extreme is the possibility in which the LDP gains the two-third majority of the Diet seats, securing the majority required for the Constitutional revision. Yet it would be conceivable but highly unlikely for the LDP members to tamper with the Constitution that has protected the very electoral system by which they obtained the Diet seats. The surest possibilities lies between these two poles, indicating the ultimate difficulty in revising the Constitution of 1947, and leaving the likelihood that, as long as the LDP is in power, its marks on Japan's defense policy will remain consistent.

An Epilogue: The Past in the Present

Since the mid-1970s, Japan has seen a surge of defense debate within. Joining in the debate are former and current government officials, politicians, academicians, and political commentators of all persuasions. In one extreme, one finds a group of individuals proposing, in effect, the creation of a Gaullist Japan.[38] They argue for the military power sufficient to deter aggression unilaterally and to project Japan's political presence. Their underlying concern is not limited to the rise of the Soviet military power in East Asia and the dubious U.S. military and political abilities to fulfill the defense commitment to Japan. Their ultimate goal lies in a Japan that fully participates in the international political system, whose rewards would include the veto power in international affairs and the corresponding national prestige. Their notion of Japan is at odds particularly with the notion of Japan, entertained by another group, that exploits the international system in which ranking among the nations on the basis of military power has been irretrievably subverted by tight international economic interdependence.[39] This second group is also cognizant that Japan's economic success has been incumbent upon the deliberate refusal to project Japan's presence militarily. Within this group, there are considerable variations. On the one hand, some argue that the pacifist Japan is an experiment to be replicated by other nations, and, on the other hand, others see in Yoshida's shrewd exploitation of the Cold War a precious lesson to learn for a nation which is neither a United States nor a Soviet Union.[40] Defense debate has obtained much of its momentum from the exchange between these two groups, allowing many more to find their places in between.

What has remained as the subtext of this debate, however, is the perennial issue of postwar Japan's quest for its new identity. A Japan which refuses to project is presence politically and militarily is, to a Gaullist, a nation which is perpetually in the custody of others and held as hostage to the unpredictable turns of international events. To a Gaullist, it is a nation whose postwar development has been nothing but a series of pathological reactions to the defeat in World War II and the Atomic Bombs. By asserting that the time has come for Japan to exit from this peculiar seclusion, the Gaullists in fact argue that Japan in its entirety, and especially since the Meiji Restoration, which launched Japan on the road toward a modern aggressive nation-state, is the normal identity that needs to be restored. On the other hand, the proponents of a pacifist Japan value its postwar efforts in successfully defining Japan's new place within the international system without the conventional link to the system, the military. For them, the identity of the nation has unfolded in these very efforts which now reward Japan with the economic prosperity and the absence of political strains. Then, finally, there are also others who view Japan's new identity as found only in completing or in perpetuating the pacifist nation as projected in the Constitution of 1947.

In other words, blended in the defense debate are the search for Japan's new identity in the past, in the present, and in the future. In these sense, defense debate among the Japanese has served to perpetuate the past in the present, and it even prevents the past from receding from the present. What is to Japan watchers the sign of Japan's intransigence on the defense issue is to many Japanese the sign of their efforts to make peace with their own past.

NOTES

1. Edwin Reischauer, *Beyond Vietnam: The United States and Asia*, (Boston, Vintage Books, 1967), especially pp. 105-39; Tetsuya Kataoka, *Waiting for a Pearl Harbor: Japan Debates Defense*, (Stanford, Hoover Institution Press, 1980), chapter 1; Taketsugu Tsurutani, *Japanse Policy and East Asian Security*, (New York Praeger, 1981), chapter 6; and Donald Hellmann, "Japan and America: New Myths, Old Realities," in Hellmann, ed., *China and Japan: A New Balance of Power*, (Lexington, D.C. Heath, 1976), pp. 19-49.

2. The most insightful analysis of this incongruity to date is an essay by Kenneth Pyle, "The Future of Japanese Nationality: An Essay in Contemporary History," *The Journal of Japanese Studies*, vol. 8, no. 2, (1982), pp. 223-263. See also Nagai Yonosuke, "Moratoriamu kokka no boeiron," *Chuo koron*, (January, 1981).

3. As the perennial issue involving contending visions for a new Japan, the Constitution of 1947 has been the subject of numerious political comments, debates, and discussion. A convenient anthology of the cricial essays on the issue is compiled by Hasegawa Masayasu and Mori Hideki, *Kempo kaiseiron*, (Tokyo, Sanseido, 1977), especially the essays in chapter 2. See also, Masataka Kosaka, *100 Million Japanese: The Postwar Experience*, (Tokyo and Palo Alto, Kodansha International, 1972), chapters 1, 2, and 3.

4. On the negotiations for the Security Pact of 1951, see Martin Weinstein, *Japan's Postwar Defense Policy, 1947-1968*, (New York, Columbia University Press), especially, chapter 3.

5. The Government was also guilty of a contrived interpretation of the Constitution, which allowed it to disclaim Japan's Self-Defense Forces as constituting the "war potentials." According to the formal definition, offered by the Government in November of 1952, the "war potentials" refer to those which are equipped with the equipments and organizations that serve the purpose of "modern warfare." Cited in Hasegawa Masayasu, *Kempo gendaishi*, (Tokyo, Aoki shoten, 1981), vol, 1, pp. 358-9.

6. For a brief yet perceptive analysis of the U.S.' orientation toward Japan at the close of World War II, see Akira Iriye, "Continuities in U.S.-Japanese Rela-

tions, 1941-1949," in Yonosuke Nagai and Akira Iriye, eds., *The Origins of the Cold War in Asia*, (Tokyo and New York, University of Tokyo Press, 1977), pp. 378-407. For a more general discussion of the U.S. policy toward the beginning of the Cold War, see John Lewis Gaddis, *Strategies of Containment: A Critical Appraisal of Postwar American National Security Policy*, (New York and Oxford, Oxford University Press, 1982), chapters 2, 3, and 4.

7. See for the witness account of this difficult time, Miyazawa Kiichi, *Tokyo-Washington no mistudan*, (Tokyo, Jitsugyo no Nihonsha, 1956), pp. 49-52.

8. *Ibid.*, p. 54.

9. Tominomori Eiji, *Sengo hoshutoshi*, (Tokyo, Nihon hyoronsha, 1981), p. 10.

10. There are many witness accounts of this, perhaps, one of the most dramatic turn of events in Japan's party history. See, for example, Hatoyama Ichiro, *Aru daigishi no seikatsu to iken*, (Tokyo, Tokyo shuppan, 1952), pp. 235-40; and *Hatoyama Ichiro kaikoroku*, (Tokyo, Bungei shunjushinsha, 1957), pp. 52-55. See also, Mitarai Tatsuo, *Miki Bukicki den*, (Tokyo, Shikisha, 1958), pp. 289-301, and John W. Dower, *Empire and Aftermath: Yoshida Shigeru and the Japanese Experience, 1878-1954*, (Cambridge, Mass., Harvard University Press), chapter 9.

11. The best analysis of Yoshida's politcal thought and behavorial pattern, as well as his political legacies to date is Kosaka Masataka, *Saisho Yoshida Shigeru*, (Tokyo, Chuo koron, 1968).

12. Because many of the former government officials Yoshida had recruited later became premiers as well as key cabinet members of various LDP governments, it is common to assume the Yoshida group stands out for its heavy reliance on the former government officials. However, there are other factions in the LDP that equally, if not more, depended upon the former government officials for their members. It is the cohesiveness among the members that seemd particularly unique to the Yoshida group. On the Conservatives' heavy reliance on former government officials, especially during the transitional period of the mid-1940s, to the late 1950s, see Robert A. Scalapino and Junnosuke Masumi, *Parties and Politics in Contemporary Japan*, (Berkeley and Los Angeles, University of California Press, 1962), chapter 3.

13. Hatoyama, *Hatoyama Ichiro kaikoroku*, pp. 111-114.

14. *Ibid.*, pp. 116-117.

15. Masumi Junnosuke, *Sengo seiji, 1945-1955*, (Tokyo, Tokyo daigaku shuppankai, 1983), pp. 435-443; Hayashi Shigeru and Tsuji Kiyoaki, eds., *Nihon naikakushiroku*, (Tokyo, Daiichi hoki shuppansha, vol, 5, 1981), pp. 327-333.

16. Although Hatoyama's pre-Purge position on Japan's foreign policy is not clear, he was at least clearly an anti-communist and pro-defense from the

very beginning of his postwar political career. See Hatoyama, *Hatoyama Ichiro kaikoroku*, pp. 38-43.

17. Donald C. Hellman, *Japanese Domestic Politics and Foreign Policy: The Peace Agreement with the Soviet Union*, (Berkeley and Los Angeles, University of California Press, 1969), chapters 2, 3, and 4; Iwanaga Kenkichiro, *Sengo Nihon no seito to gaiko*, (Tokyo, Tokyo daigaku shuppankai, 1985), pp. 35-74.

18. *Ibid*, and Hatoyama *Hatoyama Ichiro kaikoroku*, pp. 174-179, and 193-212.

19. *Sekai to Nihon*, (Tokyo, Bancho shobo, 1963).

20. See for a more negative characterizatino of this self- regulating equilibrium, Tsurutani, *Japanese policy and East Asian Security*, pp. 118-125, and Kataoka, *Waiting for a Pearl Harbor*.

21. For the intriguing mechanism of the coalition-building among the LDP factions, see Nathaniel B. Thayer, *How the Conservatives Rule Japan*, (Princeton, N.J., Princeton University Press, 1969), chapters 2, 6, and 7.

22. The most detailed account of this Ohira-Fukuda negotiations may be found in Ito Masay, *Jiminto sengokushi*, (Tokyo, Asahi sonorama, 1982), pp. 302-449. See also Kawauchi Issei, *Ohira seiken 554 nichi*, (Tokyo, Gyoseimondai kenkyujo, 1982), pp. 39-71 and Kiyomiya Ryu, *Fukuda seiken 714 nichi*, (Tokyo, Gyoseimondai kenkyujo, 1984), pp. 221-276.

23. Perpaps the most controversial statement on this issue is Eto Jun, *1946 nen kempo—sono kosoku*, (Tokyo, Bungei shunju, 1980). See also, Katsuta Kichitaro, *Heiwa kempo o utagau*, (Tokyo, Kodansha, 1981); and Shimizu Ikutaro, *Nihon yo kokkatare*, (Tokyo, Bungei shunju, 1980).

24. On the defense debate among the Japanese, see Mike M. Michizuki, "Japan's Search for Strategy," *International Security*, vol, 8. no. 3, (1983-1984), pp. 152-179; also Nagai Yonosuke, *Gendai to senryaku*, (Tokyo, Bungei shunju, 1985), chapter 1.

25. *Yosan iinkai kaigiroku*, no. 15, 1985.

26. An interview with an LDP member on March 13, 1985. The interviewee wishes to remain anonmymous.

27. An interview with a Defense Agency Official on December 10, 1985, who wishes to remain anonymous.

28. Japan Defense Agency, *Defense of Japan*, (1979), p. 70 and *Defense of Japan*, 1982, part I. See also John E. Endicott, "The Defense Policy of Japan," in Douglas J. Murray and Paul R. Viotti, *The Defense Policies of Nations*, (Baltimore, the Johns Hopkins University Press), pp. 446-466.

29. See footnotes 27 and 28.

30. See footnote 27.

31. See footnote 27.

32. This is in a way an odd proposition of a nation's defense policy as it clearly states just how far the nation's military is willing to defend it. See for example, Kataoka, *Waiting for a Pearl Harbor*, pp. 44-55.

33. An interview with a Defense Agency official on February 13, 1985, who wishes to remain anonymous.

34. On Nakasone's tenure at the Defense Agency, see Otake Hideo, *Nihon no boei to kokunai seiji*, (Tokyo, sanichi shobo, 1983), chapter 2.

35. See footnote 27.

36. *Ibid.*

37. See Otake, *Nihon no boei to kokunai seiji*, chapter 20 for Japan's defense policy under the Ohira government, which is characterized by many including Otaki as having stifled the turn of the preceding Fukuda administration toward pro-defense.

38. Mike M. Mochizuki, "Japan's Search for Strategy," pp. 166-168; Nagai, *Gendai to senryaku*, chapter 1. Kenneth Pyle, "The Future of Japanese Nationality," especially pp. 229-242.

39. The best statement of this position are Nagai Yonosuke, *Heiwa no daisho*, (Tokyo, Chuo koronsha, 1967), pp. 69-135, and "Moratoriamu kokka no boeiron."

40. Yoshikazu Sakamoto, "New Dimensions of Disarmament Processes," *Japan Quarterly*, vol 29, no. 2, (1982); Nagai, *Gendai to senryaku*, pp. 48-78.

CHAPTER 5

Prospects for Korean Security

Seung-Hwan Kim

The Korean peninsula, where the interests of the major Asian powers are at stake, is a highly inflammable region in Asia. Under the 1953 armistice agreement of the Korean War, one and a half million combat forces are concentrated along the 38th parallel, and the political hostility and military tensions between the two Koreas are explosive. An eruption of military conflict in Korea not only could jeopardize the regional balance of power, but could also ignite a global war between the superpowers.

Security in Korea is heavily affected by complex external and internal conditions. While the Asian powers exert their influence on Korea, Seoul and Pyongyang each pursue active domestic and foreign policies. Therefore, the strategic rivalries of the principal Asian powers and the changing internal conditions in the two Koreas are closely interconnected. Consequently, this study focuses upon the analysis of four distinct but related determinants of security conditions of Korea, which provide the methodological framework for this essay: the interrelationships between the Asian powers and the two Koreas, the unification policies of South and North Korea, a question of internal stability in the two Koreas, and the power balance on the peninsula. It also explores likely contingency scenarios in Korea and their implications for the Asian powers, with special attention to the importance of interests and policy options for the United States.

A thesis of this essay is that the calculus of security concerns of the principal Asian powers is vitally affected, now more than ever, by internal developments within and between the two halves of Korea. While the current strategic setting in East Asia and the major Asian powers' policies toward Korea are likely to undergo minor changes in the foreseeable future, political, economic, and military developments in South and North Korea could cause drastic changes in strategic conditions on the Korean peninsula. Throughout the remainder of this decade, Korea will continue to be a dangerous flashpoint in Asia; but in the long-term the possibility of military confrontations on the peninsula is likely to decrease.

Korea and the Major Powers

Korea is the focus of Northeast Asian security, where the interests of the four major powers (the United States, the Soviet Union, China, and Japan) intersect. The U.S.-Republic of Korea (ROK) mutual defense treaty of 1954, the defense treaty of the People's Republic of China (PRC) and the Democratic People's Republic of Korea (DPRK), and the USSR-DPRK defense treaty in 1961 demonstrate the principal powers' current strategic interests in Korea. Throughout the twentieth century, two major wars in Asia, the Russo-Japanese War in 1904-05 and the Korean War in 1950-53, embroiled East and West in military conflicts concerning the Korean peninsula. Since the end of World War II, the strategic rivalry among the four major Asian powers has shaped security conditions on the Korean peninsula, and internal developments in Korea have also greatly influenced the inter-relationships among these principal Asian powers.

The United States

Security is the dominant element in U.S. policy towards Korea. Foremost American interests in Korea lie in maintaining a stable strategic and political environment, stressing the avoidance of hegemony by any major power on the peninsula.[1] Conflict in Korea would pose a potentially grave threat to the security of Japan and to regional stability. The existence of a free South Korea is vital for the maintenance of the balance of power in the Asian-Pacific region. In view of the increasing Soviet military offensive in Asia, close U.S.-ROK strategic cooperation enhances the American capability to project its economic and strategic power in the region.

To protect these interests, U.S. policy toward Korea focuses on the prevention of the eruption of armed conflict on the Korean peninsula. The presence of U.S. combat forces in South Korea and the 1954 U.S.-ROK mutual defense treaty are an important means of preserving peace and stability in Korea, deterring communist aggression from the North. At the same time, the United States makes efforts to promote internal stability and steady economic progress in South Korea, because an outbreak of serious internal unrest in South Korea would make it tempting for North Korea to initiate a war against the South. Hence, Washington has emphasized the importance of political democratization and economic stability in South Korea.

For the reduction of tensions between the two Koreas, the United States has encouraged the successful development of South-North Korean dialogue.[2] For this reason, Washington has declined the Pyongyang's proposal of bilateral U.S.-DPRK talks or the North Korean version of trilateral talks with South Korea. The United States has also avoided either official contacts or direct trade with North Korea.

In addition, the United States has pushed for international conferences on Korean issues with China, the Soviet Union, and Japan. It has also supported the idea of the simultaneous entry of South and North Korea into the United Nations as full members and of a "cross-recognition" formula—recognition of North Korea by the United States and other allies of South Korea in return for recognition of South Korea by the Soviet Union and China. In general, the United States supports South Korea's efforts to achieve step-by-step reunification by peaceful means.

Since the early 1970s, the United States' policy for dealing with South Korea in the East Asian strategic environment has been a byproduct of the Vietnam War and U.S.-PRC rapproachement. For example, the Nixon administration applied the Guam Doctrine to South Korea by withdrawing the 7th Division (20,000 troops) in 1971. Furthermore, calling for a phased withdrawal of U.S. combat forces from South Korea, the Carter administration pulled out some 6,000 American troops in 1977 by linking troop withdrawal and human rights issues. U.S. emphasis on making human rights a prime determinant of foreign policy, along with a series of political issues including South Korea's influence-buying activities in the United States, strained the U.S.-ROK relationship.

Nevertheless, the fundamental U.S. goal of maintaining security on the Korean peninsula has remained intact. The Reagan administration has reaffirmed America's strong commitment to the defense of South Korea, stressing the continuing importance of close U.S.-ROK cooperation for regional stability throughout the 1980s. A series of summit talks between Presidents Ronald Reagan and Chun Doo Hwan in 1981, 1983, and 1985, and the resumption of ROK-U.S. security, economic, and policy planning consultative meetings, have symbolized their close strategic partnership in Asia. For their defense preparedness, the two countries have conducted "Team Spirit" military exercises in Korea in recent years. Having reaffirmed the suspension of U.S. troop withdrawal from South Korea in 1981, the Reagan administration has supported the modernization of ROK armed forces by agreeing to deploy F-16 jet fighters, sophisticated missiles, and helping to improve ROK's early warning systems.[3]

Japan

Japan shares a common interest with the United States in preserving stability and reducing tensions on the Korean peninsula to promote its security and economic interests. Due to its constitutional restrictions and the absence of defense arrangements with either of the two Koreas, Japan depends heavily upon the United States for security in Korea. The Japanese leadership is opposed to the reduction of U.S. forces in South Korea in order to prevent another armed conflict in Korea and to maintain the military balance in Northeast Asia particularly in view of the increasing Soviet military threat in the region. Within this context, Japan exerts strong influence on U.S. policies toward the Korean peninsula.

Since the normalization of ROK-Japanese diplomatic relations in 1965, economic ties between the two countries have made remarkable progress. By the late 1970s, South Korea became Japan's second largest export market and the ninth largest source of imported goods.[4] Yet, Japan experienced an uncomfortable political relationship with South Korea throughout the 1970s, which has significantly improved under the Nakasone leadership. In particular, Japan's grant to South Korea of a low-interest loan ($4 billion) by virtue of its contributions to Japan's security and an exchange of visits by Prime Minister Yasuhiro Nakasone and President Chun Doo Hwan in 1983 and 1984 were important turning points in the improvement of relations between the two countries. Overall, Japan supports the South Korean position on unification issues, as well as a "cross-recognition" formula and simultaneous U.N. entry plans for the two Koreas. Nevertheless, increasing Japanese unofficial contacts with DPRK academics and government officials and expanding trade with Pyongyang remain a sensitive issue for the Seoul government.

The People's Republic of China

China appears satisfied with the status quo and stability on the Korean peninsula. North Korea serves as an important buffer between the PRC and western powers. The eruption of another military confrontation would place China in the strategic dilemma of either supporting the DPRK and jeopardizing U.S.-PRC relations or abandoning North Korea totally to Soviet influence. During the course of war, if it occurs, North Korea's dependence upon the Soviet Union will sharply increase primarily due to the need for increased military and economic support. Indeed, in the Sino-Soviet competition for influence in North Korea, Moscow is in a much stronger position than Peking as a result of its superior military, technological, and economic capabilities. In a strategic sense, the presence of U.S. combat forces in South Korea is not detrimental to the PRC's interest. Their presence not only helps to preserve stability on the Korean peninsula, but also helps to counter Soviet expansionism in the Asian-Pacific region.

The role of Korea is of vital importance to Chinese security in the Far East. In view of the continuing Sino-Soviet dispute, Soviet-DPRK strategic cooperation against China would pose a grave threat to the security of its industrial heartland in Manchuria. Consequently, China has made efforts to maintain the close relationship with the North Korean regime.

China has been one of the DPRK's two principal allies since the early 1950s, but their relationship has experienced a series of ups and downs not only because of North Korea's opportunistic attitude in the Sino-Soviet conflict, but also because of the PRC's domestic and foreign policies. During the second half of the 1960s, for instance, PRC-DPRK relations were sharply aggravated due to the internal turmoil of the Cultural Revolution in China and North Korea's close cooperation with the Soviet Union. Beginning in the early 1970s, Sino-

North Korean relations were revamped and Pyongyang took a neutral stance in the Sino-Soviet dispute. In the late 1970s, however, the de-Maoization movement, which called for elimination of leadership personality cult and "collective leadership" in China, embarrassed Kim Il-Sung and undermined their relationship. In addition, when China concluded a peace treaty with Japan in 1978 and normalized its diplomatic relations with the United States in 1979, Pyongyang became uneasy about the possibility that the PRC's developing relationship with the West could sacrifice North Korean interests.[5] In the early 1980s, the Chinese increased their military and economic aid to North Korea, including A-5 aircraft and oil supplies, and Sino-DPRK relations have improved significantly. This support, however, has little affected the military balance on the Korean peninsula. In recent years, Peking and Pyongyang have exchanged a number of visits by high-level party and government officials including Deng Xiaoping and Kim Il-Sung.

As to the relationship with South Korea, China has quietly conducted indirect trade and informal contacts since the late 1970s. The Peking leadership recently allowed South Korean scholars, government officials, and sports teams to participate in international events in China. At the same time, as a result of unexpected events, such as the hijacking of a civilian aircraft and the defections of air force pilots and naval crews, government officials of the two countries have had a series of contacts.

For its long term interests, the PRC appears satisfied with the gradual development of economic cooperation with South Korea to a certain point. Recently, major business corporations in South Korea concluded a few joint venture projects with the PRC.[6] Nevertheless, Peking does not seem to be interested in developing diplomatic dialogue with the Seoul government due to its concern about the reactions of the North Korean regime.

The Soviet Union

Soviet policy toward the Korean peninsula is primarily a function of its complex strategic relationship with other major powers, particularly the United States, China, and Japan. In other words, it is influenced more by concern about the Sino-Soviet conflict and rivalry with the United States and Japan than by its bilateral relationship with North Korea. Long-term Soviet objectives include the expulsion of the United States from South Korea and the creation of a unified Korea dominated by pro-Soviet Communists as was the case in Vietnam in the mid-1970s, because such a situation would dramatically reinforce the Soviet position in the Asian-Pacific region. In the short-term, however, the absence of a major war on the Korean peninsula appears to be conducive to the interests of the Soviet Union. Conflict in Korea fostered by Soviet military and economic support would accelerate pressures from Japanese remilitarization, exacerbate Sino-Soviet relations, and promote anti-Soviet collaboration among the United States, Japan, and China.[7] This also would sharply aggravate the relationship with the United States, which could in turn adversely affect Soviet interests elsewhere. During the last ten years of Brezhnev's era, Moscow provided only limited military and economic support to Pyongyang despite its strategic-military offensive in Asia, a posture that, in effect, was conducive to stability on the Korean peninsula.

Nevertheless, the existence of the substantial level of tensions on the Korean peninsula may serve the Soviet interests for the reason that such a situation would help Moscow strengthen its leverage over Pyongyang particularly in view of Kim Il-Sung's opportunistic attitude in the Sino-Soviet dispute. In this connection, the presence of U.S. ground forces in South Korea may not be necessarily detrimental to the Soviet interests at this time.

Following Brezhnev's death, a series of events indicates that USSR-DPRK ties have conspicuously improved. In May 1984, Kim Il-Sung visited Moscow at the invitation of Konstantin Chernenko, his first trip to the Soviet capital in nearly twenty years. In November, Soviet Deputy Foreign Minister Mikhail Kapitsa visited Pyongyang to ratify a treaty establishing the 60km boundary between the two countries. Beginning in May of 1985, Moscow, for the first time, introduced MiG-23 jet fighters along with advanced weapons including Scud B and SAM 23 missiles to Pyongyang, and Soviet warplanes have been permitted to overfly North Korean territory en route to the Yellow Sea bordering China.[8] In August 1985, an unusually high-ranking Soviet delegation, headed by Politburo member Gaidar Aliyev and Deputy Defense Minister Vasiliy Petrov, visited Pyongyang, and three Soviet warships for the first time paid a naval port call at the North Korean port in Wonsan to celebrate the fortieth anniversary of Korean liberation from Japanese rule. In January 1986, Soviet Foreign Minister Shevardnadze visited Pyongyang and supported the North Korean position on inter-Korean relations. Furthermore, in late October 1986, Kim Il-Sung paid a call on Gorbachev in Moscow.

All these events indicate that the Soviet leadership under Mikhail Gorbachev has determined to strengthen further the Soviet position in the Asian-Pacific region through closer cooperation with North Korea, particularly in view of increasing collaboration among the United States, China, and Japan. The new military supply arrangement provided by the Soviets would not upset the military balance on the Korean peninsula.[9] Yet, this also indicates that Moscow intends to influence North Korean domestic and foreign policies in favor of the Soviet policy line, at a time when political succession in North Korea is at issue.

Conflicting Policies of the Two Koreas

Under the influence of the major powers in Asia, South and North Korea each has pursued active domestic and foreign policies. In 1972, the two Koreas attempted to work for the reduction of tensions and ultimate reunification without outside interference, but their efforts at dialogue failed in a year. Since the fall of 1984, Seoul and Pyongyang have resumed their dialogue on economic cooperation, family reunions, sports, and parliamentary exchanges after ten years of silence. The most tangible outcome of the recent talks was visits in September 1985 across the demilitarized zone (DMZ) by families separated during the Korean War. Despite these efforts, however, the South and the North still view each other with deep-seated distrust, compounded by political hostility and explosive military tensions. Indeed, up until today, no correspondence, phone calls, or news of any kind could be exchanged between the two Koreas.

There are important obstacles to ameliorating the inter-Korean relationship, as well as other conflicting policies of the two Koreas. The South Korean policy is based upon a gradual "step-by-step" approach to reunification by promoting cultural and economic exchanges during the initial stage and political negotiations later. The position outlined by the South emphasizes greater security and the guarantee of stability as preconditions in the unification process. This concept is reflected in Seoul's military-strategic policy toward the North. South Korea's posture is basically defensive and reactive, stressing deterrence—prevention of any armed conflict on the Korean peninsula. In effect, Seoul hopes for the recognition of the "two Koreas" as an intermediary stage in the process of achieving ultimate peaceful reunification.

On the other hand, the North demands excessive steps. Pyongyang stresses political negotiations at the early stage and other issues later. Since the Sixth Korean Workers Party (KWP) Congress in October 1980, the North Korean leadership has declared that the preconditions for a dialogue with the South include "withdrawal of U.S. troops from South Korea, elimination of the military fascist regime, and democratization in South Korean politics." From Pyongyang's perspective, the U.S. military presence in Korea presents the main obstacle to unification and the primary threat to its security. North Korea, therefore, has sought direct contacts with Washington, without the full participation of South Korea, to negotiate its demands.

In recent years, the Pyongyang regime has taken a more moderate stance in its domestic and foreign policies. The North Koreans have prepared tripartite talks with the United States since late 1983, and they adopted a joint venture law in the summer of 1984. Following South Korea's unexpected acceptance of Pyongyang's offer of flood relief goods, the North Korean leadership agreed to South Korea's proposal for the resumption of a dialogue in the fall of 1984.

The North Korean motivations are controversial. It is widely argued that the North Korean purpose is to attract foreign investment and trade due to the failure of their seven-year economic plan (1978-84) and to restore North Korea's international image, which was seriously damaged by the murder of seventeen South Korean government officials in Rangoon. Some observers also argue that the new North Korean approach is aimed at making their future political succession as smooth as possible by improving their economy and standard of living.

Congressman Stephan Solarz, who visited Pyongyang in 1980, stated that "anyone who knows anything about the peculiarities of North Korea would be imprudent to be confident that there has been a real change of policy in North Korea."[10] Indeed, upon scrutinizing the North Korean proposals and the North's behavior the possibility of certain risks cannot be ignored. The first is a North Korean proposal for tripartite talks. Pyongyang's plan is composed of two separate tracks: North Korea and the United States would negotiate a peace agreement to replace the 1953 Armistice Agreement, calling for the withdrawal of the U.S. troops from South Korea, and South and North Korea would negotiate a pact of non-aggression. Significantly, this proposal indicates that the North does not accept the South as a full party in talks, and that Pyongyang's desire is to obtain the U.S. recognition of its legitimacy on the Korean peninsula. Pyongyang's ultimate intention, of course, is to remove U.S. forces and make the North dominant on the peninsula, coercing the South into unity on the North's terms.

The second is North Korea's two track policy. Pyongyang has been pursuing both soft and hard-line policies depending upon changes in the internal and external situations. In the past, Pyongyang often engaged in military buildups or provocative activities, such as the tunnels under the demilitarized zone (DMZ) or the Rangoon atrocity, while pursuing a peace offensive toward the South. According to military sources, North Korea has recently deployed a large number of its troops close to the DMZ in an attempt to shorten the warning time in the event of a surprise attack on the South.[11]

Third, the North may be trying to create a more favorable international atmosphere in the hope of co-hosting the 1988 Olympic Games. If this effort fails, Pyongyang may increase provocations against the South to prevent Seoul from hosting the international event. Because the same North Korean leaders who planned and managed the Rangoon attack still remain in top positions of the party and government, this possibility cannot be excluded. Finally, North Korea may continue to pressure the United States to suspend the annual "Team Spirit" military operation which it conducts with Seoul in return for further progress in dialogue between the two Koreas. To do so, however, would risk weakening the defense preparedness of the United States and South Korea. For this reason, Pyongyang's demand was turned aside this year.

The future of inter-Korean relations will be influenced by complex external and internal factors. Unless the current strategic setting in East Asia undergoes drastic changes, the major Asian powers who have strategic interests in Korea may continue to be satisfied with the current political structure on the Korean peninsula. As long as Sino-Soviet friction, U.S.-Soviet rivalry in Asia, and Sino-U.S. cooperation continue, neither four-way nor six-way talks are apt to occur to support the unification of Korea.

The United States and Japan have pushed for bilateral talks between the two Koreas and the reduction of tension on the peninsula. Washington has flatly declined the North Korean proposal for its own version of three-way or U.S.-DPRK bilateral talks. There were important factors which convinced the North Korean leadership to come to the negotiation table to talk with the South in the past few years. Judging from North Korean approaches to the recent dialogue with the South, Pyongyang does not seem to be ready for substantial progress in North-South relations. On many occasions, Pyongyang has made either unacceptable or irrelevant demands. In January 1986, for instance, North Korea unilaterally suspended economic, parliamentary, and Red Cross talks arguing that the U.S.-ROK "Team Spirit" exercise was a provocative action against the North. Perhaps the North Korean leadership fears that rapid penetration of capitalism into North Korea—along with the exposure of the North's inferior economic and technological capabilities and its lower standard of living vis-a-vis the South—could jeopardize the infrastructure of the North Korean society and the leadership itself.[12] Therefore, the progress of inter-Korean relations, if it continues, is likely to be rather slow.

Political Stability

Another important determinant for security in Korea is the matter of political instability. An eruption of serious internal crisis in the South would make it more tempting for Pyongyang to launch an attack. In addition, an intensification of the succession struggle in Pyongyang could accelerate Northern belligerence in an attempt to seek its internal unity.

North Korea

At present, Kim Il-Sung is still firmly in command, but he is nearing the end of a long career due to his age and deteriorating health. Kim has been making steady efforts to assure the succession of his 44-year old son, Jong-Il, in order to continue his major domestic and foreign policies including the unification of Korea, and also to prevent the downgrading of his reputation after his death. Since the Sixth KWP congress in 1980, Kim Jong-Il has appeared as heir apparent and has acted as the chief administrator in North Korean politics, dealing with party, government, and military affairs on the daily basis. Only the two Kims hold positions within the three key organs of the Central Committee—the Standing Committee of the Politburo, the Secretariat, and the Military Committee. The North Korean regime has continued a major campaign aimed at creating a "cult" for Kim Jong-Il. The Soviet Union and China seem to have acquiesced to the junior Kim's succession arrangement in North Korea.

Available sources indicate that the first stage of preparation for political succession has been completed. With his father's help, Jong-Il has already strengthened his power by appointing his loyal supporters to key military and party posts. In recent years, the junior Kim in fact effected a few major reshuffles of the party and cabinet.

Yet, the prospects for internal political stability depend upon whether the junior Kim can maintain support from the party and military apparatus even after the elder Kim's demise. The political succession in North Korea will be smoother if the elder Kim can remain in power until his son fully consolidates his position in the party and the military. But if Kim Il-Sung's demise comes earlier, Pyongyang may experience complex factional struggles. The senior party and military apparatus do not seem to fully support Kim Jong-Il.

South Korea

South Korea has experienced complex political developments throughout the 1980s. Since his election in 1981, President Chun Doo Hwan has been reasonably successful in consolidating his power and maintaining internal stability in South Korea. Essential political and strategic-military posts were filled by his reliable colleagues. By sponsoring a new constitution notable for limiting the President to a single seven-year term, and by adopting various internal reforms, Chun received moderately favorable popular support. The early U.S. endorsement of Chun and his policies, along with a series of Chun-Reagan meetings since 1981, helped to create a climate of political stability in South Korea. In addition, major tragedies including the KAL incident and the Rangoon atrocity in 1983 helped to create internal unity.

Since 1985, political conditions in South Korea have undergone significant changes. After the general parliamentary elections in February 1985, the New Korea Democratic Party (NKPD), organized by hard-line supporters of Kim Dae-Jung and Kim Young-Sam, emerged as the largest and most outspoken opposition bloc in the National Assembly, and began seeking political reforms. The collapse of the Marcos regime and assumption of power by popular opposition forces in the Philippines in February 1986 has strengthened the resolve of the South Korean opposition force to challenge the government. Running parallel to the NKPD, student groups accelerated street demonstrations by demanding full-fledged and immediate political liberalization. Some student activists were increasingly violent, anti-American, and often employed the themes of neo-Marxism such as "dependency theory" or "liberalization theory."

An important source of political tensions in South Korea stemmed from the fundamental disagreements between the government and the opposition force concerning the upcoming leadership transition in 1988. The opposition NKPD demanded constitutional changes in favor of direct popular presidential elections to improve the influence of the opposition upon the policymaking process and to expand basic civil liberties. From the NKPD leaders' perspectives, any of their presidential candidates would have had little chance to win the election under the current electoral college system. Throughout 1985, the government refused to discuss the opposition proposal by insisting that discussion about constitutional reform be postponed until after the successful achievements of a peaceful power transition and the Olympic Games in 1988. The NKPD reacted by launching a petition campaign and holding a series of rallies advocating constitutional revision.

On April 30, 1986, Chun responded to the opposition demand by declaring that he would support any constitutional change endorsed by the National Assembly, and that the next election could occur under a new constitution in the event of a political agreement. He also displayed a flexible attitude by opening dialogue with opposition party leaders, including NKPD president Lee Min-Woo.

Following Chun's announcement, the key issue centered on the system of government most suitable for South Korea after 1988. Unlike the opposition NKPD, the DJP advocated a new parliamentary system of government with a strong prime minister elected by the National Assembly. In the view of the ruling party, the Presidential system would not be conducive to democratization in South Korea due to excessive centralization of political power. The NKPD, however, continued to push for a presidential system based upon a popular mandate.

Having taken diametrically opposed positions, neither the NKPD nor the DJP was likely to make major concessions to reach political compromise. Meanwhile, the power struggle was intensified among moderates and hardliners in the opposition party in late 1986, which led to the departure of Kim Dae-Jung and Kim Young-Sam from the NKPD and to the formation of their new party, called the Reunification Democratic Party (RPD), in early April 1987.

On April 13, as the prospects for the constitutional reform by consensus before the end of his presidential tenure grew dim, President Chun announced his decision to postpone further debate on constitutional revision until after the Summer Olympic Games in 1988. On June 10, the DJP nominated the party chairman Roe Tae-Woo, at the recommendation of President Chun, as its presidential candidate at the national party convention.

The opposition parties and students reacted strongly to the President's decision. The next few weeks witnessed intense street demonstrations by students and opposition forces. On June 29, pressured by public protests, Roe recommended to President Chun that he revive the constitutional revision debate and accept the opposition proposal for the presidential system of government by direct popular vote. Chun quickly approved Roe's suggestions.

The Reagan administration has encouraged both the Korean government and the opposition parties to practice moderation and to reach a compromise for the sake of political progress and internal stability.[13]

It is likely that South Korea will undergo complicated and confusing political developments in the coming years. Political stability to a large extent will depend upon the development of several important factors. Who will be elected President to succeed Chun? Will the people support him? Will the military continue to endorse fully the new President without factional struggle? What will be the political role of President Chun after he retires? Will the South Korean economy continue to make steady progress? The answers to these questions will be key determinants of the degree of future internal stability in South Korea. At this stage, there are four most-likely presidential candidates—Roe Tae-Woo, Kim Young-Sam, Kim Dae-Jung, and perhaps former Prime Minister Kim Jong-Pil. If Roe were elected President, there would be significant continuity in domestic politics. Otherwise, it is expected that tremendous change will take place in internal politics and perhaps in some aspects of foreign policy.

Prospects for Korean Security

At present, North Korea possesses a substantial advantage over the South in overall quantity of military equipment as a result of its intensive defense build-up beginning in the early 1970s. Pyongyang now allocates 20-25 percent of its GNP to military spending. The North currently retains 880 thousand-man armed forces out of a population of 20 million, which is a significant increase from 640 thousand in 1980. Most striking is the creation of a large commando force of approximately 100 thousand troops, the Special 8th Corps, whose primary mission is to create a second front in the rear area of the South. The North has continued to improve capabilities to insert them in the South, relying on light transport aircraft (AN2s), attack submarines and missile boats, and amphibious aircraft. The stockpile of North Korean military equipment in major categories—armor, artillery, ships, and aircraft—is estimated to be about three times that of the South.[14] The North holds a clear military advantage, with capabilities fashioned precisely to the battlefield's tactical contours.

Pressured by these initiatives in the North, South Korea has been expanding its military modernization program since the mid-1970s, effecting substantial increases in its military budget (currently 6 percent of the GNP). It has 600 thousand well-trained armed forces out of a population of 43 million. The South retains a qualitative advantage in military equipment, including aircraft and ground weapons, but this is not sufficient to offset its quantitative disadvantage. The military imbalance between the two Koreas seems likely to continue throughout the 1980s.

South Korea, however, enjoys far more advanced economic and industrial capabilities than the North. In 1986, for instance, the ROK GNP (U.S. $95 billion) was about four times more than that of the North. South Korean technology is far superior to that of the North in almost every field. The Pyongyang regime has been suffering from serious economic difficulties as a result of heavy defense expenditures, increasing foreign debts of approximately U.S. $3.5 billion, and lagging technology. Soviet and Chinese aid is not sufficient to enable North Korea to match South Korean economic and industrial advances.

Under such circumstances, the question is "how long, and to what extent, can Pyongyang sustain the level of massive military spending that enables it to retain its advantage over the South?" This will remain one of the most important issues in the 1980s—as will the following question: "What might the North do if it sees its window of opportunity closing?" And what extent of influence will the major Asian powers have over developments?

Threat Perception

The Korean peninsula is one of the most volatile areas in the world. Korea theoretically remains in a state of war under the armistice agreement of the Korean War signed in 1953. In this connection, the two Koreas retain large armed forces across the DMZ, and their military tensions and political hostility are explosive. From Pyongyang's perspective, the prime source of military threat to the DPRK's security is the presence of U.S. ground forces in South Korea. Nevertheless, a U.S.-ROK attack on the North is inconceivable. Both Washington and Seoul pursue defensive, essentially status quo policies, and their interests lie in maintaining stability on the peninsula. The most important role of the U.S. forces in South Korea is to deter a North Korean act of aggression.

As to the possibility of a North Korean attack on the South, there are mainly two schools of thought. One school argues that the North is unlikely to initiate a war against the South particularly under the new leadership of Kim Jong-Il. In their view, the junior Kim has a deep interest in the rapid economic development following the Chinese pattern, in view of Pyongyang's serious economic difficulties. They argue that since Kim Jong-Il emerged as heir-apparent in the Sixth KWP Congress in 1980, the Pyongyang regime has shifted to a more moderate policy line by adopting a joint venture law in 1983, proposing "tripartite talks" with the United States, and by accepting the South Korean proposal for Seoul-Pyongyang dialogue in 1984.

The other school of thought believes that Pyongyang has never abandoned its efforts to unify the peninsula by force. From their point of view, the Pyongyang regime has continued an intensive military buildup in preparation for a war, and its economic and military structure has never changed at all. They believe that, as Kim Il-Sung has already indicated, the North would not allow the South by itself to host successfully the 1988 Olympic Games.[15] The widening gap between the two Koreas' economic and technological capabilities in South Korea's favor means that North Korean military superiority is a wasting asset. North Korea, therefore, has an incentive to launch a major attack against the South while it still retains an edge in military capabilities. This school points to the fact that the North has currently deployed about 65 percent of its total forces close to the DMZ to shorten the warning time in case of a blitzkrieg on the South, and these troops are stationed in an offensive posture.

On balance, however, it seems that if Kim Il-Sung or his successor Jong-Il were convinced that they had a good chance of victory, Pyongyang may resume its efforts to unite the peninsula by force. The North Korean leadership in fact has always placed heavy emphasis on their concept of the favorable time, the so-called "decisive moment." The possibility of a North Korea attack on the South would be sharply increased if one or more of the following situations should develop:

— A weakening of the U.S. commitment to the defense of South Korea;
— A gradual U.S. withdrawal from its Asian security commitments;
— The eruption of major military conflict in other parts of the world;
— A sharp increase of Soviet military and logistic support of North Korea and closer DPRK-USSR strategic cooperation in Asia;
— An escalation of internal chaos in South Korea; or
— An intensification of the internal power struggle in the North.

Contingencies: Confrontation or Peaceful Coexistence?

Throughout the 1980s, the worst case contingency involves the eruption of high-intensity conflict in Korea. In general, there are two possible options open to the North if it decides to take military action against the South. The first option would be an all-out, surprise attack with numerically superior ground and air capabilities aimed at securing the Seoul area. Pyongyang would then have the option of seeking negotiations with the United States if the chances of capturing the rest of South Korea appeared to be unfavorable. Given the fact that Seoul is so close—only 40 kilometers away from the DMZ—a blitzkrieg appears to be a tempting prospect. Such an attack is most likely to occur if the Soviet Union sharply increases its military and logistic support to North Korea, particularly sophisticated weapons, or if major crisis in other parts of the world seriously constrain the U.S. military capability to support the South. In the event of a major East-West crisis in Western Europe and/or the Persian Gulf region, substantial U.S. resources in the Western Pacific may be transferred to those regions,[16] depleting the strategic reserve previously designed to reinforce South Korean defenses in case of a North Korean attack.

The second broad option open to the Pyongyang regime would involve a modified type of guerilla warfare. With its well trained commando units (approximately 100 thousand troops), North Korea could simultaneously dispatch large scale armed infiltrators, dressed in ROK military uniforms and using Hughes 500 helicopters covertly imported from the United States, to major cities in the South to create internal chaos by assassinating key political and military leaders and destroying major government and industrial installations. Almost simultaneously, as the South Korea command structure is paralyzed, the North Korean army corps stationed along the DMZ could immediately attack the South. Such circumstances would make it difficult for ROK and U.S. forces to offer effective resistance. This approach seems possible if internal unrest in the South leads to a major national crisis.

The best case contingency would include "peaceful coexistence" between the two Koreas as a result of a drastic change in North Korea's militant posture toward the South. In view of continuing serious economic difficulties and widening the gap between the two Korea's economic and industrial capabilities in South Korea's favor, Pyongyang may come to the conclusion that it can no longer pursue the sustained military buildup necessary to gain an absolute victory over the South in the event of its attack. At the same time, due to their broad global strategic interests, the Soviet Union and China may pressure the North Korean leadership to restrain its belligerence against the South. In addition, a strong U.S. commitment to the security of South Korea is unlikely to change in the foreseeable future. Under such circumstances, the North may decide to postpone the forceful unification policy for the time being so that it can concentrate its resources upon an economic and technological buildup rather than on military-oriented heavy industry. In that case, Pyongyang will make efforts to participate in the international community and pursue seriously the South-North Korean dialogue. Although this is the most desirable course of events, it is unlikely to occur in the near future, particularly while Kim Il-Sung is alive. It may be some time before the North Korean leadership is prepared to accept such reality.

Under the given political and strategic setting, another possible contingency involves an acceleration of tensions on the Korean peninsula in the absence of a high-intensity military confrontation. North Korea may conclude that the chances for military victory are dim, but to take no action would not be conducive to its interests. In such a case, while avoiding an open offensive, Pyongyang could step up infiltration and cross-border activities by employing commando forces in the hope of disrupting the economic progress of the South and preventing Seoul from hosting the 1988 Summer Olympic Games. This possibility continues to exist throughout the 1980s.

Implications for the Four Major Asian Powers

Open North Korean aggression could lead to major military confrontation on the Korean peninsula. Conflict in Korea would create significant dilemmas for four principal powers in Asia—the United States, Japan, China, and the Soviet Union. The United States is bound by the U.S.-ROK mutual defense treaty of 1954 to come to South Korea's defense. However, such action could jeopardize the U.S. relationship with the PRC as well as run the risk of direct U.S.-Soviet military confrontation.

Japan would be reluctant to get involved directly in the Korean conflict. The Japanese interest, however, would be seriously affected if that conflict touched off a regional or global war with the superpowers' participation. The Soviet Union and its proxies are likely to adopt a concerted coercive diplomacy toward Japan to prevent it from supplying logistic support to the United States and South Korea. In particular, U.S. use of military bases in Japan could be an important issue. Nevertheless, Japan may not tolerate a communist victory in the conflict.

China would also be caught in the dilemma. Under the Sino-North Korean defense treaty of 1961, Peking has an obligation to provide Pyongyang with military and economic support. Nevertheless, Chinese support for North Korea could inevitably threaten Peking's relations with the United States and the West, and incite negative reactions in Southeast Asia. In general, Peking would have three possible options in the event of conflict: taking a neutral position with no action, putting pressure upon Pyongyang to restrict its military action, or supporting North Korea. The most likely course for China is to take a low-key position by providing North Korea with limited economic and military support, while seeking to prevent the aggravation of its relations with the United States and Japan.

The degree of Soviet involvement will determine the nature of the conflict. Moscow, as in the early 1950s, might value a large-scale conflict in Korea as a means of distracting the United States, exacerbating Sino-U.S. relations, and reinforcing its presence in the region. Yet, the Soviet leaders would be concerned about the possibility that such a situation could embroil the Soviet Union directly in the conflict, create pressure for Japanese remilitarization, and exacerbate the relationship with the United States. Moscow would also be uneasy about the potential vulnerability of its sealanes linking Vladivostok, Cam Ranh Bay, and the Middle East as a result of the conflict on the Korean peninsula. Another consideration would be the question of Soviet military capability to support North Korea in light of its commitment elsewhere in Europe, the Middle East, and Southeast Asia. Whatever the level of hostilities, the Soviet Union will attempt to obtain maximum strategic benefit from the Korean situation.

U.S. Interests and Policy Options

In general, U.S. interests lie in maintaining a stable strategic and political environment within the context of the status quo on the Korean peninsula. To protect these interests, the United States should continue its firm military commitment to South Korea; promote internal stability in the South by maintaining close U.S.-ROK economic and political cooperation; work to rectify the South-North Korean military imbalance by helping improve overall South Korean conventional warfare capabilities; promote South-North Korean dialogue for the purpose of reducing tensions, with the ultimate goal of achieving national reunification through political accommodation; and promote international arrangements with the Soviet Union, China, and Japan such as "cross-recognition" or multilateral talks.

In the event of an eruption of serious internal turmoil in South Korea, the United States should take steps to prevent North Korea from exploiting such a situation. Possible U.S. actions include a clear warning to North Korea and its allies concerning a strong U.S.-ROK response in case of provocations and the strengthening of regional forces in and around South Korea. At the same time, Washington should initiate efforts to promote the fastest possible restoration of political and economic stability in South Korea. Indeed, to limit the possibilities of internal upheaval, the United States should encourage South Korea to develop steady political democratization. Excessive U.S. efforts to influence South Korean domestic politics would be counterproductive, because this would provoke a strong reaction and anti-Americanism among the Korean people. Instead, quiet recommendations and political consultations provided by the United States would be most effective to achieve this end.

A North Korean invasion would provoke an immediate and strong retaliation by the ROK and the United States. Yet, there would be certain constraints on U.S. actions. There is a possibility that full-scale U.S. involvement could be delayed because it has to adhere to "constitutional processes" in accordance with Article 3 of the 1954 U.S.-ROK mutual defense treaty. Under the 1973 War Powers Act, the U.S. Congress must specifically authorize the continued involvement of U.S. armed Forces in hostile action beyond a limited number of days. Moreover, in the event of simultaneous crisis in other parts of the world, particularly in Europe or the Middle East, U.S. military capabilities to support South Korea could be significantly but unpredictably limited.

If a North Korean attack occurs, the Unites States should initiate various important steps. In addition to increasing military and logistic support to South Korea, particularly air and naval capabilities, it would be in the U.S. interest to strengthen the U.S. position in the Western Pacific to deter Soviet or Chinese participation in the conflict. At the same time, it would also be important for the United States to cooperate closely with its allies in Europe, the Middle East, and Japan because if U.S. forces were to become deeply involved in a Korean conflict, the Soviets or their proxies might choose that moment to precipitate crises elsewhere.

Finally, the United States should seek to restrain North Korean military operations. North Korean logistical routes can be interrupted by blockading major Northern ports; diplomatic pressure should be placed upon the Soviet Union and the PRC to end military support to the DPRK; and collective international economic and political sanctions against Pyongyang should be pursued through multi-national organizations, particularly the United Nations.

Conclusion

Throughout the 1980s, the Korean peninsula will remain one of the most volatile regions in the world. Explosive military tensions and political hostility are likely to persist despite efforts by Seoul and Pyongyang to develop a dialogue. Security in Korea will continue to be dependent upon the external and internal situation. The strategic rivalry among the United States, the Soviet Union, China, and Japan, and their respective vital interest in Asia will heavily influence strategic-military conditions on the peninsula. Unless their interrelationships undergo drastic changes, the four principal powers will be satisfied with the current political structure and stability on the Korean peninsula. The United States and Japan will continue to encourage the realization of the "cross-recognition" formula and a "step-by-step" approach in the unification process of the two Koreas. Yet, the Soviet Union and China would be reluctant to get engaged in the multilateral talks with the United States and Japan on the Korean issues under the present strategic setting in Asia.

Within this context, the two Koreas each will pursue active domestic and foreign policies. In the not-too-distant future, both Pyongyang and Seoul are expected to experience a political succession. The leadership changes of South and North Korea will not result in major shifts in their strategic policies, although to some extent political and military tactics may be altered. In particular, there largely will be continuity in the unification policies of the two Koreas throughout this decade. For instance, under the leadership of Chun Doo Hwan's successor, the South will continue to push for a "step-by-step" approach toward gradual integration in the unification process, while maintaining internal stability and security. To achieve this end, Chun's successor will make efforts to achieve military parity with the North, while furthering economic progress.

Under the leadership of Kim Il-Jong, Pyongyang's strategic objective of unifying the peninsula on its own terms will remain intact. In the pursuit of this goal, the North is likely to continue a combination of moderate and hard-line policies to promote the strengthening of military capability and economic development until the "decisive moment" arrives. Therefore, the possibility of North Korean attack against the South cannot be totally ruled out.

As time elapses, however, the window of opportunity for North Korea will be gradually closed. Perhaps, by the turn of this decade, if stability on the peninsula prevails, the ROK forces will be able to provide effective deterrence to the North Korean aggression without substantial U.S. military support, although the North may still retain a marginal edge in the overall military balance. Sometime in the 1990s, Kim Jong-Il may be fully convinced that the North has little

chance to achieve a victory over the South in the event of war; Pyongyang is
decisively overwhelmed by the South in the economic and technological
arenas; and that internal conditions in the South, as well as the policies of the
four major Asian powers, are unfavorable to the North Korean efforts to unify
the peninsula by force. In that case, the Pyongyang leadership will have to assume a sincere attitude in the dialogue with the South to discuss the unification
issues. The North, at the same time, will have to adjust to its major domestic
and foreign policies. The important tasks facing Kim Jong-Il will include the
rapid economic development and the further consolidation of his power, for
which the revamping of the military and economic structures is essential. In this
respect, Pyongyang will emphasize the improvement of the standard of living
and consumer goods rather than the military buildup. North Korea also will
have to participate in the international community by opening up further channels with the West for economic and technological cooperation, while seeking
the U.S. recognition of DPRK's legitimacy on the peninsula. Such developments would require the adjustment of the principal Asian powers' policy
toward the Korean peninsula. At that point, all the parties involved would tackle
the issues of "cross-recognition" and the two Koreas' simultaneous entry into
the United Nations into a more realistic and sincere manner.

In sum, the principal factor determining the resolution of various pending issues relating to the two Koreas is the question of "time." Whether these issues
are resolved sooner or later will have a great influence on "how" they are
resolved. Therefore, both South and North Korea will seek to exploit the "time"
to their own strategic advantage. In the meantime, the two Koreas will continue
their intensive competition in the political, military, economic, ideological, and
cultural arenas.

NOTES

1. For a comprehensive study on the subject of U.S. policy toward Korea,
see Claude A. Buss, *The United States and the Republic of Korea: Background
for Policy* (Stanford: Hoover Institution Press, 1982).

2. Paul Wolfowitz, "Recent Security Developments in Korea and U.S.
Policy." A speech delivered at the Council on U.S.-Korean Military and Security
Studies in Washington, D.C. on August 12, 1985.

3. For details, see the "Joint Communique Following the Meeting Between
the President of the United States and the President of the Republic of Korea"
released by the White House on February 2, 1981 and the Joint Communique
of the 13 Annual U.S.-ROK Security Consultative Meeting on April 30, 1981.
See also the Joint Communique of the 18 Annual U.S.-ROK Security Consultative Meeting on April 3, 1986, *Korea Herald*, (April 5, 1986).

4. Bae-Ho Hahn, "Policy Toward Japan," in *The Foreign Policy of the Republic of Korea* (New York: Columbia, 1985), edited by Youngnok Koo and Sungjoo Han.

5. Harry Harding, "North Korea and the Republic of China." A paper presented at the "Conference on Northeast Asia in the 1980s: Issues and Opportunities," Seoul, Korea, in November 1983.

6. *Asian Wall Street Journal*, (January 20, 1985).

7. Seung-Hwan Kim, *Contingencies on the Korean Peninsula: Confrontation or Peaceful Coexistence?* (Washington, D.C.: Center for Strategic and International Studies, 1983). CSIS Contingency Report No. 10.

8. *Hankook Ilbo* (Seoul), (December 30, 1985); *Korea Herald* (Seoul), (January 24, 1986); and *Korea Newsreview*, (March 29, 1986).

9. *Washington Post*, (August 14, 1985).

10. A speech delivered by Stephan Solarz at the Northeast Asia Council Forum at the Georgetown University Center for Strategic and International Studies on April 23, 1984.

11. See the text of the press conference with ROK Defense Minister Lee Ki-Baek in Seoul, Korea on March 20, 1986. *Korea Herald*, (March 22, 1986).

12. Seung-Hwan Kim, "Is There a Korean Summit in the Cards? *Asian Wall Street Journal*, (December 2, 1985).

13. Testimony by Gaston J. Sigur, Jr., Assistant Secretary of State for East Asian and Pacific Affairs, at a Hearing before the U.S. House of Representatives Subcommittee on Asian and Pacific Affairs on April 16, 1986. See also Stephen J. Solarz, "After Manila, Is Seoul Next?" in the *Washington Post*, (April 27, 1986). See also Gaston J. Sigur, Jr. *Korean Politics in Transition*, U.S. Department of State, Current Policy No. 917, February 6, 1987; and "Korea: New Beginnings," an address by Gaston J. Sigur, Jr. before the Foreign Policy Association, New York, July 21, 1987.

14. *The Military Balance 1985-1986*, (London: IISS, 1985). William C. Sherman, "The Interests and Policies of the United States in the Korean Peninsula." A paper presented at the conference on "Tensions in the Korean Peninsula" at the Hoover Institution in California on November 18-20, 1984.

15. *Korea Herald*, (March 28 and April 23, 1986).

16. The Reagan administration for instance established priorities for the use of American military power in the event of a global war with the Soviet Union in 1982. For details, see "Reagan Moves on Military Priorities," *New York Times*, (May 25, 1982) and "Persian Gulf Oil Region Near Top of U.S. Defense Priority List," *Washington Post*, (June 2, 1985).

CHAPTER 6

The Philippines after Marcos

Larry A. Niksch

After two decades as President of the Philippines, Ferdinand Marcos relinquished his power in February 1986. His authoritarian style of government allowed him to use the resources and institutions of his country to benefit himself as well as his inner circle of friends and supporters. The legacy he has bequeathed to his successors is composed of formidable challenges at all levels—social, political, and economic.

President Corazon Aquino's job will not be easy in the immediate post-Marcos era. She must strive to reconcile her divided compatriots and encourage them to support her new administration. Concomitantly, Aquino will have to contend with a bleak economic situation, an active communist insurgency and severely corrupt political institutions. The prospect that she will remedy all of these internal problems—and solidify her base of political support—is not guaranteed.

Nevertheless, President Aquino is not alone. The United States and the Philippines have developed a special relationship over a span of twenty years. The change in administration of this strategically located country will not alter important U.S. security interests here. The Reagan administration has reiterated its desire to maintain the U.S. presence in the Philippines. Clearly, the U.S. has a vested interest in assisting the new government in rectifying the excesses and abuses of the former regime and building a democratic and popularly supported government.

This essay demonstrates that only in a stable, non-communist dominated Philippines will the U.S. assure the preservation of its security interests. The first section describes the U.S. military bases in the Philippines. The next part examines the nature of country's internal crisis, dealing specifically with political, economic, and military issues. The final section looks at the way in which the U.S. can play a positive role in helping the new administration bring about a stable and prosperous Philippines. Only by actively assisting the Aquino government can the U.S. preserve its vested interests in the Philippines.

The U.S. Military Presence in the Philippines and
Western Pacific Security

The role of the United States in the Philippines during the last few years has been controversial. Nevertheless, a broad consensus has existed in the United States that the U.S.-operated military bases in the Philippines support a number of U.S. security and military policy objectives in the Western Pacific. Among these are:

(1) The maintenance of a military balance among the major powers in the Western Pacific, especially with respect to the growing Soviet military role;

(2) A secure alliance with Japan, the strongest non-communist power in East Asia;

(3) Closer relations and increased cooperation with China against the Soviet Union and its allies in East Asia;

(4) Control of key sea and air transport routes connecting the United States and Northeast Asia and the Indian Ocean-Persian Gulf region.

American operated bases in the Philippines are among the most important of U.S. facilities overseas in terms of size and functions.[1] Subic Bay Naval Base, with over 7,000 U.S. military personnel and a Filipino work force of about 20,000, is the key logistical center for the U.S. Seventh Fleet in the Western Pacific. Approximately 65 percent of the fleet's repair work is done at Subic. The base can perform dry docking of all Seventh Fleet ships, except carriers and battleships. In time of crisis, Subic would be the main support base for additional carrier task forces deployed into the Japan-Korea region, the South China Sea, and the Indian Ocean. Subic's storage capacity for petroleum (110 million gallons, spare parts, and ammunition) make it the largest U.S. naval supply depot outside the United States.

Subic has two adjunct facilities: the Naval Communications Station at San Miguel and the Naval Air Station at Cubi Point. The Naval Communications Station is one of the Navy's principal communications sites worldwide and provides tactical communications for Seventh Fleet operations. Cubi Point provides maintenance and repair facilities for aircraft from U.S. carriers. It also support P-3C anti-submarine patrols over the South China Sea and the Indian Ocean.

Clark Air Base, about fifty miles northwest of Manila, is the largest U.S. Air Force-operated installation outside the United States. Its runways and hangar space can accommodate any combat and transport aircraft in the U.S. inventory. Clark has a petroleum storage capacity of 25 million gallons and 200,000 square feet of ammunition storage space. Two tactical fighter squadrons of F-4s are permanently stationed at Clark. Clark is the home of the Crow Valley weapons range, where Air Force, Navy, and Marine units throughout the Western Pacific conduct combat exercises up to eight times a year. Clark also serves as a conduit through which supplies, aircraft, and personnel flow to

Subic and the Seventh Fleet. The Air Force operates daily flights of C-5 and C-141 transport aircraft through Clark to the U.S. base at Diego Garcia.[2]

The bases' support functions have been made important by the vast geographical distances covered by the Seventh Fleet and the many military missions that would be directly assisted from Subic and Clark. The geographical distances are immense: from the northwest Pacific to the western Indian, including Southeast Asia and the Southwest Pacific. The actual and potential missions supported by the two bases include carrier and tactical aircraft movement to South Korea in the event of a North Korean attack; wartime operations in the Northwest Pacific against Soviet forces; security for the southern sea and air transport routes to Japan from Hawaii via Guam; carrier operations in the Indian Ocean; logistical support deployment of the Rapid Deployment Force and land-based aircraft into the Persian Gulf region; and air and naval involvement in the defense of Thailand.

The Stakes for the U.S. in the Philippines

The dramatic events surrounding the fall of Ferdinand Marcos and the assumption of power by Corazon Aquino have produced various reactions in the United States and East Asia. These reactions ranged from sighs of relief, to downright euphoria, to concern over the impact of the Philippine crisis on the internal stability of other countries. The Philippines, long viewed as the "odd man out" in Asia, had come to occupy center stage in the last years of Marcos. This was, unfortunately, not due to any great achievement by the Philippines; rather, it resulted from the acute deterioration within the country.

From the perspective of the United States, the country's internal deterioration of continued political polarization and radicalization may ultimately lead to a communist takeover and the emergence of a new center of Marxism-Leninism in the East Asian region.[3] The crisis awakened in the United States an awareness of its multiple interests in its former colony. Americans have become more aware of the unique relationship between the two countries. They watched, especially in the last weeks of the Marcos government, as Filipinos demonstrated the close cultural ties to Americans and their strong sensitivities to American actions. U.S. officials and other observers grew alarmed over the fate of Filipinos as communist insurgents revealed their repressive intentions in regions where they were strong or dominant.[4] No group was more concerned over the plight of their homeland than the over one million Filipino-Americans.

American experts also began to see adverse implications for U.S. interests in the East Asian region if the Philippines' deterioration continued or if a communist takeover occurred. The Philippines' ASEAN neighbors could be threatened by a massive outflow of Filipino refugees. A communist takeover could spark regional conflict over issues like refugees, territorial disputes, and

the emergence of an anti-communist resistance in the Philippines. A radicalization of the Philippines and an ouster of the United States likely would threaten
the unity of ASEAN. The United States would be less able to play the role of
regional balancer in Southeast Asia—not only among the big powers, but also
among the ASEAN states themselves, with their differing views of how to deal
with China, Vietnam, and the Soviet Union.

The potential implications for big power relations emerged more often in
U.S. statements.[5] A communist takeover of the Philippines, and a subsequent
ouster of U.S. bases, would have provided the Soviet Union with a major
strategic gain in the Southwest Pacific. Moscow could have been expected
under such conditions to accelerate its military buildup in the South China Sea.
A permanent Soviet military role in Vietnam would have been assured. If access to Subic and Clark bases became available to the USSR, the Soviets would
have seized the opportunity without hesitation. Soviet political influence undoubtedly would have risen in some ASEAN states, and U.S. credibility would
have suffered a severe blow in Southeast Asia. At the same time, China would
not have sat idly while Moscow achieved dominant power status in the region.
China could be expected to escalate its role in Southeast Asia and perhaps move
to "solve" the Taiwan problem.

The United States would face the difficult task of constructing alternative
military bases along the Saipan-Tinian-Guam-Palau line. New military
facilities and increased levels of mobile naval forces would cost tens of billions
of dollars.[6] U.S. failure to commit the money in an era of reduced deficit spending would result in a major pullback of the Seventh Fleet to Hawaii.

Regardless of the military alternatives available to the United States, U.S.
interests in strengthening anti-Soviet defenses in the Northwest Pacific would
grow. Washington undoubtedly would view increased capabilities to isolate
Soviet forces in Siberia as one way to compensate for a shift in the military
balance due to a U.S. ouster from the Philippines. The United States no doubt
would look to Japan to accelerate its military buildup and defense responsibilities in the Northwest Pacific. Washington in particular would seek an enhanced Japanese contribution to the security of that part of the Hawaii-Japan
transport route extending north from Guam.

U.S. defense capabilities in the Northwest Pacific and Northeast Asia would
not suffer if the United States built comparable naval and air facilities in Guam,
Saipan, and Tinian. This would be especially true if naval facilities on these islands could take over the logistics support currently performed by the Subic
base. If, however, this was not done, the United States probably would not be
able to deploy additional aircraft carriers to the Western Pacific to meet contingencies in Korea or involving the Soviet Union.

The New U.S. Interest

This multi-dimensional set of interests gives the United States a substantial stake in the success of the new Aquino government in restoring the Philippines' political and economic health—even if changes eventually are made to the U.S. military presence in the Philippines. Other states in the region have a similar stake in maintaining stability in the Philippines because they share these common interests.

More than any other country, however, the United States has acquired an additional interest (commitment may be a more appropriate term) in assisting the new government due to the large role it played in bringing about the demise of the Marcos government. Consequently, the U.S. must preserve its various interests in the Philippines by engaging in a concerted effort to help stabilize the political environment throughout the transition to a democratic form of government. From the time the Reagan administration launched its campaign in January 1985 to pressure President Marcos for reforms, the United States supported those forces within the society that had turned against the government or would eventually do so. These forces include the political opposition, the leadership of the Catholic Church, and the military reformists. U.S. encouragement probably contributed to the decisions of most members within these groups to challenge Marcos through the political processes available, and not to enter into alliances with the Communist Party and its front organizations.

U.S. charges of a fraudulent presidential election helped to seal President Marcos' isolation after February 7.[7] The U.S. government supported the Enrile-Ramos rebellion through such acts as the White House pronouncements of February 22, 23, and 24; allowed rebel air units to use Clark Air Base;[8] advised President Marcos to relinquish his power; and communicated the U.S. position to Filipino military commanders in metropolitan Manila. Filipinos no doubt would have risen against the regime at some point without American involvement; but the timing, the amount of bloodshed, and the outcome might have been radically different.

The Nature of the Internal Crisis

The government of Corazon Aquino must now confront itself with the legacy Marcos bequeathed it. The same issues that produced the crisis in the last years of the former regime, but which the old regime largely ignored, remain to be solved—political polarization, the breakdown of political institutions, a declining economy, and a communist insurgency movement that has become a significant force.

Marcos' style of personalized rule left many government institutions weakened in terms of functional independence, quality of personnel, and public support. This is true of the former parliament, the courts, and the military. It is especially true of local government, which was a vital center of Filipino political life and community activity prior to Marcos' imposition of sterile rule, due to declining popular identification with Marcos-appointed officials; popular participation in politics has declined considerably. In addition, government employees at the grass roots level usually receive little training to perform adequately in their jobs. The economic crisis has also adversely affected the efficiency of local politics because of the reduced financial support they receive from Manila. In short, local government today suffers from an acute crisis at the same time communist insurgents are attempting to undermine it.

The economic crisis is composed of several elements, all of which are inextricably linked and inter-related.[9] The inability of the Philippines to pay its foreign debt resulted in a cutoff of foreign capital which Philippines businesses had used to finance imports. The business sector has been crippled, operating at well below 50 percent of capacity. Unemployment is at a rate of 20 percent, according to the Aquino government, and underemployment approaches 50 percent of the adult work force. Little new investment has accrued since late 1983. The Marcos government was forced to impose austerity measures largely in response to the debt situation and the rising inflation rates for private borrowers to over 30 percent. The business sector suffered even more as credit dried up. Even when new credit became available in 1985, businesses made little use of it. Businessmen lacked long term confidence, and many had turned against Marcos politically. Some began to describe not investing as a "patriotic act."

Falling international prices for sugar and coconut exports have hit the rural sector equally hard. Living standards declined for large segments of the rural population (one-third of all Filipinos are dependent on the coconut industry), and acute hardships and malnutrition have developed in certain regions. The sugar-producing island of Negros, for example, has become a cauldron of economic breakdown, starvation, and, consequently, a target for the communist insurgency.

International lending agencies, bankers, and economists criticized the Marcos government of mismanaging the budget and of turning over key economic sectors to friends of President Marcos (the so-called "crony capitalists"). In addition, they criticized the large government expenditures granted to subsidize "crony" enterprises that were unsound financially and allowing "cronies" to establish debilitating monopolies over the sugar and coconut sectors. They decried the allocation of large sums of public money on unnecessary projects and resented the government's clearly biased development programs which favored Manila and surrounding areas of Luzon. Marcos' government further minimized the earnings of producers by establishing price controls on food products. Together, these factors served to exacerbate an already bleak economic situation; the potential for domestic strife remained high. The statistics speak for themselves: Gross National Product declined by over five percent in 1984 and over three percent in 1985; per capital income fell by even greater rates.

In October 1984, the International Monetary Fund (IMF) approved credits totaling about $615 million to rescue the Philippines economy. However, the IMF attached tough conditions with the credits which included tight budget and monetary targets and a full float of the peso. The IMF also made disbursement of the credits dependent on the government reaching agreements with foreign lending banks about debt rescheduling and new credits. Agreement was reached in May 1985. It provided for new loans of $925 million and $1.75 billion in new trade credits through the end of 1986. The banks also agreed to the rescheduling of $5.8 billion in principal payments owed by the Philippine government and private borrowers. The new loans and credits have been disbursed in segments, conditional upon government's success in meeting the IMF's performance criteria.

As the economy began to stagnate after 1979 and political turmoil rose, the communist insurgency made major gains. The strength of regular forces of the New Peoples Army (NPA), the armed wing of the Communist Party of the Philippines (CPP), is estimated at 16,000 to 20,000. The CPP has established political organizations in over 20 percent of the 41,000 barangays (the lowest level governmental units in the country). The CPP exercises political influence in various degrees over approximately 25 percent of the population. The insurgency operates at various levels in nearly every one of the Philippines' seventy-three provinces. The CPP has expanded urban operations and infiltration of social and sectoral groups to a significant degree since 1982.[10] Bayan, a key front organization, emerged in 1984 as a political grouping of the left, and became a potent political force in 1985.

Six main factors appear to have contributed to the growth of the insurgency and communist political influence:

(1) the weakness of local government and law enforcement at the level of the Philippines' 1,534 towns;

(2) the declining living standards in the towns, particularly falling real incomes, unemployment, malnutrition, and lack of medicines and adequate medical care;

(3) the breakdown of traditional social structures and support systems in places such as Mindanao and Negros;

(4) the growth in Communist organizations at the local level that have become skilled in penetration, establishing links with people in the barangays, and convincing people that the government is responsible for their problems and worsening conditions;

(5) military abuses of civilians, which alienate civilians from the government and the armed forces; and

(6) the political unpopularity of the Marcos government with important groups in the cities.

CPP strategy consists of three components—party building, armed struggle, and united front building. Party building is the organizational foundation for the other two and the source of ultimate political control. CPP-controlled organizations in the barangays develop in stages, and when successfully they eventually reach a level where they replace the legal authorities and support the formation of armed guerrilla units for the NPA.

The NPA performs several functions: (1) the killing of town mayors, policemen, barangay officials, and the individuals who oppose the insurgents; (2) the acquisition of arms; (3) the forcing of the Philippines armed forces to abandon outposts and operations in the countryside; and (4) eventual attacks on major military bases and the large cities.

The CPP conducts its united front strategy through the National Democratic Front (NDF). The united front strategy focuses on the cities. The CPP seeks to influence politically aware segments of the urban society, place its operatives in sectoral organizations, set up front organizations as a spearhead of urban discontent, and direct the united front toward the CPP's tactical goals of increased militancy and violence against the government. Besides the CPP's united front activities, armed communist units in urban areas have engaged in assassinations of government officials, police, and military personnel.

The CPP has problems including shortages of weapons and other resources, command and control of units over wide geographical areas and separate islands, and weak ideological commitment to communism among the rank and file insurgents. Nevertheless, the CPP has become adept at political organization building and taking advantage of the numerous weaknesses and mistakes of the Philippine government and armed forces.

During the Marcos period, the counterinsurgency strategy of the Philippine government was primarily military and emphasized the establishment of security in areas where the communists were active. It usually came into play after the insurgency was well established in the area and had committed overt acts of violence. The strategy has had three main elements:[11]

(1) Town mayors and barangay captions form Civilian Home Defense Forces (CHDF) and secure arms from the armed forces for the CHDF. CHDF units often act as bodyguards for local officials.

(2) Regular AFP forces move units into trouble spots. The Constabulatory (PC) normally reacts first. The army and marines deploy units into the most severely infiltrated areas. The AFP conducts operations with the goals of eliminating armed NPA units, apprehending CPP/NPA personnel and their supporters, and controlling roads and other transportation routes.

(3) The AFP conducts intelligence operations at different levels. It aims to locate and apprehend CPP national and regional leaders, identify CPP cadre and supporters in the towns and rural barangays, and gather information on sectoral and political organizations to determine CPP/NDF influence.

Government and military officials have talked about a broader counterinsurgency strategy to include dialogues with civilians, civic action, and economic development. The kinds of programs occur only sporadically. Consequently, the government and the AFP face severe problems which they must overcome in order to defeat the insurgency:[12]

(1) *Lack of security at the grass roots*: Barangay, town, and police officials often do not cooperate in communicating information on insurgent activities. This is due to such factors as institutional and personal rivalries, fear of the NPA, fear of military units entering the towns, and lack of awareness of CPP activities. Police units usually are ineffective in intelligence gathering and arresting operations. Policemen are poorly trained, and they often lack transportation and communication equipment. The Marcos government did little to improve their performance.

CHDF units receive little training, or sometimes no training at all. Recruitment standards of the CHDF are applied unevenly. The CHDF has few resources aside from weapons. In many towns, it apparently does not function most of the time.

(2) *Poor military-civilian relations*: Relations between the AFP and civilians have been strained in many regions. Civilians raise two issues: abuses and corruption. Their comments point to fundamental problems in the Constabulatory: visible corruption and abuses such as drunken behavior of PC personnel and checkpoint shakedowns of civilians; and covert torture and execution of suspected insurgents and supporters. The army and the intelligence agencies reportedly have been involved in torture and execution cases. Many of these incidents occur during interrogation of suspects. Some individual units and commanders have had better reputations with civilians. The Philippines marines appear to have good relations with civilians in many of their operational areas.

(3) *Lack of sufficient military resources*: The AFP suffers from a severe deficiency of material resources. This erodes moral and contributes to military misconduct. Commanders often have little or no transportation equipment and not enough radios to equip platoons and squads. Food and clothing are in short supply. Medical care is minimal in military bases and is generally unavailable for troops in the field. Pay allows only a subsistence existence for military families. Commanders lack the resources to conduct civic action programs for civilians.

(4) *Inadequate training*: With the exception of the marines and a few individual army units, training in the AFP is of questionable quality. There is little standardized training in the army and PC. Since there are few central training camps, recruits often are trained in the units with which they sign up. The army and PC conduct little training.

(5) *Weak political unity among non-communist groups*: The CPP had based its recent efforts to escalate united front activities in the cities on the assumption that the Marcos government would not reach accommodation with the non-communist political opposition groups that emerged after the Aquino assassination. The CPP was correct in this calculation. Marcos, and even the most conservative elements in the opposition, remained hostile towards each

other to the end. President Marcos showed little willingness to accept political reform measures.[13] Some opposition groups cooperated with CPP front elements as a means of escalating pressure on the government. This state of affairs worked to the advantage of the CPP's united front strategy in the cities.

The Aquino Government After 18 Months: Tremendous Problems and Limited Progress

The Aquino government has struggled with the same problems as faced by the Marcos government, but it has taken a different approach based on democratization and limited economic and military reforms. It has achieved some positive results—the greatest being in democratization and lesser successes in dealing with the economy and the communist insurgency. Nevertheless, the Philippines remains in a permanent state of tension, and its future is very much in doubt.

Political Restructuring

The Aquino government has made substantial progress in putting into place a democratic political system at the national level based on a democratic constitution and elections for national officials. Moreover, the Philippines enjoys a broad range of political and civil liberties under Aquino.

The new constitution, drafted in 1986 by a constitutional commission, features a presidential system of government with an elected president limited to one six-year term. It allows President Aquino to serve a six-year term ending in 1992. The constitution also provides for a two-house Congress composed of two hundred elected members of the House of Representatives, fifty appointed members and 24 senators elected on a nationwide basis.

A national plebiscite was held on the constitution on February 2, 1987. President Aquino campaigned hard for a "yes" vote. Opposition came from communist-influenced groups, groups associated with the former Marcos government, and supporters of former Defense Minister Juan Ponce Enrile, whom Aquino had fired the preceding November. Voters approved the constitution by a margin of over 76 percent. The large affirmative vote reflected Aquino's popularity with the public and the desire of Filipinos to see democracy restored at the grass roots through free elections.[14]

The Philippines held congressional elections in May 1987. The opposition charged widespread fraud, but most observers believe that the elections were generally honest. Pro-Aquino candidate swept the Senate, but the results of the House races showed a more diverse mix of winners. Old-line political families that had lost power under Marcos re-emerged in the elections. The Congress

convened in July 1987, and Aquino now will have to share power with a legis-
lature holding considerable power.

The Aquino government still faces the tough task of revitalizing local
government, which suffered decay during the later Marcos years. The Aquino
government has made only limited progress in breaking up the fiefdoms of local
political bosses in specific parts of the country. Its policy of replacing nearly
1,600 local elected officials with appointed Officers in Charge has been controversial. The Aquino government has set elections for provincial and
municipal officers for late 1987 and elections for barangay officials for early
1988. Many experts on Philippine politics and the Communist insurgency argue
that elections are crucial at the local level to restore political competition, ac-
countability of government and popular identification with local administrations. The government, nevertheless, displays reluctance to hold local elections,
postponing them on several occasions. Officials in Manila probably fear that
pro-Marcos former officials and communist-backed candidates may win many
offices.

Challenge from the Military

Elements from within the Philippine armed forces (AFP), sometimes allied
with pro-Marcos civilians, have sought to take power from Aquino on several
occasions. There have been three overt coup attempts and a number of credible
reports of plots against the government. The origins of the situation have been:
(1) the existence of several politically-oriented factions in the AFP, including
one major group (the Guardians) considered loyal to former President Marcos;
(2) Marcos' involvement in several plots from his exile in Hawaii;[15] (3) the am-
bition of Enrile to dominate the government while he was Defense Minister
under Aquino (March-November 1986); (4) the influential role of the armed
forces reform movement (RAM), especially its leaders in the Defense Ministry
who had ties to Enrile; (5) dissatisfaction within the AFP over Aquino's policy
toward the communist insurgency and over the lack of improvement in the low-
level physical resources available to units in the field; and (6) President
Aquino's aloofness from the military except for top commanders loyal to her.

The Aquino government has dealt successfully with these threats for several
reasons. Aquino has broad popular support. Most Filipinos support her
democratization program, and the overwhelming vote in February to approve
the new constitution was a rebuff to critics of the constitution within the AFP.
The armed forces leadership under General Ramos and the bulk of the troops
have remained loyal to Aquino. Finally, the U.S. government has supported the
Aquino government fully; U.S. views have influence in the AFP.[16]

In the aftermath of the congressional elections and the convening of the new
Congress, the Aquino government appears stronger in relation to its opponents
in the AFP. Key, pro-Marcos plotters are in custody or are fugitives. Rafael

Ileto, the new Defense Minister, has started to break up the military factions. Civilian opponents have begun to emphasize participation in electoral politics.

Economic Restructuring

The Aquino government has emphasized the need to restore economic growth and alleviate unemployment and poverty. It has encouraged domestic and foreign private investment as the main engine of growth in the manufacturing sector. It has promised to end the preferential treatment which the Marcos government extended to favored businesses owned by Marcos friends and family members, and it has launched a program to sell government-owned enterprises to private businesses. The government has disbanded the Marcos era monopolies that controlled the purchase and export of coconuts and sugar. The government has adopted tax reforms aimed at encouraging exports by ending export taxes and stimulating domestic demand by lowering individual income tax rates.

The Aquino government also had changed fiscal policy away from austerity budgets to what it calls "growth budgets." In addition to tax reforms, the government has increased spending and has accepted higher budget deficits.

The Aquino government has stressed foreign financial assistance as the key means of financing higher expenditures and budget deficits. It sought nearly $1.1 billion in foreign economic aid in 1986 and secured pledges of about $1 billion by the end of 1986. The government asserts that the Philippines will need between $6 billion and $7 billion in foreign aid during the six year period, 1987-1992.

The government has succeeded in working out new loan arrangements with the International Monetary Fund, the World Bank, and foreign lending banks. Such arrangements are crucial to help finance the $27 billion foreign debt, which eats up 40-45 percent of the Philippines' export earnings and 40 percent of the national budget annually. An accord in March 1987 with foreign banks provided for the re-scheduling of $10.3 billion of debt. Filipino officials believe these arrangements will reduce the debt/export earning ratio to 25-30 percent.

The economic decline ended in 1986, as the economy grew by a miniscule one-tenth of one percent. Economic forecasters predict a recovery in 1987, although many forecast a 4-5 percent growth rather than the 6.2 percent growth rate predicted by the Philippine government.[17] First quarter growth in fact was over six percent, confirming that a recovery is underway. The recovery is fueled primarily by rising export earnings for coconuts, which has resulted in larger incomes and consumption by coconut farmers. (Nearly one-third of the population earns some portion of income from the coconut industry). Government pump-priming also has increased domestic demand. Prospects for growth also stem from low inflation, falling interest rates, and an improved current account balance.

The Philippines' ability to sustain growth beyond 1988 is more uncertain. It will require significantly more private investment. So far, both Filipino and foreign private investment has remained at low levels since Aquino came to power—insufficient to sustain a long-term recovery.[18]

Businessmen have cited the continuing political and insurgency situations as a major disincentive to investors. Besides coup plots and communist attacks and taxation of businesses, businessmen remain concerned over the large number of labor strikes and the kidnapping of foreign businessmen and technicians by insurgent groups and criminal elements.

Rural Poverty and Unemployment

In large part because of the communist insurgency, the Aquino government has stressed the need to ameliorate the severe poverty and unemployment in the rural areas where most Filipinos live. So far, its main accomplishment has been in the coconut sector, where the dismantling of the Marcos coconut monopoly and the lifting of export taxes have contributed to the improved incomes of coconut farmers.

In three other areas, however, the Aquino government has accomplished much less. First, the government has had little impact on malnutrition and starvation among 700,000 children on the island of Negros. Voluntary agencies and United Nations agencies are active in Negros, but the effort has been insufficient to reduce significantly the prevailing conditions.

Second, the government has intended that much of its increased budget expenditures will finance rural works projects. The government has asserted that this program will provide jobs to one million rural Filipinos in 1987. The rural works program has been delayed, however, reportedly due to bureaucratic inefficiencies in the drawing up of project plans, problems in securing competent contractors, and corruption within the Ministry of Public Works. As a result, prospects for the rapid creation of jobs in 1987 have dwindled.

Third, the government has said that it will institute a land reform program intended to distribute land to landless workers, whose numbers are estimated at eight to ten million. The government produced a plan before the convening of the new Congress but left important details for the Congress to legislate. Many observers doubt whether there actually will be a massive land re-distribution. Major obstacles exist including the likely high cost of a program, resistance from politically- powerful landowners, and the attitude of the new Congress.[19]

Dealing with the Communist Insurgency

The Aquino government's approach to the communist insurgency has contained misperceptions and underestimates of the strength of the communist movement in the Philippines, but the government has had some successes with a broader political approach toward the problem. Aquino government spokes-men initially predicted that the insurgency would quickly collapse with the demise of Marcos. President Aquino proposed a cease-fire and the negotiation of a political settlement with the communist leadership. In order to make this offer attractive, the AFP adopted a defensive stance in most parts of the country, including a withdrawal from some distant rural areas into major towns and reduced patrolling in rural areas generally.[20]

The CPP agreed to negotiate, but CPP leaders stated that the insurgents would not lay down their arms in any settlement. NPA attacks continued, in-cluding well-publicized ambushes and raids. However, the two sides signed a cease-fire agreement in late November 1986, provided for a sixty-day truce.

After the cease-fire went into effect on December 10, 1986, communist negotiators put forth proposals to form a coalition government; nationalize key, industries; institute land re-distribution; integrate the NPA into the AFP; remove local police from AFP supervision; and terminate U.S. base rights and agreements with the United States. The Aquino government rejected these demands and offered to discuss communist participation in democratic elec-tions, reintegration of former insurgents into civilian life, land reform, and in-dustrial policy. The communists broke off the talks late in January, however, and refused to renew the cease-fire, which expired February 8, 1987.

Although the Aquino government failed to secure a lasting truce and negotiated settlement, it succeeded with its cease-fire and democratization policies in strengthening its political support from the more affluent elements in the cities (the middle class, the intelligentsia, students, civil servants, profes-sions, etc.). The communist front organizations, which had developed rapidly in the cities in the last two years of the Marcos government, were further weakened as a result.[21]

The Aquino government has had less success in the countryside. Few NPA rank and file have surrendered. The NPA, in fact, grew by an estimated nine percent in 1986, and the number of infiltrated barangays continued upwards.[22] The rate of growth in 1986 apparently was lower than in 1985 and 1984, but conditions persisted in the countryside that create opportunities for the com-munists.

The communists have escalated the level of violence since the end of the cease-fire, including assassinations in Manila. The CPP, despite its setbacks in the cities, believes that time remains on its side and that Aquino's popularity with the people will wane in the long term.

The Communist Party indicates that it will seek more material and political support from abroad, including support from communist countries and leftist groups in Western Europe, Australia, and the United States. There are reports that the Soviet Union has started to supply arms to the NPA, but evidence so far is lacking. Politically, the CPP can be expected to work hard to get insur-gent members or sympathizers elected to municipal and barangay offices in fu-ture local elections.

The insurgency likely will remain on a plateau in the rest of 1987 and 1988. It may grow little, but it will not collapse. Developments after that will depend largely on whether the Aquino government begins to alleviate socio-economic conditions in the countryside, carries out an election strategy that limits communist gains at the local level, and improves the effectiveness of local government and the armed forces in counterinsurgency and related functions. If the government does not succeed in these tasks, the insurgency could start to expand again in the rural areas by the end of 1988. Renewed CPP/NPA growth also would threaten the government's base of support in the cities, as urban opinion probably would turn against the government and new political opportunities could emerge for the CPP.

Military Reform

President Aquino stated soon after taking office that if the communists did not agree to a negotiated settlement, they would face a reformed and revitalized AFP. The government and the AFP leadership under General Ramos have instituted reforms, but any objective evaluation of the AFP would still emphasize the problems and deficiencies.

Ramos has made numerous personnel shifts in the upper echelons of the AFP command, and he has begun to replace mid-level brigade and battalion commanders. U.S. officials generally regard the replacements as competent military professionals. Ramos has moved units and personnel out of Manila into the field.

Most observers believe that the task still is formidable. They state that more personnel changes will be required down into the middle ranks of the command structure. Younger officers with good records will have to be promoted rapidly, according to this view. The shortage of competent non-commissioned officers will have to be addressed.

The government, too, will have to redress the severe resource deficiencies of the AFP and upgrade training considerably. So far, few of the over sixty regular army and marine battalions have been put through a multi-week retaining course. Provision of food, medical care, and clothing remain very inadequate.[23] The AFP, too, will have to create an internal system of justice to deal effectively and sternly with incidents of military abuses of civilians and corruption within the ranks. Abuses of civilians reportedly have declined in number, but the increase of military operations in the post-cease-fire period raises the danger that the AFP could resume some of the practices of the Marcos era. The poorly trained civilian home defense forces and the emergence of anti-communist vigilante groups are added elements of the human rights problem. They reflect on the condition of the police in the rural towns, which should have the responsibility for local security and law enforcement. The police are badly in need of training and new equipment.

The U.S. Role

U.S. policy since the advent of the Aquino government has had two conflicting elements. The Reagan administration and the Congress have been very supportive of the Aquino government in public statements and private diplomacy. The Reagan administration in particular has backed Aquino strongly in the face of the plots and coup attempts against her. U.S. officials reportedly have warned Filipino military officials that the United States will not support any effort to overthrow the Philippine government and will not back any regime that comes to power through such means.

The United States, however, has not been able to provide material assistance to the Philippines commensurate with its original promises or close to Filipino expectations that such aid would be forthcoming. The American role in the events leading to the fall of Marcos helped to raise expectations in the Philippines that the United States would provide extensive aid to the new government, which entered office facing the formidable economic and insurgency problems. President Reagan reinforced these expectations in his statement of January 30, 1986:

If the will of the Filipino people is expressed in an election that Filipinos accept as credible—and if whoever is elected undertakes fundamental economic, political and military reforms—we should consider, in consultation with the Congress, a significantly larger program of economic and military assistance for the Philippines for the next five years. This would be over and above the current levels of assistance.[24]

The reality of executive branch and congressional actions on aid have been different. After high profile action to increase aid for fiscal year 1986, congressional legislation and Reagan administration's actions for FY 1987 and FY 1988 appear to be producing a decline in aid toward levels similar to the last years of the Marcos government. The Marcos era pattern of adding slightly more economic aid to the original amount requested and cutting military aid by a commensurate amount also has re-appeared.

Two obstacles have stood in the way of a major increase in U.S. aid to the Philippines. First, general budget restrictions have resulted in Congress cutting overall foreign aid levels. Within a few days of Aquino's assumption of power, Representative David Obey, chairman of the House Appropriations Committee's Subcommittee on Foreign Operations, told Secretary of State Schultz that Congress would make major cuts in the Reagan administration's foreign aid request for FY 1987.[25] Congress, in fact, did cut the total aid significantly and also reduced categories of aid that included aid to the Philippines.

For Economic Support Funds (ESF), Congress reduced the Reagan administration's request from $4.09 billion to $3.55 billion. With regard to major categories of military aid (grant assistance and foreign military sales credits), Congress cut the Reagan administration's request of $6.66 billion down to $4.94 billion.

Preliminary congressional action on FY 1988 aid continues the pattern. The Senate Foreign Relations Committee's authorization bill cut ESF from the requested $3.55 billion to $3.49 billion. The Committee reduced major categories of military aid from the requested $5.75 billion to $4.96 billion.

The budget cuts resulted in a loss of some flexibility regarding aid to the Philippines, but this loss has been greatly exacerbated by congressional action—with Reagan administration support—to exempt Israel and Egypt from taking any share of the cuts. These two countries are the largest recipients of ESF and military aid, and their exemption from reductions increases the percentage of ESF and military aid to them as against other recipient countries.

Thus, of the $3.55 billion in ESF appropriated for FY 1987, Israel and Egypt received $2.15 billion, or over 60 percent of the total. The Senate Foreign Relations Committee's bill for FY 1988 again specified that Israel and Egypt would receive no less than $2.15 billion, despite a further cut in overall ESF.

A similar pattern has prevailed for military aid. Israel and Egypt received $3.1 billion in the FY 1987 aid legislation, or 63 percent of total military aid. The Senate Foreign Relations Committee's FY 1988 authorization specified $3.1 billion to them, a similar percentage as in FY 1987.

The Philippines under Aquino, in effect, has been left in competition with twenty-seven other major recipients of ESF for remaining ESF funds after allocations to Israel and Egypt. The Philippines also is in competition with twelve other major recipients of military aid and numerous smaller recipients.[26]

Actions by the Reagan administration and Congress for FY 1986 gave a brief indication of an intent to raise aid to a level of over $400 million per year as compared to about $200 million annually in the last two years of the Marcos government. The Reagan administration announced a supplemental aid package for FY 1986 which contained an additional $100 million in ESF, which would supplement $125 million already approved for the fiscal year. It also contained $50 million in supplemental grant military assistance to the Philippines. This was in addition to the previously approved $40 million in grant aid and $15 million in foreign military sales credits.

The Reagan administration subsequently added another $75 million by taking ESF from proposed allocations to other countries. As a result, ESF to the Philippines in FY 1986 reached $300 million. This, coupled with increases in development assistance and P.L. 480 food aid, boosted economic aid to $379 million, compared to $175 million in FY 1985 (of which ESF totaled $140 million).

The Reagan administration's proposal had little difficulty passing Congress in June 1986. However, greater difficulty for FY 1987 aid as the impact of budget cuts and country allocation priorities became more pronounced. In July, the full House approved an additional $200 million in ESF to the Philippines for FY 1986. The Senate did not act on the measure; but after President Aquino's dramatic address to Congress on September 18, the House passed a joint resolution to appropriate an additional $200 million in ESF for FY 1986.

Senate leaders, however, balked at including extra aid in the FY 1986 budget, and it was decided to place the $200 million in the continuing appropriations resolution for FY 1987. The House cleared the measure easily, but it ran into difficulty in the Senate. The Senate rejected two amendments to add the money before passing a third amendment. There was little opposition to the aid itself, but there was opposition to the first two amendments' provisions to take the money from proposed ESF allocations from other countries except Israel and Egypt. The amendment, which the Senate finally passed on October 3, specified that the money would come from an account that financed various international programs rather than from bilateral programs.

The Reagan administration then added an extra $50 million in ESF for the Philippines during its country allocation exercise. However, it did not take the money from the already reduced allocations for other countries. Instead, it reduced military aid to the Philippines by $50 million, from the $100 million it had allocated in its original submission to Congress.

Officials of the Reagan administration calculated that it could restore the $50 million military aid in a supplemental appropriation bill submitted to the 100th Congress. This calculation so far has proven erroneous. The House in April 1987 struck out the entire foreign assistance section of the supplemental, including the $50 million for the Philippines.

Economic and military aid for FY 1987 thus showed significant slippage from FY 1986 aid. Total economic assistance was $272 million, and military aid was $52 million (including $2 million in training funds). The Reagan administration's request for FY 1988 and initial congressional action shows likely further reductions. The Reagan administration requested $124 million in ESF, $110 million in military aid (minus $2.6 million for training), and $13.6 million in development assistance and P.L. 480. The Senate Foreign Relations Committee's authorization bill added $38 million in ESF to $162 million and reduced the military aid request by $22 million back to $88 million.

In short, by FY 1988, U.S. aid levels to the Philippines likely will have fallen to levels only slightly higher than that of FY 1985, the last full fiscal year of aid to the Marcos government. This raises the important question of whether foreign aid is a suitable program for meeting future financial obligations to the Philippines in return for renewed U.S. military base rights after 1991 when the present bases agreement expires. The Aquino government can be expected to demand much higher U.S. financial support than the $900 million which the United States has promised for the FY 1985-1989 period. Prominent Filipinos speak of $1 billion per annum or more. Under present conditions, it is doubtful that the U.S. government could use the foreign aid program to meet significantly larger monetary commitments.

President Aquino has stated that she will respect the agreement on U.S. base rights until 1991 when the present agreement expires; after that, she says, her options are open. Opinions on the bases differ among her closest advisers and in the new Congress. The issue is controversial in the larger body politic. Surveys indicate that a majority of Filipinos presently support a continuation of the U.S. military base presence but that opinion is closely divided among the more affluent and influential Filipinos. The Communist Party and its full or part-time allies on the left can be expected to launch a vigorous campaign against the bases in 1988 when U.S.-Philippine negotiations likely will begin.

In drafting the new constitution, the Philippine constitutional commission rejected proposals to prohibit American bases after 1991. The commission, however, did insert two clauses into the constitution that (1) makes any future bases agreement subject to approval by the Senate of the Philippines, with the option to hold a national plebiscite; and (2) declaring that "The Philippines, consistent with the national interest, adopts and pursues a policy of freedom from nuclear weapons in its territory."

The negotiations likely will be the most difficult yet on the bases. Besides the issue of U.S. financial commitments, other controversies no doubt will include the extent of Philippine involvement in base operations, criminal jurisdiction over U.S. servicemen, the outbreak of AIDS among Filipino women who work in bars frequented by U.S. servicemen, and U.S. rights to store nuclear weapons in the bases.

Conclusion

The outcome of the Philippine crisis has yet to be determined. Whatever the result, however, it will clearly affect U.S. military security interests in the Northeast Asian-Northwest Pacific region. The ability of the U.S. to manage the crisis will also influence the populations of Japan, South Korea, Taiwan, and China. The U.S. must initiate a significant economic contribution to the Philippines. Given the exigencies of the international economic situation, Washington may also want to call on South Korea, and even Taiwan (with its $35 billion in foreign exchange reserves) to make up for the badly needed financial assistance that the U.S. cannot provide due to domestic political and economic constraints. U.S. policies towards the Philippines will be monitored closely by Congress and the Administration at least for the short term. The U.S. has too much at stake in the success of the Aquino government and its reforms to abandon this important ally. Through prudent policies, and not to mention a little bit of luck, U.S. short term investments will hopefully be paid off with long term stability and prosperity in the Philippines. It is only under such domestic circumstances that the U.S. will preserve its important security interests in the Western Pacific.

NOTES

1. U.S. Congress, Senate, Committee on Foreign Relations, *United States Foreign Policy Objectives and Overseas Military Installations*, 96th Congress, 1st Session, (1979), pp. 134-64.

2. *Ibid.*

3. U.S. Department of State, Developments in the Philippines: Statement by Paul D. Wolfowitz, Assistant Secretary for East Asian and Pacific Affairs, before the Senate Foreign Relations Committee, (October 30, 1985).

4. *Ibid.*

5. *Ibid.*

6. For a recent study of basing options, see: U.S. Congressional Research Service, *Philippine Bases: U.S. Redeployment Options*, by Alva M. Bowen, (Washington, D.C. 1986).

7. Statement by the U.S. Presidential Delegation to the Philippine Presidential Election, (February 10, 1986).

8. *Washington Post*, (March 3, 1986).

9. For the most thorough analysis of the crisis, see Emmanuel S. De Dios (ed.) *An Analysis of the Philippine Economic Crisis*, (Manila: University of Philippines Press, 1984).

10. For a detailed study of the communist insurgency, see: U.S. Congress, Senate, Committee on Foreign Relations, *Insurgency and Counterinsurgency in the Philippines*, S. Prt. 99-99, 99th Congress, 1st Session, (GPO, 1985).

11. *Ibid.*, pp. 28-32.

12. *Ibid.*, pp. 32-48.

13. Larry A. Niksch, "Marcos Turns a Deaf Ear to Reform Proposals," *Far Eastern Economic Review*, (June 27, 1985), pp. 40-41.

14. James Clad, "Vote for Stability," *Far Eastern Economic Review*, February 12, 1987, pp. 10-11.

15. *Washington Post*, July 9 and 10, 1987.

16. *Business Day*, February 20, 1987; *Washington Times*, January 28 and 30, 1987 and July 14, 1987; *Manila Evening Post*, June 23, 1986.

17. Wharton Econometrics, *Asian Economic Outlook*, April 1987, pp. 127-138.

18. *Ibid.*

19. "Philippines: Whose Land," *Far Eastern Economic Review*, March 5, 1987, pp. 32-37.

20. *Business Day*, September 29, 1986; *Manila Bulletin*, September 29, 1986.

21. *Business Day*, March 31, 1987. The CPP leadership reportedly undertook an evaluation of its key front organizations after the cease-fire and concluded that a number were no longer reliable.

22. Testimony of Assistant Secretary of Defense Richard Armitage before the House Subcommittee for Asian and Pacific Affairs, March 17, 1987.

23. For a detailed description of conditions in an army battalion on Samar, see Tom Marks, "Cease-Fire Maneuvers," *Soldier of Fortune*, May 1987, 48-84.

24. White House Press Statement, January 30, 1986.

25. *New York Times*, March 5, 1986.

26. For a list of recipients, see the letter from Assistant Secretary of State J. Edward Fox to Speaker of the House Thomas O'Neill, December 15, 1986.

CHAPTER 7

The Isolation of Island China

Stephen P. Gibert

As President Reagan enters his last year in office, his administration's Northeast Asian policy is still characterized by some degree of uncertainty. As compared with the first eighteen months of Republican government, however, the last five-plus years have seen a clearer perception of U.S. interests. As a generalization, it might be said that the first eighteen months saw the administration trying to reconcile the personal views of the President and those of his close associates with the ambiguous legacies of the past. While the tone and approach toward Northeast Asia of the Reagan government reflected more self-confidence and a greater emphasis on reasserting American leadership in the national security area, in all important particulars initial policy reflected continuity rather than a sharp break with the past, insofar as Asia and the Western Pacific were concerned. The issue of Japanese rearmament remained, with the Japanese still refusing to make meaningful contributions to mutual security. The consternation which greeted President Carter's ill-considered 1977 decision to remove U.S. ground forces from Korea had subsided and the U.S.-South Korean security relationship remained intact. Relations with the People's Republic of China continued to have its ups and downs, with no visible and sustained movement in any particular direction. On the whole, however, PRC-American relations continued to progress satisfactorily. As for the Republic of China, the Taiwan authorities, although certainly more pleased with the Reagan government as compared with its predecessor, could not but contrast the rhetoric of the Republican leadership prior to the 1980 election with its cautious and hesitant post-election policy.

In the years since the low-point (from Taipei's perspective) of American-Taiwan relations—the August 17, 1982 U.S.-PRC Joint Communique which committed the United States, under certain conditions, to gradually terminate security assistance to Taiwan—Washington's Northeast Asian policy has shown more steadfastness of purpose and has evolved into a more realistic appreciation of the requirements of American security policy in the Western Pacific in general and with regard to the problem of divided China in particular. In brief, despite some unresolved issues—especially with regard to the quantity, quality and type of arms transfers, and Taiwan's growing surplus in its trade with the United States—American-Taiwan relations since August 1982 have been placed on a more substantial basis than at any time since President Carter's December 1978 decision to terminate Washington's diplomatic relations with Taipei and institute diplomatic ties with the People's Republic of China.

This generally satisfactory state of affairs results from the fact that all of the crucial decisions affecting relationships between Taiwan and the United States occurred in the period from December 1978 to August 1982. Since that time, there have been negotiations about the amount of security assistance, not whether there will be U.S. military aid for Taiwan; there have been disagreements over the conduct of the "informal" relations between the two countries, not whether the United States will end diplomatic ties with the island state; and there have been criticisms in the U.S. Congress and media of authoritarian rule on Taiwan but wide acknowledgement of substantial progress in Taiwan toward democracy. Finally, there has been increasing concern in both Taiwan and the United States over Taiwan's growing trade surplus with the United States. Few suggest, however, that this problem has resulted from deliberate trade policies by the Taiwan government.

In short, since August 1982, there have been problems in relations between Taiwan and the United States but no fundamental changes in the arrangements established in the period between 1978 and 1982.

This essay will first describe briefly the confused and uncertain China policy which the Reagan government inherited in 1981. Subsequently, important milestones in the ambivalent U.S. relations with the two Chinas from January 1981 until the August 1982 Joint Communique will be noted. The third section of the paper will address the current state of American-Taiwan relations and the problems that remain between the U.S. and Taiwan governments. This essay will conclude with comments about the future prospects for the continuation of satisfactory relationships between the United States and Island China.

The Dual Legacy

The Reagan Administration inherited a very confused and uncertain China policy when it took office in 1981. Two legacies had been bequeathed by previous actions of the President and Congress concerning the China problem. The first may be called the "Carterite approach" and had as its basis the conditions agreed to between the Carter administration and the People's Republic of China in late 1978 which permitted the exchange of diplomatic relations between Washington and Beijing in January 1979. With regard to Taiwan, the Joint Communique of January 1, 1979 stated that "The Government of the United States of America acknowledges the Chinese position that there is but one China and Taiwan is part of China." And in a separate statement, also issued on January 1, 1979, the U.S. government terminated diplomatic relations and the

Mutual Defense Treaty between the United States and the Republic of China and announced the forthcoming withdrawal of U.S. military personnel from Taiwan within four months. As to the security of Taiwan, the United States was "confident that the people of Taiwan face a peaceful and prosperous future."[1] No mention was made as to the basis of Washington's confidence; this was significant in the light of the PRC statement that "the way of bringing Taiwan back to the embrace of the motherland. . . is entirely China's internal affair."

It is true that the PRC had also claimed a right to decide how China was to be reunified in the negotiations with President Nixon in 1972 and in that earlier Joint Communique stated that "the liberation of Taiwan is China's internal affair in which no other country has the right to interfere. . ." Three aspects, however, distinguish sharply between the Carter agreement of 1979 and the Nixon agreement of 1972. First, the U.S. in 1972 "reaffirmed its interest in a peaceful settlement of the Taiwan question" and, with that prospect in mind, agreed to "progressively reduce its forces and military installations on Taiwan as the tension in the area diminishes."[2] In contrast, the U.S. in 1979 did not "reaffirm its interest in a peaceful settlement of the Taiwan question."

The second difference concerns U.S. military forces on Taiwan. In 1972 the U.S. made their progressive reduction contingent upon the diminution of the PRC threat to Taiwan, while in 1979, the U.S. government made an unconditional pledge to remove all American military forces from Taiwan within four months. Accordingly, the claim of both the U.S. and the PRC in the Joint Communique of 1979, that the normalization agreement was reaffirming the 1972 Shanghai agreement, is only partially correct. The difference in the two agreements is the principal reason why for seven years after 1972 normalization did not occur. In short, President Carter had met the three conditions Beijing had put forward for normalization—the derecognition of the Republic of China, the termination of the Mutual Defense Treaty, and the withdrawal of all U.S. military forces from Taiwan. Presidents Nixon and Ford had not agreed to these terms and had insisted, in addition, that reunification be peaceful.

Perhaps more important than the wording of the two communiques were the motives of the Nixon and Carter administrations. In the case of Nixon, the "opening to China" was clearly intended to facilitate American withdrawal from Vietnam. From the intervention of China in the Korean War until the Nixon trip to China in February 1972, successive American governments had viewed the PRC as the principal threat to peace in Asia. The U.S. intervention in Vietnam had been justified primarily on the basis that behind North Vietnam lay China. The enormous American investment in Vietnam, it was universally agreed, was disproportionate to any possible U.S. interests in Southeast Asia. Still, as long as defending South Vietnam was part of a larger policy of containing China it could be justified. A domino theory, in short, presumed China was interested in playing dominos.

That the PRC and not the Soviet Union was perceived as the principal threat, indeed almost the only threat, to the peace in Asia is most clearly revealed in

President Nixon's well-known article in the fall 1967 issue of *Foreign Affairs*. Most Asian governments, wrote Nixon, "recognize a common danger, and see its source as Peking." Red China's "threat is clear, present, and repeatedly and insistently expressed." China is "the world's most populous nation and Asia's most immediate threat." Accordingly, the U.S. "cannot afford to leave China forever outside the family of nations, there to nourish its fantasies, cherish its hates and threaten its neighbors. There is no place on this small planet for a billion of its potentially most able people to live in angry isolation." The United States should persuade China that it must change just as American policy eventually succeeded in changing the Soviet Union by shoring up Western Europe. As to the Soviet Union in Asia, Nixon remarked parenthetically, that "although the U.S.S.R. occupies much of the land map of Asia, its principal focus is toward the west and its vast Asian lands are an appendage of European Russia."

Hence the Kissinger visit in 1971 and the Nixon trip to China in 1972 were intended to start the process of defusing the perceived Chinese threat in Asia. This in turn would permit American withdrawal from Vietnam and the implementation of the "Nixon Doctrine" which called for a world-wide reduction of U.S. forces overseas. In fact, including Vietnam, approximately 700,000 U.S. military personnel were withdrawn from overseas—all from Asia—between the time Nixon assumed the presidency and the fall of Saigon in April 1975.

In contrast to President Nixon's obvious interest in achieving some sort of rapprochement—however limited—with the PRC, one searches in vain for a particularly urgent foreign policy reason for President Carter's decision to normalize relations with China. Except for Korea, the U.S. had no ground forces stationed on the Asian continent so troop reduction was not an issue. Carter did not have a "grand design" such as that envisioned by Kissinger's "pentapolar world." There was no need to extricate the U.S. from an unpopular conflict. In sum, the irony of the situation is that Nixon really needed the opening to China for sound national security reasons, yet did not make the concessions to Beijing which Carter willingly made. One aspect the Nixon and Carter policies had in common, however—neither based his China policy primarily in terms of "playing a China card" against the Soviet Union. Nixon did not regard the Soviet Union as an Asian power. Further, he believed that Moscow had accepted a policy of detente. As for President Carter, he thought the U.S. suffered from an "inordinate fear of communism,"[3] and, according to Secretary of State Vance, that the United States and the Soviet Union shared similar aspirations. Furthermore, at the time of the recognition of the PRC, Washington was at an advanced stage of arms control negotiations with Moscow. It is true, of course, after the Soviet invasion of Afghanistan in December 1979, that President Carter's policy toward Moscow considerably hardened. Earlier, in 1977 and 1978, Secretary of State Vance and the Department's view that American relations with Beijing and Moscow could be simultaneously improved had prevailed. But the discovery of the Soviet combat brigade in Cuba in August

1979 and various Soviet moves in Southern Africa and the Horn of Africa and the possibility—perhaps probability—that the SALT II agreement would not be approved by the Senate, thus causing further deterioration in American-Soviet relations, inclined the Carter administration toward cooperation with China against the U.S.S.R. As a former member of the National Security Council staff later wrote, "[National Security Adviser] Brzezinski and [Secretary of Defense] Brown wished to cultivate the Sino-American relationship to become a permanent part of Moscow's calculations. . ."[4] Nevertheless, it was not until Reagan assumed office that the "China card" became an important and perhaps principal element of Washington's policy toward the People's Republic.

Perhaps it was the very absence of a compelling rationale that led the Senate and the Congress in general to react so strongly and negatively toward the legislation which the Carter administration submitted to the Congress in early 1979, in order to provide the legal basis for the future unofficial relations with the people of Taiwan. As expressed by Senator Frank Church, Chairman of the Foreign Relations Committee, the legislation proposed by the Carter government was "woefully inadequate to the task, ambiguous in language, and uncertain in tone."[5] Even liberal Senators Cranston and Kennedy, although stating they thought the Carter agreement was "adequate" for the security of Taiwan, introduced a resolution to "spell out" U.S. interest in Taiwan's security. This was done, said Cranston, since some members of Congress did not perceive the Carter government's proposed legislation as sufficiently concerned about Taiwan's security, and also because he and Kennedy wanted to correct any misperception, presumably on the part of the PRC, that its recognition could "automatically be translated as abandonment of Taiwan."[6]

Thus began the other part of the dual legacy President Reagan inherited with regard to the China problem: the Congressional approach, which was to eventuate in the Taiwan Relations Act (Public Law 96-8), signed into law by President Carter on April 10, 1979.[7]

The Taiwan Relations Act (TRA) is so well-known that no elaborate explanation of its provisions are required. Briefly, with regard to Taiwan's security, the TRA declares that peace and stability in the Western Pacific are in the political, security and economic interests of the United States and are matters of international concern. Further, the American decision to establish diplomatic relations with the PRC rests upon the expectation that the future of Taiwan will be determined by peaceful means and any effort to use other than peaceful means, including boycotts or embargoes, would be a threat to the peace and security of the Western Pacific and of grave concern to the United States. The U.S. would maintain the capability to resist any resort to force or other forms of coercion that would jeopardize the security, or the social or economic system of the people of Taiwan. On the critical question of arms for Taiwan, the TRA said it would be U.S. policy to provide Taiwan with defensive arms and such defense articles and services in such quantity as would be necessary to enable Taiwan to maintain a "sufficient self-defense capability."

In making arms transfer decision, the President and Congress "shall determine the nature and quantity of such defense articles and services based solely upon their judgment of the needs of Taiwan. . . " These provisions, as have often been noted, go far beyond the 1954 U.S.-ROC Mutual Security Treaty. Despite this, the TRA was passed by a vote of 339-50 in the House of Representatives and 85-4 in the Senate on March 29, 1979. Thus was established what one observer has called Washington's "two-track solution" to China policy: on the one hand, the improvement of strategic, political, economic, and other relations with the People's Republic of China and, on the other hand, the maintenance of historically friendly ties with the Republic of China on Taiwan.[8]

Under President Carter, however, it is clear that the first track—good relations with the PRC—took precedence. Congress could and did stipulate the underlying premises for U.S. policy toward Taiwan but it was up to the President "to prescribe such rules and regulations as he may deem appropriate to carry out the purposes of this Act."[9] To be sure, as in this and other cases, Congress authorized the relevant committees to monitor the implementation of the law.[10] But effective implementation of the TRA, as is the case with other laws, especially in the foreign policy and national security areas, depends upon the cooperative attitude of the President and his administration, as experience with both the TRA and the War Powers Act of 1973 fully attest. In the American political system, it is quite difficult to stop an American president from pursuing courses of action he wishes to follow and virtually impossible to compel him to undertake policies to which he is opposed. And, although President Carter signed the TRA into law, and on June 22, 1979, issued an Executive Order to implement the act, the fact of the matter is that he was opposed to it.

In view of this attitude, it is not surprising that the Carter administration undertook several measures which were not consistent with the spirit of the Taiwan Relations Act. For example:

— In August 1979, Vice President Mondale disclosed in China that the administration intended to change its official civil air agreement with Taiwan to unofficial status in order to secure a civil air agreement with the PRC.[11]

— A one-year moratorium on U.S. arms sales to Taiwan was imposed, lasting until January 1980.[12]

— The Carter administration did not express concern when the International Monetary Fund and the World Bank decided to expel the ROC from membership.[13]

— In January 1980, the Department of State instructed the U.S. Customs Office that no goods bearing the label "Made in the Republic of China" would be admitted to the United States. Rather, the label had to read "Made in Taiwan."[14]

— Prior to 1979, the ROC had fifteen consular offices in the United States. This was reduced to only nine under the Coordinating Council for North American Affairs, established, in lieu of an embassy, to conduct

Taiwanese affairs in the United States. There was also a significant reduction in U.S. personnel for the American Institute in Taiwan as compared with the disestablished U.S. embassy. American officials were discouraged and even forbidden, in some cases, from journeying to Taiwan.[15]

— In May 1980, members of the Joint Economic Committee of the U.S. Congress were allowed to go to Taiwan only if the crew of the U.S. military plane wore civilian clothes and if the plane stayed in Taiwan only long enough to load and unload its passengers.[16]

— Officials of the Republic of China were forbidden official visits to the United States, despite the continuance of many relationships between the two countries.[17]

It is true that these various actions (in most cases) were not expressly forbidden under the TRA, although not permitting goods into the United States under the Republic of China label was probably a violation of Section 4(A) of the Act. But it is equally clear that the administration interpreted the meaning of the continuation of American relations with Taiwan on an "unofficial" basis in the most narrow sense of the word. And clearly, contrary to Congressional intent, American policy decisions with regard to Taiwan were certainly affected by the administration's view as to reactions in Beijing. Altogether, it seems likely that had President Carter won reelection in 1980, American relations with Taiwan would have continued to deteriorate. This seems especially likely when it is recalled that the perceived need to "play the China card" increased as relations with the Soviet Union worsened and certain more detente-oriented members of the Carter government, such as Secretary Vance and Arms Control Director Paul Warnke, were replaced with more anti-Soviet officials.

The Policy of Muddling Through: Reagan's First Eighteen Months

In an interview in the evening of August 20, 1984, on the floor of the Republican Presidential Convention, liberal Senator Lowell Weicker urged the listening TV audience to forget the conservative rhetoric embodied in the 1984 Republican Party platform. Rather, said the Senator, wait for the policies of the second Republican administration. These policies would bear little relation to the platform and its rhetorical echoes in the ensuing Presidential campaign.

This was advice that could have been usefully offered to both Beijing and Taipei during Candidate Reagan's first presidential race in 1980. If one believed the speeches of the day, it would have appeared that a new conservative government in Washington would seriously reappraise American policy toward the so-called "China problem," upgrading in some ill-defined way U.S. relations with the Republic of China on Taiwan and permitting relationships with the People's Republic of China to deteriorate correspondingly.

When one recalls the language in the Republican platform of 1980, Beijing's fears and Taipei's hopes are understandable. While reaffirming Washington's intention to continue diplomatic relations with the PRC, the China resolution deplored "the Carter Administration's mistreatment of Taiwan, our long-term ally and friend," pledged "concern for the safety and security of the seventeen million people of Taiwan," and stated that the Republican administration under Ronald Reagan would strengthen relations with Taiwan and "give priority consideration to Taiwan's defense requirements."[18] And Mr. Reagan suggested that, if elected, he would place U.S. relations with Taiwan on an official basis. Also, on August 25, 1980, Candidate Reagan publicly expressed his "special feelings" for the Republic of China and spoke, albeit vaguely, about "upgrading" American relations with Taiwan.[19]

Beijing apparently believed there was, indeed, a distinct possibility that the Reagan administration might "tilt" significantly more toward Taipei than had the previous three American administrations and especially that of President Carter. In such circumstances, the PRC could have become more placating, hoping to convince the Reagan government that the PRC could be relied upon as a tacit partner of the United States in Asia even if not an ally. Conversely, Beijing could "test the water" with the new government in Washington by sharpening its attack on the U.S. relationship with Taiwan and, in general, becoming more harshly critical of American global policies. The PRC chose the latter course, going on the offensive even before Reagan was elected, telling Vice Presidential Candidate Bush, who had gone to China in August 1980 to soothe PRC feelings about the future Republican administration's policy, that "we [the PRC] hold that any remarks and comments which have the effect of retrogression from the current, the present state of Sino-United States relations, would do harm to the political basis on which our relations have been built and would be detrimental to the interests of world peace."[20] Subsequently, the Chinese threatened not to attend Reagan's inauguration if the Taiwan officials were invited. This ploy worked; not only were Taiwan officials not invited, the Reagan administration began a slow retreat from its pro-Taiwan stance, culminating in the U.S.-PRC Joint Communique of August 17, 1982.

Taipei also had been led to believe that the new government in Washington might translate Reagan's "special feelings" for the ROC into concrete steps to upgrade the Washington-Taipei relationship. Taiwan officials recalled that Reagan during the 1980 campaign had refused to endorse the Shanghai Communique of February 27, 1972, which stated, *inter alia*, that the United States government did not challenge the PRC position that "there is but one China and Taiwan is part of China." Furthermore, Mr. Reagan also had refused to give his support to the normalization agreement of January 1, 1979, which repeated much of the language of the Shanghai Communique. Instead, Candidate Reagan said the Taiwan Relations Act would be the basis of his government's future policy toward the China problem.

Under these circumstances, it is not surprising that the ROC government was displeased with developments in 1981. First, as noted earlier, the Reagan government decided not to include Taiwan's representatives at the Presidential inauguration. Second, in March 1981, the Reagan government acknowledged that it was not going to "upgrade" relations with Taiwan and announced that the administration did indeed support the Shanghai Communique.

These developments were followed by the June 1981 visit of Secretary of State Alexander Haig to Beijing to reassure the Chinese leadership that, irrespective of contrary sentiments previously expressed, the Reagan government was committed to an expansion of already developing relations between the two countries. To underscore this pledge, Haig used the occasion of his trip to proclaim official U.S. willingness to sell arms to China and to be more flexible in applying controls on U.S. high technology exports to the PRC.[21]

Various high-level meetings between PRC and American leaders occurred throughout the period extending from Secretary Haig's visit in June 1981 until the August 1982 Joint Communique. In addition, responding to Soviet overtures, there was a noticeable attempt on the part of the PRC to "play the Soviet card" against the United States by, once again, linking the United States and the Soviet Union together as "hegemonial powers." Beijing also sought to portray itself as reasonable on the Taiwan issue by advancing a nine-point proposal for the peaceful return of Taiwan to Mainland China.[22]

The Reagan administration during this period, as it had even before it took office, reacted in such a way as to indicate uncertainty and indecisiveness as to how to approach relations with the two Chinas. On the one hand, in January 1982 Assistant Secretary of State John Holdridge journeyed to Beijing to inform PRC leaders that the U.S. would continue co-production with Taiwan of the F-5E fighter aircraft rather than transfer the FX or any other more advanced combat aircraft sought by the ROC government. On the other hand, President Reagan continued to maintain he was not interested in playing a "China card" against Moscow or a "Soviet card" against the PRC; rather, said the President, the U.S. would pursue its own interests. This included implementing the Taiwan Relations Act.

While this pledge seemed straightforward enough, in fact, once again, the Reagan administration showed confusion and uncertainty. This took the form of two letters from President Reagan in April of 1982 to Deng Xiaoping and Zhao Ziyang in which the President made three basic points: first, the U.S. understood and respected PRC opposition to American arms transfers to Taiwan; second, Washington anticipated that Taiwan's needs for defensive arms would diminish as progress was made on a peaceful solution to the unification problem and Taiwan's future; and third, that the U.S. regarded Beijing's nine-point proposal as a significant move on the PRC's part to achieve progress toward a solution of the unification problem.[23] This was followed in June by a visit to China by Vice President Bush, presumably to carry forward the talks which were to lead to the low point (from Taipei's perspective) of American-Taiwan relations during the Reagan administration—the August 17, 1982 U.S.-PRC Joint Communique.

The Joint Communique was consistent with the Nixon Shanghai Communique and the Carter PRC recognition agreements, and implemented the promises President Reagan made in his letters of April 5, 1982. On the important issue of U.S. arms transfers to Taiwan, the Joint Communique went further toward meeting Beijing's demand for the termination of such military aid. Specifically, in Point 6 of the Joint Communique "... the United States Government states that it does not seek to carry out a long-term policy of arms sales to Taiwan, that is, arms sales to Taiwan will not exceed, either in qualitative or in quantitative terms, the level of those supplied in recent years since the establishment of diplomatic relations between the United States and China, and that it intends to reduce gradually its sales of arms to Taiwan, leading over a period of time to a final resolution."

Concurrent with the Joint Communique, both the United States and China issued separate statements. The American statement claimed, regarding future U.S. arms sales to Taiwan, that the Joint Communique was "fully consistent with the Taiwan Relations Act." This statement was clearly not true; the Chinese statement that "... interpretations designed to link the present Joint Communique to the 'Taiwan Relations Act' are in violation of the spirit and substance of this Communique ..." is an accurate assessment of the contradiction between the TRA and the 1982 Communique. As Senator John Glenn commented, "The communique announced today discards that very carefully crafted framework, the heart of the TRA, in favor of an arms sales formulation negotiated under Chinese threats of a retrogression of United States-PRC relations."[24]

There is little doubt that the Reagan government agreed to the Joint Communique because of the influence of the "China card" players in his administration. At the risk of oversimplification, it may be said that three different groups of people have held high office in the foreign policy and national security areas under President Reagan. The first group included members of the permanent government bureaucracy and "holdovers" from the Carter administration. These officials, on the whole, did not share the somewhat sentimental feelings the President felt for the Republic of China on Taiwan. To the extent they were involved in China policy, they tended to favor broadening the U.S. relationship with the People's Republic, and accepted the utility of the "China card" as a useful foreign policy gambit.

Two different groups of officials were appointed to key national security positions under President Reagan. The first group consisted in large part of people who had been relatively minor officials during the Nixon-Ford-Kissinger era and were brought back into government primarily at the instigation of Secretary of State Alexander Haig. Haig and his subordinates were not so much anti-communist as they were anti-Soviet. Thus "playing the China card" against the Soviet Union seemed to them an eminently sensible policy. Undoubtedly it was Haig's influence that led President Reagan in May 1981 to say that arms sales to the People's Republic was a natural development. In June 1981, Haig announced in Beijing that restrictions on American arms transfers to China would be lifted. Throughout his eighteen months at the helm of U.S. foreign policy, Secretary Haig worked to improve relations with the PRC; if this came at the expense of Taiwan, then it was unfortunate, but a price the United States should pay to counter the Soviet Union.

The second group who came to power in 1981 may be called, for want of a better term, "Reaganauts." In contrast to Haig's view, these people were not simply anti-Soviet; rather, they were anti-communist. Their anti-communism included the PRC; they thus were suspicious of the efficacy of the "China card" and, like President Reagan himself, felt a sense of loyalty to the Republic of China on Taiwan. But, so long as Secretary of State Haig held office, this group was unable to exercise much influence on China policy. While it is true that the August 1982 Joint Communique came after Secretary Haig left office, it resulted from a process which could not easily be modified. The Joint Communique thus marks a high point (or low point, depending upon one's perspective) of the Reagan government's attempts to foster strategic cooperation between Washington and Beijing during his first administration.

While the precise words of the August 1982 Communique certainly contradict the Taiwan Relations Act, it quickly became apparent that the Reagan government intended to interpret its China policy in such a way as to remain an arms supplier for Taiwan. First, the Taipei authorities revealed that Washington had informed them in July about the impending agreement and had reassured the ROC that the United States had not agreed to set a date for terminating arms sales to Taiwan nor would the administration violate the TRA by consulting Beijing on U.S. arms agreements with Taiwan. Additionally, there was no intention on the part of the United States to revise the Taiwan Relations Act. Finally, despite its previous statements of praise for the PRC nine-point proposal, Washington said it would not attempt to persuade Island China to enter into reunification talks with Mainland China.[25]

The Reagan administration also moved to allay doubts in Congress. Private meetings were held between NSC Adviser William Clark and key Congressional leaders, who were told that, despite the letters to Beijing and the wording of the Joint Communique, the President was not considering a termination date for arms sales to Taiwan, and that the Reagan government remained fully supportive of the Taiwan Relations Act.[26]

Thus American relations with Taiwan continued its uneven, ambivalent, and ambiguous course, continually subject to the vicissitudes of Washington's sometimes warm, and sometimes cool, relationship with Communist China. But, on the whole, there was a distinctly more forthcoming relationship with Taiwan after the August Communique than there had been during the first eighteen months of the Reagan administration.

Current Issues

There are two issues which contain the potential for serious damage to Taiwan-American relations: United States security assistance to Taiwan and United States-Taiwan trade relations. A third problem is not really an issue between the two countries—internal political conditions in Taiwan itself—but, given the emphasis in the United States on democratic values, it could affect American policy toward the island country, should Taiwan not continue its progress towards a more open and pluralistic society.

With regard to the important issue of security assistance, the Reagan administration informed Congress only two days after the August 1982 Communique that it intended to sell Taiwan sixty F-5E and F-5F aircraft, valued at $622 million, over the next several years.[27] And in November some $97 million worth of armored vehicles were sold to Taiwan.[28] This was followed by additional aircraft sales totalling approximately $31 million in February 1983.[29] In March 1983 the Reagan government moved still further toward supporting the arms needs of Taiwan when it was announced that future weapons sales would be indexed for inflation.[30] This rather disingenuous move enabled the U.S. to claim that, on the one hand, it was complying with the August 1982 Communique and, on the other hand, to provide increased aid to Taipei. This was followed in July by approval of a number of weapons and spare parts requested by Taiwan.

As a result, Taiwan still continues to receive substantial amounts of military equipment from the United States. Foreign Military Sales Agreements (FMS) between the two countries were valued at approximately $289 million in FY 1981, $472 million in FY 1982, $653 million in FY 1983, $664 million in FY 1984, $699 million in FY 1985, and $511 million in FY 1986.[31] In addition, during these years, Taiwan was able to purchase through licensed commercial channels military items valued at about half a billion dollars. While FMS agreements declined from $699 million in FY 1985 to $511 million in 1986, the value of U.S. commercial sales has been increasing, rising from approximately $54 million in 1985 to $228 million in 1986.[32] This is undoubtedly because commercial sales receive less public scrutiny than government-to-government transactions; commercial figures are not reported to the Congress by the U.S. Defense Security Assistance Agency and must be estimated by United States customs receipts.

In addition to indexing military sales to Taiwan to inflation and of military items, the Reagan administration also has adopted the position that technological transfer and assistance to Taiwan does not come under the restrictions agreed to in the Second Shanghai Communique; this interpretation has been protested by the PRC but without success. As a result, the United States is assisting Taiwan in undertaking a major improvement in its military forces. Four efforts are now underway which will substantially improve Taiwan's defensive capabilities in the 1990s. These projects include about a dozen frigates to replace Taiwan's overage destroyers, modern tanks for the Army, various missiles, and an advanced fighter aircraft.

While official sources in the United States and in Taiwan will not provide details of these projects, it is known that all four contemplate significant American technological assistance. The frigates will be built in Taiwan with design and construction help from either the Todd Pacific Shipyard Corporation or the Bath Iron Works. The new engines for the Army tanks are of the type produced by the U.S. Teledyne Continental Motors, with tank assembly bodies furnished by General Dynamics, which is also assisting with the development of Taiwan's fighter aircraft.[33]

Despite the considerable help the United States has provided Taiwan, the Reagan administration did not agree to furnish the requested Harpoon anti-ship missile nor an advanced fighter aircraft to replace the aging Northrop F-5E. In the late 1970s, Taiwan had decided to forego the opportunity to purchase the F-5G, an early version of the F-20, in the hopes of acquiring the F-16 built by General Dynamics. In 1982 the Reagan Administration, in an effort to cultivate closer ties with the PRC, announced that Taiwan did not require an advanced fighter of the capabilities of either the F-16 or F-20. After that decision, Taiwan accelerated its funding for the research and development of an indigenous fighter (IDF). In March of 1986, it became publicly known that the United States was helping Taiwan develop the IDF. The assistance being offered Taipei in building the IDF, however, is sharply circumscribed. While the U.S. has agreed to assist Taiwan build a fighter that is an improvement on the F-5E, the IDF's capabilities are not supposed to exceed those of the F-16 or even the F-20. General Dynamics has been licensed to act as a consultant, but the "rules of consultation" are carefully drawn. General Dynamics cannot provide "full-service" consultations, it can only approve or disapprove certain designs. If a variable-geometry wing configuration is proposed, for example, General Dynamics engineers can point out its flaws, but cannot recommend alternative designs. Despite these constraints, the new Taiwan fighter is progressing satisfactorily and is expected to be deployed about 1990.[34]

In summary, while there are problems between the United States and Taiwan over implementing the Taiwan Relations Act, the Reagan Administration, despite its agreement with the PRC in 1982, has been concerned about Taiwan's security and has undertaken the steps necessary to see that Taiwan's military forces remain strong. And the PRC, although it has protested various actions from time to time, has acquiesced in a broad interpretation of the Shanghai Two Communique.   •

Of greater potential difficulty in American relations with Taiwan is the trade imbalance (in Taiwan's favor) between the two countries. The U.S. stock market collapse in October 1987 is generally attributed to the closely-linked Federal budget and trade deficits. The budget deficit stood at $61.3 billion in 1980 and $145.9 billion in 1982. It then grew to $204 billion in 1986; this

Table 7-1
Taiwan's Trade with the United States

Unit: US $ millions

	Exports		Imports		Total Trade		
Year	Amount	% of Total Export	Amount	% of Total Import	Amount	% of Total Trade	Surplus or Deficit
1976	3,038.7	37.2	1,797.6	23.7	4,836.3	30.7	(+) 1,241.1
1977	3,636.3	38.9	1,963.8	23.1	5,600.1	31.3	(+) 1,672.5
1978	5,010.4	39.5	2,376.1	21.5	7,386.5	31.1	(+) 2,634.3
1979	5,652.3	35.1	3,380.8	22.9	9,033.1	29.3	(+) 2,271.5
1980	6,760.3	34.1	4,673.5	23.7	11,433.8	28.9	(+) 2,086.8
1981	8,163.1	36.1	4,765.7	22.5	12,928.8	29.5	(+) 3,397.4
1982	8,758.9	39.4	4,563.2	24.2	13,322.1	32.4	(+) 4,195.7
1983	11,333.7	45.1	4,646.4	22.9	15,980.1	35.2	(+) 6,687.3
1984	14,867.7	48.8	5,041.6	23.0	19,909.3	38.0	(+) 9,826.1
1985	14,770.3	48.1	4,746.5	23.6	19,516.8	38.4	(+)10,023.8
1986	18,994.4	47.8	5,416.3	22.4	24,410.7	38.2	(+)13,578.1

Source: Taiwan's Customs Statistics, furnished by the Coordination Council of North American Affairs.

dramatic growth was associated with the 1982 recession, large tax reductions, and slow growth in GNP. As a percentage of GNP, the Federal deficit rose from less than one percent in 1979 to about five percent in 1986.[35]

The budget deficit, in turn, contributed significantly to the trade deficit, which totalled about $144 billion is 1986 and is projected to be about $156 billion in 1987. Sharply increased U.S. imports made the United States the major "engine of growth" for the world economy. This especially benefited Taiwan, whose growth in GNP in 1986 was estimated at more than ten percent, making it one of the world's fastest growing economies.

Taiwan's economic growth was largely propelled by exports to the United States. As indicated in Table 7-1, Taiwan's exports to the United States multiplied by six times in the 1976-1986 decade, with a trade surplus with the United States rising nearly every year, reaching about $13.6 billion in 1986.[36]

It is obvious, as the decline in world stock markets brought home, that Taiwan's large trade surplus with the United States must be reduced. Unless the trade problem is solved, as Senator Richard Lugar, the former chairman of the Foreign Relations Committee noted while visiting Taipei in August 1986, there will be a "rising tide of protectionism in the United States."[37] Unfortunately, that improvement has not happened; Taiwan's trade surplus with the United States continued to increase in 1987.[38]

The basic reasons for the trade imbalance between the two countries are not easily amenable to solutions. First of all, Taiwan is a small country of only about nineteen million people and therefore cannot absorb a large volume of American products. It is inevitable that the U.S. market of 240 million is a target for Taiwanese exporters. Thus for many years, the United States has been the number one trading partner for Taiwan and in 1986 became America's sixth largest trading nation. In that year, U.S. products made up about one-fifth of Taiwan's total imports while Taiwan's exports to the United States accounted for only about four percent of total U.S. imports.

A second factor is the different stage of industrial development of the two countries. Taiwan is a newly industrializing nation and therefore has cheaper labor costs as compared to the United States. Taiwan supplies a wide variety of products to developing countries which lack the technological capability to produce them and furnishes similar goods to the advanced industrial nations, principally the United States, whose labor costs prohibit competitive production. Many of Taiwan's exports, in fact, are produced by American corporations which have located in the island country to take advantage of low labor costs.

A third basic reason for the trade relationship has been close political ties between the United States and Taiwan, which has fostered many interactions between the two nations. Taiwan's very survival as an independent state would have been in jeopardy were it not for its long security relationship with the United States. It is thus natural that trade between the two countries would flourish.

The Taiwan government is anxious to reduce its trade surplus with the United States and has sent twelve Special Procurement Missions to the United States since 1978 to buy American products. Results, however, have been modest; a total of some $8 billion worth of U.S. products have been purchased by these missions. The current (1987) Special Procurement Mission intends to spend about $2.4 billion in the United States.[39] Whether such efforts are sufficient to curtail protectionist sentiment, now clearly rising in the United States, remains to be seen. It is certainly in Taiwan's interest to reduce its trade surplus with the United States as much as it possibly can, irrespective of whether or not principal causes of the problem are of Taiwan's making. Failure to solve the trade problem will almost certainly affect adversely the security relationship between the two countries, so vital to Taiwan's future.

As compared to security assistance and trade issues, the third problem—human rights and democratization in Taiwan—has not significantly affected U.S. policy toward Taiwan. After all, these questions are really Taiwan's concerns and strictly speaking are not issues between the United States and Taiwan. Nevertheless, the furtherance of democracy and the protection of human rights are enduring goals of the U.S. government and the American people as represented by the Congress. Other countries may protest that such policies constitute interference in their domestic politics. Be that as it may, authoritarian governments which engage in violations of human rights and impose martial law on their citizenry must expect adverse consequences for their relations with the United States, whether they like it or not. Especially under President Carter, human rights was elevated to an important consideration in determining American relations with other counties, especially those nations allied to the United States and where Washington felt it could exercise some influence. The U.S. Congress first required annual human rights reports on countries receiving American economic or military assistance and subsequently for all member states of the United Nations, whether or not they received American aid. In the case of the PRC and Taiwan, American human rights policies should have redounded to Taiwan's benefit since Taiwan's human rights record is incomparably superior to that of the People's Republic—indeed, it is almost insulting to mention the two cases together. But political and strategic considerations have operated to focus more attention on the occasional problems on Taiwan than on the calculated and flagrant abuses of elementary human rights practiced in Mainland China. As in the case of South Korea versus North Korea, it would appear that this is an illustration of the double standard applied to American allies about which the former U.S. ambassador to the United Nations has so eloquently written.[40]

With regard to Taiwan, however, recent Department of State reports have been generally favorable. To the extent there has been criticism in the U.S. Congress, it has usually concerned the lesser role accorded to native-born Taiwanese in the governance of Taiwan and the existence of martial law, since the establishment of the Republic of China on the island of Taiwan in 1949.[41]

The issue of greater participation of native-born Taiwanese in the governance of Taiwan is gradually being solved as political leaders born on the mainland are being replaced by persons born on the island. Children of "mainlanders" are not generally considered Taiwanese but this is a legal fiction complicated by intermarriage and the rise of a new generation. While the current collective leadership of the ruling Kuomintang party is likely to remain in power, the apparent constitutional successor to 77-year-old President Chiang Ching-kuo is a native Taiwanese, Lee Teng-hui. In 1987, 255 of the 319 seats in the Legislative Yuan are still held by mainlanders, by virtue of their election in 1947. But many of these legislators are over eighty years of age; many seats in the Legislative Yuan will soon be contested and, unquestionably, native Taiwanese will gradually assume political power.

In July 1987, Taiwan ended martial law. Other steps toward democratization included the termination of trials of civilians by military courts, the release of a number of political prisoners, and placing new censorship responsibilities in the hands of civil instead of military authorities, along with the establishment of new guidelines.[42] And in September 1987, Taiwan also lifted the ban on travel to the People's Republic of China, which had been in place since 1949.

There is no question but that Taiwan is making substantial progress toward liberalization and democracy. Nevertheless, the human rights issue remains a problem in Taiwan-American relations. Especially troubling was the killing of

Henry Liu, an American citizen of Chinese descent, in October 1984. There also have been allegations of Taiwanese harassment directed at Chinese-Americans who have been critical of the Taiwan government.[43]

On balance, the Republic of China on Taiwan is identified with free market, democratic regimes in contrast to the idiocratic, one-party command economies of the communist states. Assuming that Taiwan continues its progress toward democracy, the human rights problem should fade away as an issue in its relations with the United States.

Future Prospects

President Carter's decision in December 1978 to end formal diplomatic relations between the United States and the Republic of China on Taiwan, and to recognize the People's Republic of China, was a severe blow to the Republic of China. This decision was not made for moral reasons, despite President Carter's well-known penchant for invoking morality in the conduct of American foreign policy. The decision was not based on trade; nor was it based on cultural affinity nor on historic ties. Rather, it was a power-politics decision based on the natural desire to establish ties with the world's most populous nation. Other governments had made the same choice earlier; others were to follow in the wake of Washington's new policy. Island China by 1987 maintained diplomatic ties with only twenty-two countries; of these, only three—South Korea, South Africa, and Saudi Arabia—are considered important to Taiwan. It was, in short, the enormous disparity in power between Taiwan and the People's Republic of China that precluded a "German" solution for divided China.

Despite its remarkable economic and political progress, Taiwan has become to some extent a "pariah nation" in world politics, along with South Africa, Israel and (to a much lesser extent) Pakistan. With the exception of South Africa, this pariah status is wholly unjustified, resulting from great power rivalries, Third World prejudices and the vicissitudes of international politics. These "vicissitudes" were given a significant boost by the American decision to switch recognition from Taipei to Beijing; no amount of euphoria over recent improvements in Washington-Taipei relations or paeans of praise for the Taiwan Relations Act can obscure the fact that Taiwan's diplomatic status in the world community has suffered severe erosion. It is true that, in addition to diplomatic relations with twenty-two countries, as noted above, the R.O.C. has non-formal relations with over one hundred others and maintains membership in many international organizations. Nevertheless, a different American president from the present incumbent and a different Congress than that of 1979 could certainly modify, and even eliminate completely, the Taiwan Relations

Act. Taiwan should bend every effort, accordingly, to become as self-sufficient in arms production as feasible.

Taiwan also needs to continue the process of encouraging the participation of native-born Taiwanese in its political stuctures. Further democratization and additional progress on human rights will earn it sympathy, if not diplomatic ties, with the Western world, especially the United States. This will make it much less likely that a future Congress will dilute the critically important Taiwan Relations Act.

Taiwan's enormously robust economy remains its strong suit in international politics. But vigorous efforts should be made to minimize Taiwan-American trade frictions.

Taipei should also continue the cautious expansion of contacts between the island and the mainland, so long as these are consistent with the preservation of Taiwan's sovereignty. Such relations—even if they seem to be of little consequence— make it less likely that Beijing will resort to force to reunify China.

At some point—perhaps a generation from now—it seems inevitable that the Taiwan government will have to make some fundamental decisions about the future of the island republic. In the meanwhile, it is to be hoped that the United States will continue to support Taiwan and to insure that future choice by the people of Taiwan is freely made.

NOTES

1. Department of State Bulletin (January 1979), pp. 25-26.

2. *Ibid.*, (March 1972), p. 435.

3. See his April 1977 speech at Notre Dame University.

4. Michel Okensberg, "A Decade of Sino-American Relations," *Foreign Affairs* (Fall 1982), p. 190.

5. U.S. Senate, Committee on Foreign Relations, Taiwan: Hearings, (GPO, 1979), p. 1-3. The Senate was also angered over the administration's secrecy concerning China and that the Senate received word of Carter's decision only several hours before the public announcement.

6. U.S. House of Representatives, Committee on Foreign Affairs, Implementation of Taiwan Relations Act: Issues and Concerns (GPO, 1979), pp. 2-7.

7. The full text of the TRA may be found in *Ibid.*, Appendix 3.

8. Martin L. Lasater, *Taiwan: Facing Mounting Threats*, (The Heritage Foundation, 1984), p. 1, passim.

9. Section 13 of the TRA.

10. Section 14 of the TRA, which placed primary responsibility for Congressional oversight with the Senate Committee on Foreign Relations and the House Committee on Foreign Affairs.

11. U.S. Congress, Foreign Affairs Committee, Executive-Legislative Consultations on China Policy, 1978-79, (GPO, June 1978), p. 27.

12. James Soong, "Divided China: The View from Taipei," *International Security Review*, (Summer 1982), p. 207.

13. *Ibid.*, p. 208.

14. *Ibid.*

15. *Ibid.*, p. 209.

16. King-yuh Chang, "Partnership in Transition: A Review of Recent Taipei-Washington Relations,"*Asian Survey* (July 1981), p. 612.

17. *Ibid.*

18. Committee on Resolutions, Republican Platform, (Detroit: July 14, 1980), p. 71.

19. *New York Times*, August 26, 1980.

20. Quoted in O. Edmund Clubb, "America's China Policy,"*Current History*, (September 1981), p. 252.

21. It was not until two years later, however, that technology restrictions were relaxed after the PRC was reclassified as a "friendly but not allied country."*Washington Post*, June 21, 1983.

22. This proposal was promptly rejected by the ROC officials. For a listing of the nine points and Taiwan's explanation of its reasons for rejecting them, see *China's Reunification: Is the Nine-Point Proposal a Yesable Solution?* (China Mainland Affairs Research Center, Taipei: 2nd edition, July 1982).

23. *New York Times*, May 10, 1982.

24. U.S. Senate, Committee on Foreign Affairs, U.S. Policy Toward China and Taiwan (GPO, 1982), p. 3.

25. Lassater, *op. cit.*, p. 53.

26. Robert Downen, *The Tattered China Card*, (Council for Social and Economic Studies, 1984), p. 80.

27. *Washington Post*, August 20, 1982. This included $240 million in equipment for 30 F-5E and 30 F5F fighters, to be paid to the Northrop Corporation for providing the plans. These 60 were in addition to the same 200 Taiwan had already acquired through an initial co-production agreement.

28. *New York Times*, December 1, 1982.

29. Lassater, *op. cit.*, p. 54.

30. *Washington Post* (March 23, 1983).

31. Defense Security Assistance Agency, Foreign Military Sales, Foreign Military Construction Sales and Military Assistance Facts (GPO, 1986), pp.3-4.

32. *Far Eastern Economic Review* (July 30, 1987), p. 17.

33. *Ibid.*, pp. 15-16.

34. Personal interview with officials of the Coordination Council for North American Affairs, October 2, 1987. This is the unofficial "embassy"of the Republic of China [Taiwan].

35. George Wilson, *The East Asian Success Story,* unpublished paper presented at Kyung Hee University, Seoul, Korea, September 16, 1987. See especially pp. 17-18.

36. Because of different accounting methods, U.S. calculations show the trade deficit to be somewhat larger than Taiwan's figures presented in Table G-1. The 1986 U.S. trade deficit with Taiwan may be as high as $16 billion.

37. *Free China Journal* (August 25, 1986).

38. At the time of writing, 1987 figures were not available but quarterly estimates revealed a widening gap in Taiwan's favor.

39. Statement by Vincent Siew, Director General of the Board of Foreign Trade, Republic of China (July 21, 1987).

40. Jeane Kirkpatrick, "Dictatorships and Double Standards," *Commentary* (November, 1979).

41. See, for example, U.S. House of Representatives, Committee on Foreign Affairs, Martial Law on Taiwan and United States Foreign Policy: A Study in Human Rights, (GPO, 1982).

42. *Washington Post* (July 15, 1987).

43. Robert G. Sutter, *Taiwan and the Killing of Henry Liu: Issues for Congress*, Congressional Research Report 85-42 (February 1, 1985).

CHAPTER 8

Military Balances in Northeast Asia

Sarah M. Taylor

Four major possible arenas for military conflict within Northeast Asia exist today. One of these is the Sino-Soviet Border; a second, the divided Korean Peninsula; a third, Japan, which sits astride the strategic straits leading out of the Sea of Japan; and the fourth, the sea lanes of the Western Pacific, access to which is vital for all the national actors in Northeast Asia. The following assessment of the balance of military power in Northeast Asia builds on a discussion of the military forces which can be brought to bear on these four arenas.

The assessment of military force rightly should include more than a description of the numbers and qualities of available equipment and manpower. A nation's military forces need to be considered in terms of what is required of them. On the other hand, such requirements may be difficult to determine. While certain military requirements have a kind of objective reality growing out of the legitimate need for self-defense, geographic circumstances, and the strength of opposing forces, a nation's goals for itself and its perceptions of friends and potential opponents are also powerful influences shaping its own assessment of its military requirements. Therefore, the discussion below explores, to the degree possible in this length of survey, probable motivations and interests of the national actors in each conflict arena, as well as the more objective elements affecting their defense requirements. Additionally, the discussion offers some assessment of the effects of national unity and economic power on the military balance in these four arenas. Military power is dependent to a great degree on both of these factors, most simply because one cannot fight without national unity, however it may be achieved, and one needs money to buy weapons and support a conflict.

The national actors in Northeast Asia are the Soviet Union, China, Japan, Taiwan, North Korea, and South Korea—all present by virtue of geography— and the United States, a player by virtue of its trade interests, its world wide rivalry with the Soviet Union, and its net of Asian defense alliances and relationships born in the aftermath of the Korean and Second World Wars. The years since those wars have witnessed a dramatic growth in Northeast Asian regional power and a relative decline in U.S. power in the area. The greatest growth of regional military power has been in North Korea and in the Far Eastern TVD (Military Operational Theater) of the Soviet Union. To a large extent, this burgeoning of military might has been overshadowed, however, by the rapid economic expansion of Japan, Taiwan and South Korea and by the current dynamism of the international relationships among Northeast Asian states and the U.S. The Soviet Union and North Korea have remained outsiders to these healthier regional trends. In the end, their awkward diplomacy and emphasis on the primary importance to themselves of military power in the region has fostered the continuing U.S. military presence, nurtured U.S.-Japanese-Chinese-South Korean friendship and cooperation, and helped prod the U.S. toward a necessary modernization and strengthening of its Pacific forces.

Sino-Soviet Border

The current balance of forces along the Sino-Soviet border unquestionably favors the Soviet Union. While China is too large and densely populated to make all out invasion by the Soviets a reasonable proposition, a limited thrust into Chinese territory would be well within the capabilities of Soviet forces stationed in the area. Although the Chinese possess a minimal nuclear force of sufficient strength to deter Soviet nuclear strikes, the invisible factor which works to balance Chinese and Soviet strengths along the border is Chinese friendship with the United States and her allies.

Along the Sino-Soviet border the Chinese maintain perhaps twice the manpower of Soviet forces and larger numbers of attack aircraft. (See Figure 1.) However, the Soviets are vastly superior in the quality of their weaponry, both on the ground and in the air. They have almost five times the number of tanks and armored vehicles as the Chinese along this border. Ninety percent of Soviet fighter/attack aircraft and interceptors are now late generation,[1] including MiG-25 Foxbats, MiG-21 Foxhounds, and SU-24 Fencer fighter bombers, the last with a combat radius of 1,800 km. Total Soviet long-range bomber strength is presently over 300 aircraft, 80 of which are Backfires. These have an unrefueled range of 3500 km and both nuclear and conventional attack capability.

Much of the Soviet air power is located at more than 140 airfields in the maritime portion of the Far East Military District, the eastern most of the military districts in the Far East TVD.[2] The fields lie in the area between Chinese Manchuria and the Sea of Japan. Thus, the bulk of Soviet aircraft are centrally located to threaten either Japan or China, and can reach South Korea and the Pacific sea lanes as well. Currently about 50 of the existing air bases are being upgraded, with second or third runways being added. Until recently most have been "austere" with few facilities.[3]

In contrast, the majority of Chinese aircraft, F-6s and F-7s, are based on older Soviet MiG-19 and MiG-21 designs. They lack nighttime and-all weather capability,[4] electronic warfare gear, and long range air-to-air missiles. The Chinese also have no long range bombers. Further weaknesses along this front

Table 8-1

FORCES ON THE SINO-SOVIET BORDER

	SOVIET	CHINESE	
Divisions	53	105	
MBT	14,500	2,700	
Bombers	310	0	
FTRs/Interceptors	1,350	5,120	(total includes 620 light bombers)

REGIONAL NUCLEAR FORCES

	SOVIET	CHINESE
ICBM	380	6
IRBM	171	60
MRBM	0	50

Source: International Institute for Strategic Studies, *The Military Balance, 1986-87*

include not only fewer and older style tanks, but a dearth of effective anti-tank and anti-armor weaponry. In addition, as demonstrated by the fighting in Vietnam in 1979, lack of mechanization in the PLA prevented both troops and logistics from keeping up with the ground speed of the Vietnamese.[5] The Soviets on the northern border are certainly better equipped to supply and support a modern war, therefore, than the Chinese.

In addition, the nuclear forces of the Soviet Union are overwhelmingly larger and more sophisticated than those of the Chinese. (See Figure 1.) The Chinese have an ICBM capable of reaching Moscow, but they have comparatively few of them. Their ICBM survivability is questionable, although both camouflage, such as hiding them in caves, and mobility, hauling missiles on trucks, have been used to counter this. The Chinese bomber force is wholly inadequate as a possible delivery system. At the same time, the Chinese, along with the rest of Asia, must face the 170 or more SS-20 missiles now located east of the Urals. Compounding Chinese problems is a very poor long range detection and early warning system for their northern borders.[6] While the Soviet forces along this front are undoubtedly well equipped with biological and chemical weapons as well as with tactical nuclear weapons, at best the Chinese have only a modest retaliatory capability in these categories.[7]

Several reasons lie behind the heavy concentration of forces along the Sino-Soviet border. In Soviet eyes, China, although weak militarily, has become an increasingly independent and potentially dangerous neighbor at every step of its development since the Sino-Soviet split about 1960. The Chinese detonated their first nuclear device in 1964, and then turned unpredictable and erratic through the Cultural Revolution. They began a reconciliation with the West in 1972 and by the end of the decade were flirting with a Western military alliance. Now, finally, the reorganization of the economy and political life suggests the potential for major economic growth, perhaps the most dangerous possibility of all to the Soviets.

Of course, what the Soviets chronically fear is not only strong, independent neighbors, but the possibility of a second front opening in the Far East should war break out in Europe. China is not capable of challenging the Soviet Union alone, but if the Soviet Union were weakened by a prolonged struggle with the United States, or if China should join the U.S. in opposing the Soviet Union in the Far East, then clearly China becomes a serious threat. Therefore, it is necessary for the Soviets in the Far East to have sufficient forces to challenge not only the U.S. with its allies, but also the Chinese, either concurrently or in succession. In addition, parts of the border with China are still in dispute. It was along this border that fighting broke out in 1968-69 with strong Chinese provocation. The major east-west rail line connecting the European and Eastern sections of the Soviet Union runs within 30 miles of the Chinese border. Finally, the neck of land leading down to Vladivostok, the most important Siberian port, while heavily militarized, is only about 200 miles wide.

For the Chinese, historically the threat has been from the north. Repeatedly during their history, in periods of internal weakness, "barbarians" from the north have invaded to conquer large portions of the northern half of the country. Currently, the Soviets have five of their border divisions stationed inside Mongolia and thoroughly dominate that country. At their closest these forces are within about 400 miles of Peking. Soviet forces also line the borders of Manchuria where currently much of China's heavy industry and energy production is located. Finally, along the Western part of their common border, the land is sparsely populated and generally less developed. The people are largely ethnic minorities with strong historical and cultural ties across the border into the Soviet Union and historically a nomadic lifestyle. Their reliability as loyal Chinese citizens has traditionally been suspect for the Han Chinese. All these factors suggest for the Chinese the threat of the thing Soviet forces are in fact most capable of doing at this time: a quick thrust into China for a limited territorial gain, the most likely place being Manchuria where the industrial loss would simultaneously weaken China and aid in Soviet development of Siberia.

The Soviet response to their problems with China has been almost entirely a military response, to this point. Over the period since the Sino-Soviet split the Soviets have systematically increased and upgraded their forces along the border. Some of these forces—the SS-20s and the aircraft—are directed also against Japan and U.S. forces in East Asia. However, the manpower and tanks are solely aimed at the Chinese. In addition, a second railroad line, the Baikal-Amur Mainline, has been added further north of the Trans Siberian Railway. While its primary purpose may well be regional development, its supply of an alternate route between Tayshet, west of Lake Baikal, and the Soviet ports on the Sea of Japan at a further distance from the Chinese border must also be considered a military asset.[8]

The Chinese response to its weak position along the Sino-Soviet border has been predominately diplomatic and political. In their opening to the West the Chinese have sought to create potential allies, from among the United States and its European and Asian allies. Simultaneously they have worked to reduce the impression that they themselves pose a threat to their neighbors. Deng Xiao Ping has said repeatedly that what China needs is peace and stability in which to pursue economic growth and that any substantial strengthening of military power must take a back seat to economic development. In addition, the Chinese have been relatively open about their military weaknesses. Their need to modernize and the areas in which they must do so are no secret.

Diplomatic efforts on both the Chinese and Soviet sides to lower the level of tension between them have moved forward slowly since 1979 when the Chinese press stopped berating the USSR for its "revisionism." Meanwhile trade between the two has grown and cultural exchanges have been reinstituted. In March 1986, agreements were signed arranging the return of Soviet advisors to China, for the first time since 1960, to help with the modernization of industrial equipment originally installed by the Soviets.[9] Of course, open rivalry between the two countries still exists for influence in Southeast Asia, where the Chinese aid anti-Vietnamese rebels in Cambodia and maintain their heavy force along the Sino Vietnamese border, and with the Soviet's deep involvement in economic and military aid to Vietnam.

The Chinese and Soviets have competed for many years for influence in North Korea. Currently the Soviets appear to have gained the upper hand there with their agreement to send MiG-23s to Kim Il Sung and the subsequent granting of overflight rights to Soviet aircraft. Additionally, reports exist of the Soviets being granted access to North Korean harbors.[10] Influence on the Korean peninsula is directly relevant to the strategic problems both the Chinese and Soviets face in Manchuria and Siberia. With strong Soviet influence in North Korea, Chinese Manchuria would be almost 2/3 surrounded by Soviet dominated territory. With strong Chinese influence there the isolation of Vladivostok and the nearby developing industrial areas of Soviet Eastern Siberia would become even more complete.

The second major thrust of Chinese policy to counter its weakness in the face of the Soviet Union has been domestic. Economic, political, and social reforms have been initiated to provide an underpinning for developing their military strength. At the very least the economy must grow sufficiently to pay for any substantial military modernization and to allow for the adoption and absorption of the requisite high technology. Both of these are beyond present Chinese capability on the broad scale necessary to make Chinese forces equal to Soviet forces. At the same time the Chinese are focussing their efforts on a few important defense factors to maximize the effect of the money they do spend. These programs are not only key to their defense problems but also practicable to institute in terms of current domestic policies.

First, efforts are being made to settle Han Chinese into border areas, to develop those areas economically, to increase local ethnic participation in the government and to allow for ethnic groups to maintain to some extent their own separate cultures. Secondly, efforts are being made to develop industry outside of Manchuria, particularly energy production. Thirdly, the military itself is being modernized. This effort focuses on streamlining the PLA and making it more professionally competent on a continuing emphasis of naval and nuclear force modernization programs, and on some military cooperation with the Western powers. Thus manpower in the PLA was to be cut in 1985-86 from about four million to about three million, higher education requirements have been introduced for officers, the PLA is largely withdrawing from manufacturing for the civilian economy, its political role and influence are gradually being eroded, and the emphasis on widespread militia training, once necessary for "people's war," is apparently being dropped.

Meanwhile there has been an intensive effort by the Chinese to learn about what is required for their military modernization from the U.S., Japan, and European powers. This has involved exchange visits of high ranking officers, some training programs, observations of military exercises, extensive "shopping trips" for possible purchases of new technologies and weapons systems, and a few actual purchases of key systems. Additionally, in the line of more direct military cooperation with Western powers, naval visits of some European vessels have been allowed. Furthermore, the United States and China are reported to be jointly operating listening posts in western Xinjiang Province to monitor Soviet missile testing and military communications, providing some alleviation of the early warning problem for the Chinese.[11]

Both the Chinese Navy and Nuclear forces have continued to grow and modernize over the past ten years at a comparatively faster rate than the ground and air segments of the PLA. Part of the reason for this may be domestic/political, that neither pose the threat to the civilian center of authority that would be posed by a fully modernized army or air arm. At the same time, these two efforts have strategic rationale. Largely by virtue of the fact that it has nuclear forces, China can begin to stake its claim as one of the great powers, despite its economic and other military weaknesses. Additionally, faced with overwhelming U.S. and Soviet power, nuclear and conventional, the cheapest way toward some kind of deterrence has been to possess at least a minimal nuclear deterrent, which the Chinese have now achieved.[12] They continue to work on their delivery systems, in particular, solid fueled missiles and a MIRV capability, the latter which can be deduced from their having launched three satellites simultaneously atop one rocket in 1981.[13] Their naval program includes two Xia class SSBN with four scheduled to be built.[14] These presumably mark the initial stages of an effort to provide a secure second strike capability.

The present Chinese policy of deemphasizing the Soviet threat and making friends with the West must be considered successful. The Chinese appear to be gaining the time they want to develop their economy. However, it is important to remember that Soviet strength along the Sino-Soviet border is delicately balanced against a combination of factors; world opinion, Chinese forces, and the current lack of pressing Soviet motivation for a strike into China. Should any of these factors change for the worse, particularly should Soviet motivations change, the force balance as it stands would be grave indeed for the Chinese.

The Division of the Korean Peninsula

Broadly speaking, the military situation on the Korean Peninsula favors the North Koreans on the ground and the South Korean and U.S. combined forces in the air. A major deterrent to renewed war on the peninsula is the presence of U.S. forces in South Korea and the dependence of North Korea on Soviet and/or Chinese aid, as well as their mutual defense treaties with those two nations. Thus no drive over the DMZ can be prosecuted in either direction without the prompt involvement of a major power on the other side.

Along the Korean DMZ, North Korea currently has an advantage of about two and one half to one in tanks, and four to one in artillery and heavy mortars. North Korean army personnel number perhaps 200,000 more than South Korean. (See Figure 2.) Northern ground equipment, most of it manufactured indigenously, is generally considered superior to that used by the South. In addition, of North Korean forces, about 100,000 are ranger commandos trained for insertion into the south, with one of their most probable targets being allied air power. Tunnels have been dug to help accomplish their infiltration southward, and the North Koreans also have a large fleet of older, slow, low-flying aircraft and small boats to be used for the same purpose.[15] The North has a number of diesel submarines which could presumably be used to harass Southern shipping. The South itself have none, but have some 22 ASW aircraft and 10 ASW helicopters.[16]

In contrast, U.S. and South Korean combined forces on the peninsula are considered to have superior air power. The Soviet Union began delivery of MiG-23s to the North in 1985, and perhaps a total of 40-45 will be supplied.[17] At the same time the U.S. is sending 36 F-16s to the South Koreans. Allied air defense in South Korea is quite strong in aircraft and warning technologies, but remains weaker in ground-based anti-air weaponry. In the North much of the air defense equipment has been buried in caves and aircraft are kept at hardened sites.[18] Additionally, the Soviet Union has been supplying more sophisticated air defense missiles such as the Scud SS-1, AA-7 Apex, and SA-3 Goa.[19]

The situation along the Korean DMZ remains one of the most tense areas of military confrontation in the world. The threat to the South is clear and has been repeatedly dramatized over the past years through major incidents such as the bomb-assassination of South Korean leaders in Rangoon in 1983, and through more frequent instances of attempted infiltrations of commandos into the south. Many in the South fear that Kim Jong Il, in an effort to consolidate power after his father dies, may choose a military adventure southward as a way of doing so. Analyses by both Koreans and Japanese conclude that Kim Jong Il, not his father, was responsible for the Rangoon bombing.[20] Additionally, the hosting of the Asian Games and then the Olympic Games in Seoul, major diplomatic triumphs for the South Koreans, may prove to be provocations for violence on Kim Il Sung's part.

The South is faced with a major strategic problem in that Seoul, the capital, lies within 40 km of the DMZ. This city is home to nearly one quarter of the Korean population and much of the nation's thriving industry and commerce. Seoul is vulnerable to any quick thrust across the DMZ by the North. The North Koreans have chosen to emphasize this problem within the past several years by moving large numbers of troops into about 100 underground bunkers, 12-18 miles from the DMZ. This has reduced the warning time of an attack for the South from about 24 hours to 6 hours. The pace of North Korean military exercising has also been increased.[21]

In the North, the U.S. troops in the South are seen as a direct threat, as well as an affront to Korean nationalism. At the same time, the North Koreans are faced with a deteriorating military situation in the long term. The total population of the South (forty-two million) is much larger than their own (twenty million). South Korea is becoming economically and technologically strong enough to increasingly bear the load of its defenses independently. Within ten to fifteen years Southern military capability may well be substantially larger than that of the North and the restraining presence of the United States forces may no longer be necessary. The economic growth trend may slow but shows no signs of fundamentally changing. Meanwhile, the less well developed economy in the North shows no signs of blossoming and leaves North Korea heavily dependent on outside military aid, particularly for higher technology items.

The response of the South to the threat from the North has been multifaceted. It begins with a reliance on U.S. military aid and the presence of U.S. forces in the South, where U.S. and South Korean forces operate under an American led joint command. These forces rely on a forward defense and on their superior air power to achieve quick control of the air battle and halt any North Korean advance as close to the border as possible.[22] The possibility that U.S. tactical nuclear weapons would also be used can not be ruled out. Domestically, the South has traditionally relied on a population with strong anti-communist sentiment and memories of the Korean War as a highly effective defense against the kind of infiltration which Kim Il Sung has regularly attempted. At the same time, the South has counted heavily on the rapidly increasing standard of living to maintain loyalty and to minimize dissent within the country. Domestic policy has included a concerted and largely successful effort to develop the economy, allowing eventual independence from U.S. aid. At least 50 percent of the South's military equipment is now produced locally. Currently, the South Koreans are embarked on an ambitious modernization program for this equipment. Additionally, the South has pursued, over the past several years, an aggressive foreign policy aimed at gaining trade plus diplomatic support for South Korea in its rivalry with the North.

North Korean response to the threat from the South has been to spend heavily on military equipment, and build up an industrial base geared to the production of military goods. North Korean society is kept highly regimented and a very high proportion of the population is in the military. Estimates of the percent of GNP spent on the military run from 13 to 30 percent per year over the past fifteen years. One out of twenty-five people is in the military and as much as 25 percent of the population has at least some reserve commitment.[23] Diplomatically, the North Koreans have remained isolated from most of the world. Their major dealings have been with China and the Soviet Union as a counter-balance to the U.S. presence in the South. Their military ties with radical states such as Iran and Libya and the presence of their military advisors and trainers in African and Caribbean states have helped to perpetuate their isolation. Diplomatic moves toward peace talks or reunification talks, until 1984, specifically required the withdrawal of U.S. troops or excluded the ROK. Such moves in the past have been so frequently connected with violence that they are met now with extreme skepticism by the U.S. and South Korea.

Talks between North and South, halted in 1973, began again in 1985. They have been dealing with economic and humanitarian issues, as a prelude to reducing tensions on the peninsula. An important outcome was meetings held in September 1985 between some families separated by the Korean War. There have been moves toward a meeting between President Chun Doo Hwan of the South and Premier Kim Il Sung.[24] However, since at the very time these negotiations have been taking place, North Korea has continued its forward redeployment of troops, it is difficult to believe that the military confrontation is going to be sublimated into some other form. The major factor that continues to maintain the uneasy peace on the peninsula is continued dependence by both North and South on the United States, the Soviet Union, and China, none of which wish to see war break out.

The Position of Japan Astride the Straits

At present, Japanese forces alone are not capable of defending Japan against Soviet attack. The Japanese currently rely heavily on the U.S. both for conventional and nuclear defense. Soviet nuclear forces and air power directed against Japan are the same forces that threaten China; that is, some of the 200 SS-20s east of the Urals and some of the 2000 or so fighters and bombers stationed in Siberia are meant for Japan. Japan maintains no nuclear capability, of course, and must rely on the U.S. nuclear forces for deterrence. Japanese air power is somewhat out of date and entirely defensive in character. They have no long range bomber and their fighter aircraft have no aerial refueling capability. One hundred-forty of the total of 250 fighters and interceptors are aging F-4s and F-104s. More modern Japanese aircraft are 60 F-15s and 50 F-1s.[25] The Air Self Defense Force continue to use the Nike-J for their surface to air missiles and need better anti-air guns and warning radar.

Current U.S. air forces stationed in Japan to some extent make up for these deficiencies. The U.S. has 74 F-15s and F-16s stationed on Honshu and a Marine Air Wing in Okinawa. It is likely that these aircraft would need to be rapidly reinforced when possible, and supplemented by carrier air and by the B-52s on Guam, in any full blown conflict with the Soviets. (See Figure 3.)

Soviet forces have been built up in the islands north of Hokkaido quite dramatically since the signing of the Sino-Japanese Friendship treaty in 1978. Sakhalin, 42 km from Wakkanai on the northern tip of Hokkaido, is one site. The Kurile Islands are another, particularly Etorofu, within 150 miles of Hokkaido. On Etorofu is now stationed a 10,000-16,000 man composite division of regular army equipped with tanks, APCs, long range 130mm cannon and ground attack helicopters. Forty MiG-23s stationed at Etorofu and cruise missiles with nuclear warheads have also been placed there, from which the Japanese bases of Senzai and Misawa are within range.[26] Recent additions to the Soviet Pacific fleet include the Aleksey Kosygin, an atomic powered landing ship with a carrying capacity of 35,000 to 40,000 tons. It is capable of landing the equipment for a full division on its 100 barges.[27] This substantially increases Soviet amphibious capability in the area, which would presumably be directed against northern Hokkaido in order to secure La Perousse strait. At least one division of 8,000 naval infantry is stationed near Vladisvostok. Their amphibious capability includes 18 or more smaller vessels.

Four of the 12 Japanese Ground Self Defense Force divisions are stationed in Hokkaido to counter these Soviet forces. This is a total of 31,000 troops, and the divisions in Hokkaido include Japan's only armored division. Exercises in Hokkaido in 1984 suggested defenses there are still inadequate. A heavily outnumbered defending force was defeated in less than twenty minutes in a simulated invasion. The results indicated the inadequacy of Japanese GSDF anti-armor, anti-aircraft and tanks to cope with a Soviet assault.[28]

In the GSDF today, roughly 1/2 of the battle tanks are the newer type 74. There are about 700 HAWK surface to air missiles of which about 75 percent are Improved HAWK.[29] Recent acquisitions include 22 AH-IS attack helicopters, which represent the beginnings of the GSDF's first anti-tank helicopter force,[30] an urgent need given the type of attack the Soviets could be expected to mount against Hokkaido.

All of the Japanese Self Defense Forces suffer further from sustainability, logistics, and communications deficiencies. The Air Self Defense, for example, has enough missiles to load its aircraft for only 1 1/2 missions. Stocks for the naval forces are so low that all destroyers could load up only once.[31] Such shortages inhibit exercises and training, and would be crippling to Japanese forces facing an actual assault. Other weaknesses include the lack of a credible reserve system, poor cooperation between the SDF services and a surprisingly poor communications system given Japanese capabilities in this area.

Nevertheless, Japan presents a considerable strategic problem for the Soviet Union. Year around access by Soviet ships going to or from Eastern Siberia requires passage through one of the straits around Japan and such Soviet shipping is of considerable economic and military importance. The port of Vladivostok is the major naval base for the Soviet Pacific fleet for supply and repairs. At the same time, the port is the major point for trans-shipment of military supplies into the heavily militarized area to the north. Furthermore, Soviet development of the economic resources of Siberia depends on the shipment of supplies into Siberia by sea and the export of lumber or other products by the same route. The Trans-Siberian Railroad carried only about 20 percent of the two-way shipment of goods in 1978.[32]

In addition, Japan borders the Sea of Japan, within much of the Soviet Pacific fleet is expected to shelter should a major war occur. Soviet SSBNs will probably hide in the Sea of Japan and Okhotsk to preserve a second strike capability. Their freedom of operation would be limited by U.S. and Japanese air and sea power based in Japan and by surveillance facilities located there also. Finally, U.S. facilities in Japan constitute a direct, conventional threat to the Soviet homeland.

On the other hand, Japan, by its geography, is particularly vulnerable to attack. The islands present an attractive and nearly indefensible target for nuclear strikes. They are small, densely populated, highly industrialized and lie close to the Asian mainland. Even an entirely conventional attack could be quickly devastating and difficult to defend against, there being little opportunity for a defense in depth. Furthermore, Japan is vulnerable to blockades or disruptions of shipping as the economy is heavily dependent on exports and high percentages of vital commodities are imported, such as energy (70 percent) and food (50 percent).[33]

The nation currently most likely to take advantage of these vulnerabilities is the Soviet Union. There is historical animosity between the two countries. The Soviets, for example, occupy islands north of Hokkaido, the "Northern Territories," which the Japanese consider to be part of Japan. More importantly, the Soviets are likely to want to seize the northern part of Hokkaido during any major conflict with a third country in order to assure themselves of passage through the straits. The Soviets would be further likely to threaten Japan with nuclear or conventional air strikes or disruptions of shipping in order to pressure Japan into neutrality during a U.S./USSR confrontation.

The Soviet reaction to problems with Japan has been the military build-up in Siberia, particularly on Southern Sakhalin, Etorofu, and the neighboring islands. Basing on the Kamchatka Peninsula has also become more important and may be aimed at reducing somewhat Soviet dependence on the use of the Japan straits. In addition, the visibility of Soviet forces around Japan has been increased in recent years, with more Soviet violations and near violations of Japanese airspace, and naval maneuvers in proximity to Japan.[34] Soviet diplomacy in dealing with Japan has been deliberately negative in tone, although Mr. Gorbachev may represent a change. The Soviets have been uncooperative in fishery talks, unwilling to arrange high level meetings with Japanese officials and completely unwilling to acknowledge Japanese concern over the Northern Territories. In addition, there have been thinly veiled threats to use nuclear weapons against Japan should the Japanese fail to abandon their U.S. alliance in the face of war.[35]

After WW II, it was clear to the Japanese government, that, given its strategic vulnerabilities, it would have to ally with the United States if it was to avoid Soviet domination. The Japanese began in a nearly totally dependent position militarily and have very gradually increased the degree of responsibility they take in their own defense. Since the late 1970s, this trend has accelerated as cooperative planning and exercising with U.S. forces has increased rapidly. Defense issues, once entirely taboo in public debate, are now discussed openly. While Japanese defense spending has not yet been allowed to break the 1 percent of GNP per annum cap imposed by the cabinet in 1976, defense spending has been increasing more rapidly than other elements of the government budget, and has remained as close as possible to the 1% mark. Despite their dependence on the U.S. for much of their defense needs the Japanese have avoided becoming totally dependent on imported weapons systems. While a certain number are imported, generally from the U.S., some are produced in Japan under license. Others have been indigenously developed and manufactured, such as the T-74 tank and the SSM-1 surface to surface missile.

Planning for the remedy of deficiencies in the Japanese Self Defense Forces is extensive and addresses the very issues raised above. More money is being used to build weapons stockpiles. The GSDF defense of Hokkaido is being reorganized. A new fighter plane is being developed under contract by Japanese companies. Meanwhile F-1s and F-4s are to be upgraded and further F-15s added to the ASDF. The Patriot Missile is on order for the ASDF and Aegis for the MSDF. Some use of satellite communications by the military has begun.[36] Over the horizon radar are planned for Iwo Jima and Okinawa.[37] At the same time, the limits on spending do not allow these developments to take place fast enough for the Japanese to quickly take over those defense roles reserved for them in U.S.-Japanese agreements. Defense of the islands from an invasion or from sea and air bombardment remains problematical even with the help of U.S. forces, as does the control of the straits. Finally, as will be discussed below, Japanese Maritime SDF is a long way from being able to defend the sea lanes between Japan, Guam, the Philippines, and Taiwan.

Diplomatically, the Japanese have tended to be cautious about offending the Soviets and have attempted without much success to pursue more normalized relations with them. However, the Japanese have not been willing to ease their pressure on the Northern Territories issue or to lessen their military cooperation with the United States. Furthermore, Japanese participation in development projects in Siberia, another major goal for the Soviet Union, was largely halted as part of the sanctions introduced after the Soviet invasion of Afghanistan.

The emphasis of Japanese foreign policy in Northeast Asia, as elsewhere, has generally been economic. Largely through trade, Japan has been able to maintain at least minimal contact with North Korea and a fairly close if highly unofficial relationship with Taiwan while at the same time pursuing closer relationships with both China and South Korea. This economic emphasis, and Japan's perceived attitude of sitting on the fence on strategic East/West issues has caused some problems in its relationship with both the U.S. and South Korea, both of which would like Japan to come down more firmly on their side. However, under Prime Minister Yasuhiro Nakasone, Japan has articulated a more forceful support of the U.S. military presence in Northeast Asia. Japanese efforts to improve this relationship and their own military preparedness have not gone unnoticed in the United States. Similarly, both President Chun, of South Korea, and Nakasone have worked to reduce the antagonism in the relationship between their countries. Thus Japanese cooperation with the U.S. in Northeast Asian contingencies, particularly in defense of South Korea, does not seem as problematical as it was even three years ago.

The Western Pacific

The defining component of geopolitics in East Asia is the Pacific Ocean. There is an important subtlety to this statement of the obvious that is often neglected. The control of the Pacific's vast stretches and narrow passages is of critical concern to virtually every nation in the region because the economies of all the states, even the continental ones, are fundamentally insular. There is relatively little commercial activity across national frontiers. However, despite the fact that all significant commerce in finished products as well as raw materials comes by sea, there are only two rival naval forces that contest the

Figure 8-1

Balance of Major Naval Forces
in the Pacific Theater

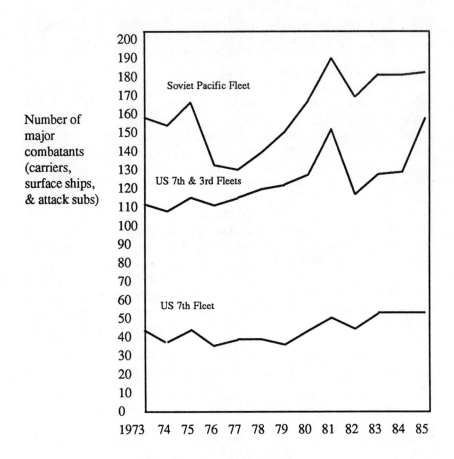

Source: International Institute for Strategic Studies, *The Military Balance*,
1973-74 thru 1984-85

Table 8-2

EAST ASIA/PACIFIC FORCES

	US 7th Flt.	US 3rd Flt.	Total	Soviet Pacific	US standing
SHIPS					
Aircraft carriers	2	4	6	2	4
Helicopter carriers	1	5	6	0	6
Battleships	0	1	1	0	2
Cruisers	5	13	18	15	3
Destroyers	8	21	29	25	4
Frigates	12	35	47	54	-7
Attack submarines	9	40	49	83	-34
SSBNs	0	7	7	32	-25
Amphibious ships	5	20	25	20	5
AIRCRAFT					
ASW	36	81	117	70	47
Fighter					
Navy	174	232	406	70	336
Marine	53	133	186	0	186
Air Force	240	0	240	1160	-920
Bombers					
Air Force					
Heavy	14	0	14	0	14
Medium	0	0	0	100	-100
Navy					
Heavy	0	0	0	0	0
Medium	0	0	0	100	-100

John M. Collins, *U.S.-Soviet Military Balance,* Congressional Research Service Report No. 87-128-S (Washington: April 3, 1987); International Institute of Strategic Studies, *The Military Balance 1986-87* (London: Autumn 1986); and "The Naval Balance in the Indian-Pacific Ocean," *Naval Forces Special Issue: The Naval Balance '87* No. II/1987 Vol. VIII

control of the Pacific: the American and Soviet Pacific fleets. Until quite recently, the American 7th and 3rd Fleets sailed the Pacific unchallenged.

In both the popular and expert press much has been made of the growth of the Soviet Pacific Fleet, now the largest of the four Soviet fleets. But there is virtual unanimity among Western naval analysts that even if the larger Soviet fleet were commanded by a modern Nelson, it could not wrest control away from the United States. While this may be true, it may also be irrelevant for it begs the question of where these two navies might clash should war break out. What this section will examine is less the forces themselves than the strategies which guide their deployment.

Soviet naval policy in the Pacific has closely mirrored changes in broader Soviet national strategy. In the late 1960s Soviet strategic assumptions underwent a significant transformation. Prior to 1966, Soviet planners almost fatalistically assumed that a world war would automatically and quickly escalate to the level of cataclysmic nuclear war. After 1966, the Soviets have considered the possibility that war, should it come, might be protracted and fought with conventional forces.[38]

This possible change in Soviet thinking was in part prompted by NATO's shift from "massive retaliation" to "flexible response" and by the American emphasis on "assured destruction," both of which could be interpreted as an American reluctance to resort to strategic nuclear weapons except in response to a direct attack on U.S. soil. These changes in strategic assumptions paralleled a change in the technology and tactics of waging strategic war at sea. The 1960s witnessed a minor revolution in the conduct of nuclear war by naval forces; from carrier borne aircraft the mantle of responsibility in the American fleets for nuclear strikes passed to the nuclear-powered ballistic submarine. Initially this change made strategic defense of the Soviet Union a vastly more demanding task. Also, by the latter half of the 1960s the modest range of the early Polaris missiles, which required that they be launched from areas close to the Soviet coast, was replaced by the much longer ranged Poseidon.

These developments led to a commensurate change in both operational requirements and force structure for the Soviet navy. The pre-1966 emphasis on anti-carrier and counter-SSBN operations was shifted to creating secure "bastions" for the Soviets' own nascent long-range SSBN force(the "Yankee" class entered service in the late 1960s and the "Delta" class SSBNs in the early 1970s). The acceptance of a possibly protracted war necessitated a complementary change in naval design as well as mission. Whereas before this transformation in assumptions Soviet forces had only to weather a preemptive strike and then deliver their weapons, they now had to be capable of sustained operations needed to gain and maintain command of large sea areas contiguous to the Soviet Union, such as the Norwegian Sea, the Sea of Japan, and the Sea of Okhotsk. Such operational requirements demanded long endurance capability, large magazine loads, and underway replenishment capability. Put simply, Soviet naval design had to switch from small coastal ships to large ocean-going vessels.[39]

The shift to a more capable Soviet blue water navy began in 1971 with the adoption of the ninth five year plan by the 24th Party Congress. The plan provided that all follow-on cruiser, destroyer, and frigate class ships would be scaled up in size. In addition, the plan authorized a class of heavily armed nuclear-powered battlecruiser, the Kirov-class. A similar scaling up process was applied to amphibious vessels, reflecting the new requirement for a long-range heavy assault lift suitable for seizing key islands, such as Hokkaido, or long stretches of coastline, as in Norway.

The new classes of ships began to attract significant attention as more and more of them found their way from Black Sea shipyards to the Pacific Ocean. Beginning in 1978 the Soviet Pacific Fleet joined the ranks of the world's truly powerful navies. In that year the "Vasiliy Chapavev," a Kresta-II class cruiser, docked at Vladivostok; it was the first major surface combatant to join the Pacific fleet in over four years, but it would not be the last. In the following year Soviet naval power in the Pacific theater increased substantially as the Kiev class aircraft carrier, "Minsk," transferred to the Pacific with a task force comprising two Kara class cruisers, the landing ship "Ivan Rogov" and a new underway replenishment ship. The next four years saw the arrival of two more cruisers and another carrier task force.

In the West an early interpretation of this naval expansion was that the newly enlarged and improved Pacific fleet is meant to challenge the United States for control of the SLOC in East Asia. This is now not thought to be the case, however.[40] First, Soviet naval writers have given scant attention to interdiction of the SLOC. When thought has been devoted to SLOC interdiction it invariably stresses the role of submarines and naval aviation, not surface ships.[41] While the Pacific fleet closely approximates the Northern fleet in numbers of surface ships, it does not come close in the category of submarines. The Northern fleet has well over half of all Soviet submarines and fully two-thirds of all nuclear powered attack submarines. If there is to be a major campaign to interdict the SLOC, it will be in the North Atlantic, not the Pacific.

Second, one needs to consider the "Gorshkov reversal." Western analysts have long been aware of a distinctly Soviet way in war and nowhere is this more true than in the planned role of surface ships in naval combat. Admiral Gorshkov, architect of the modern Soviet navy, attributed the defeat of the German U-Boat campaign in both world wars to a failure to support the submarines by utilizing surface ships and aircraft to attack Allied antisubmarine warfare(ASW) units. Since under today's conditions the greatest threat to Soviet SSBNs is U.S. attack submarines, most surface combatants built after the mid-1960s have been designed principally for ASW operations in support of submarines. In the West the tactical rule of thumb in design and operation is for submarines to operate in support of surface ships and their missions.

Third, SLOC interdiction and distant power projection mandates that, institutionally, the navy have a rather independent role in the formation and execution of national strategy. While the U.S. Navy may represent such a confident and independent bureaucratic actor, its principal adversary does not. Consistently ranked last in the order of precedence among the five Soviet military services,[42] the Baltic, Black Sea, and Pacific fleets are all subordinated to the army commanders of various theaters of operation, and the commander-in-chief of the navy has no operational control, but functions as an administrator and advisor. Admiral Gorshkov's attempt to carve out an unique and independent mission for the navy failed well before his ouster in late 1985; the second edition of his *Sea Power and the State*(1976) backed away from his earlier claim to "naval preeminence within the armed forces and instead made obeisance to the 'unified strategy,' which, in essence, reaffirmed the Soviet navy's traditional subordination to a strategy dominated by continental considerations."[43]

None of this is to say that the Soviet Pacific fleet will not try to interdict the Pacific SLOC. Rather the point is that interdiction is not the primary mission to which the Soviet navy in the Pacific is devoted and, consequently, it will be carried out in the main by the Pacific fleet's least capable forces. An extensive Western study of the SLOC issue in the late 1970s concluded that the Soviet navy would probably dedicate mainly torpedo-armed, diesel-electric submarines to SLOC interdiction.[44] Such units would pose a sharp threat initially to merchant shipping, but relatively little to carrier battle groups. The primary threat to American carriers in the Pacific will come from Soviet naval aviation. Given however, the lack of long-range fighter support for Soviet bombers, the deployment of sophisticated fighters to Japan and South Korea, and the deployment of Aegis radar systems with American task forces, the threat to the Pacific sea lanes appears to be manageable.

While it is quite likely that during war the United States Navy will find the vast majority of the Soviet Pacific Fleet not far from its home ports, in peacetime the units of the Soviet Pacific Fleet are to be found in distant waters. Making good use of the facilities at Cam Ranh Bay, the Soviet Pacific Fleet has greatly extended Moscow's diplomatic reach as well as its days at sea. Port calls and large, highly visible exercises and maneuvers have begun to reverse Moscow's diplomatic fortunes in the Far East. The Soviet Union has quickly made it clear that it seeks to end its isolation from the world's most dynamic economic zone and chip away at American influence in East Asia by wooing the mini island states in the deep reaches of the Pacific. As the editor for *Jane's Fighting Ships* notes, "Find an island state in the Pacific and you'll probably find an industrious Soviet diplomat offering aid, airfields, advice. This is no burgeoning magnanimity but reflects a stern determination to move in where others have indulged in benign neglect."[45]

Fishing treaties, tourism agreements, and diplomatic recognition by themselves do not threaten the military balance in the Western Pacific; it is what they portend that gives the U.S. and its allies pause. As Australia's former prime minister Malcolm Fraser observed, "It will start as a fish-processing facility. But that will have some refueling facilities, which will require repair facilities and, in turn, an airfield. Then it's a base."[46]

Unlike Soviet naval design and operational strategy, American naval policy has not undergone any radical revision. In large part, this constancy is a function of geography as much it is national strategy. While Soviet naval tacticians have had to wrestle with escape from confined waters , American planners have had to overcome the Pacific's immensity. In the world of the military planner it has been an axiom since Clausewitz that the power of the offensive diminishes with distance in an almost geometric progression. For example, in the years preceding World War II both American and Japanese naval planners calculated that a fleet would lose 10 percent of its combat effectiveness for every 1000 sea miles travelled from its base.

So long as the United States wished to influence events along the Asian littoral, this attrition of geography has imposed a "forward strategy" on the United States. The U.S. meets its forward strategy requirements through a "dual anchoring" policy. The two "anchors" in the Western Pacific are the bases in Japan(Yokosuka, Saesbo, and Okinawa) and the bases in the Philippines(Subic and Clark). East Asia is thus divided into two principal theaters of operation: Northeast Asia and Southeast Asia. The two sets of bases are widely dispersed, unencumbered by narrow chokepoints, and provide the United States with interior lines of communication, which facilitate the rapid transfer of force from one theater to another.

The United States has recently modified this strategy to endorse early and sustained operations against Soviet SSBNs in their ocean bastions.[47] This "horizontal escalation" attempts to exert significant leverage upon the Soviets to accept a ceasefire by altering the nuclear balance. While a variety of pointed criticism has been directed at this "maritime strategy," perhaps the most significant one for the military balance in the Western Pacific is that in attempting to hold Soviet strategic assets at risk, the U.S. Navy sails into confined waters and the teeth of a prepared, combined-arms defense. While few question the American navy's ability to defeat their Soviet opponents far out to sea, more than a few question the strength of American superiority when pitted against significant land-based air power and sizable naval forces. It is generally assumed that four carrier battle groups would be required for an attack on a Soviet bastion; unexpectedly heavily losses could jeopardize other missions that the U.S. Navy must perform. Perhaps the best current assessment of the military balance in the Western Pacific was given in 1983 by Vice Admiral M. Stasser Holcomb, then commander of the 7th Fleet: "No question, we have an edge in the Indian Ocean. We have a marked edge in the South China Sea. . . . I maintain that the strengths of the 7th Fleet, properly applied, would prevail over the Soviet Pacific Fleet."[48]

Conclusions

The Soviet Union undoubtedly possesses overwhelming military power to face either the Chinese or Japanese alone in Northeast Asia. Soviet superiority in quality and quantity of weaponry, in logistics and supply and in nuclear forces exists along the border as well as to the north of Japan. The Chinese and Japanese have relied heavily on their friendship and alliance with the United

States to balance Soviet power. At the same time, both are pursuing internal reform movements to modernize their military establishments within the limits set by the needs of other national goals. Diplomatic efforts on the part of both nations to strengthen their ties to other Asian and European nations have to a great extent been successful. Neither nation faces the Soviet Union unsupported or dependent solely on the U.S.

U.S. reliance on ties with Japan and China in the Far East is equally necessary. Commitments in the Indian Ocean and Persian Gulf area have to some extent reduced U.S. naval presence in the Western Pacific. Additionally, long lines of supply and communications over the Pacific would severely handicap the United States in any Northeast Asian conflict without the use of the bases in Japan. At the same time, the U.S. and Japan rely on Chinese forces to tie down some of the Soviet air power stationed in the Far Eastern TVD and, to a lesser extent, some of Soviet ground forces.

The balance on the Korean Peninsula can be considered separately. The forces currently stationed there roughly offset each other and could not be diverted to other Northeast Asian conflict arenas without inviting aggression in Korea. In particular, U.S. air power is still of prime importance in aiding the South to balance the superiority of North Korean ground forces. The presence of U.S. troops on South Korean soil also helps counter Seoul's vulnerability to a quick thrust by the North Koreans across the DMZ. However, the North Koreans, too, are dependent on their alliances with the Soviets and the Chinese for weapons and aid. Neither the Soviets, or the Chinese have been willing recently to underwrite an open invasion of the South. Therefore, at present North Korean hopes for reunification of the peninsula must be centered on subversion and taking advantage of social unrest in the South.

What emerges from this discussion is a remarkably consistent picture of the Soviet Union and North Korea, isolated diplomatically and economically in Northeast Asia, and relying heavily on military power to strengthen their positions. On the other side of the fence are the U.S. and its friends and allies. Their diplomatic and economic relationships strengthen the military ties that are necessary to balance Soviet and North Korean force. All rely heavily on economic prosperity to maintain national unity in the face of any outside threat. The importance of their ties to each other, however, does not mean that a formal three or four part military alliance including China should be seriously pursued. The current ambiguity in Chinese ties to the U.S., Japan and South Korea generally serves the interests of these parties very well. A formal alliance among them would be sufficiently threatening to the Soviets as to be inadvisable, in peacetime, could it be achieved.

The driving factor in Northeast Asian military developments is the inherent weakness of the Soviet position geographically, especially when coupled with the Soviet's understandable determination to continue economic development of Siberia. Within Northeast Asia, the Soviets face two fronts, the Chinese and the Japanese/U.S. The uncertainties of alliances and participation make any calculation of the necessary force to meet these two fronts even more than usually problematical. This encourages any Soviet predilections for overkill. Additionally, Soviet access to the Western Pacific sea lanes is crucial, yet these are dominated economically and diplomatically, and to a lesser extent militarily, by their antagonists. Under these circumstances, the build-up to the present state of Soviet forces seems inevitable and the greatest probability is that it will continue at least to some degree.

The fact that this build-up can be accounted for in these terms does not make it any less threatening to the other Northeast Asian actors. None of their forces are adequate either, for the tasks they propose to do, especially when each defense problem is considered separately. The Chinese need more modern forces along their northern border; the Japanese home islands need more modern defenses; the straits and the sea lanes must be able to be defended; and the list goes on. Therefore, further build-up on their side also seems necessary and inevitable.

Is there a way to arrest this apparently perpetual pressure to escalate the size and capability of Northeast Asian military forces? Probably no perfect way exists. However, the alliances and friendships among the Western powers and China, Japan, and South Korea, do allow their forces to remain smaller than would otherwise be necessary. At the same time, keeping force increases incremental, which is virtually mandated by Japanese and U.S. politics and by the Chinese economic situation, helps to reduce pressure on the Soviets to increase their forces dramatically. One could also hope that the Soviets, having begun to achieve by their Far Eastern build-up a more secure military position in the area will slow the rate of that build-up. In the meantime, perhaps they and the North Koreans can be teased or tempted out of their isolation into a more constructive participation in the vibrant economic and political life of Northeast Asia.

NOTES

1. Lt. Col. Ralph A. Cossa, "Soviet Eyes on Asia," *Air Force Magazine*, (August 1985), p. 56.

2. "30th Air Army—the Soviet Far East Air Force," *Jane's Defense Weekly*, (March 9, 1985), p. 407.

3. "Soviets Building New Runways in Far East," *Jane's Defense Weekly*, (December 14, 1985).

4. Jack Anderson, "Maybe China Can't Use U.S. High-Tech Items," *Washington Post*, (August 20, 1983), p. E21.

5. Harlen Jencks, "China's 'Punitive' War on Vietnam: A Military Assessment," *Asian Survey*, vol. 19, no. 8, (August 1979).

6. Jack Anderson, *op cit.*

7. "The Military Balance 1985-86", (London: IISS 1985) p. 111; "There are Unconfirmed Reports of Tactical Nuclear Munitions..." and "Chemical Warfare Units Admitted by China," *Jane's Defense Weekly*, (August 31, 1985), p. 384.

8. James T. Westwood, "Soviet Maritime Strategy and Transportation," *Naval War College Review*, (Jan-Feb 1986).

9. Richard Nations, "Revisionism Revised," *Far Eastern Economic Review*, (April 10, 1986), p. 35.

10. Adrian Buzo, "Order on the Frontier," *Far Eastern Economic Review*, (March 20, 1986).

11. "...But the Military Ties Are Growing," *Wall Street Journal*, (May 5, 1986), p. 32.

12. Richard Nations, "Joining The League," *Far Eastern Economic Review*, (April 24, 1986), p. 15, and Gerald Segal, "China's Nuclear Posture for the 1980s," *Survival XXIII*, (Jan-Feb 1981).

13. "A New Long March in China," *Economist*, (January 25, 1986), p. 31.

14. *The Military Balance 1985-86*, (London: IISS, 1985)

15. N. F. Wilkner, "What the Hell is Kim Il-Sung Up To?" *Armed Forces Journal International*, (September 1984) p. 103.

16. *The Military Balance 1985-86*, (London: IISS, 1985)

17. Don Oberdorfer, "U.S. Vows Balance in Korea Zone," *Washington Post*, (August 14, 1985).

18. Benjamin Schemmer, "North Korea Buries its Aircraft, Guns Submarines, and Radars Inside Granite," *Armed Forces Journal International*, (August 1984).

19. "SA-3 SAMs in North Korea," *Jane's Defense Weekly*, (January 25, 1986).

20. William Chapman, "North Korean Leader's Son Blamed for Rangoon Bombing," *Washington Post*, (December 3, 1983), p. A20.

21. Bill Gertz, "N. Korea Troops Near Border Alarm U.S." *Washington Times*, (May 2, 1985), p. 5.

22. Rick Atkinson, "Hostility Along Korean DMZ Vented in Battle Over Trivia," *Washington Post*, (May 16, 1984), p. A16.

23. *The Military Balance 1985-86*, (London: IISS, 1985)

24. Ron Richardson, "Towards the Summit," *Far Eastern Economic Review*, (December 5, 1985), p. 46.

25. *The Military Balance 1985-86*, (London: IISS, 1985)

26. "Deployment of Soviet Missiles in Asia," *Jane's Defense Weekly*, (February 15, 1986), p. 232.

27. Akihiko Ushiba, "Huge Landing Ship Deployed to Soviet Far East," *Sankei Shimbun*, (Tokyo, July 15, 1984), p. 1.

28. "Soviet forces defeat Japanese in 17 minutes," *Jane's Defense Weekly*, (January 12, 1985).

29. *The Military Balance 1985-86*, (London: IISS, 1985)

30. "Japanese Defense Budget Extends Growth Despite Strong Opposition," *Aviation Week and Space Technology*, (March 18, 1985), p. 72.

31. John Burgess, "Japanese Military Growing Despite Political Limits," *Washington Post*, (August 14, 1985).

32. James T. Westwood, *op. cit.*, p. 47.

33. John S. DeMott, "At the End of a Floating Pipeline," *Time*, (August 1, 1983), p.43.

34. Japan Defense Agency, *Defense of Japan 1984*, p. 36.

35. Celestine Bohlen, "Gorbachev Warns Japan on U.S. Plans," *Washington Post*, (August 6, 1985), p. 10.

36. "Japanese Comes Satellite," *Jane's Defense Weekly*, (March 30, 1985).

37. "Japan's interceptor plan," *Jane's Defense Weekly*, (October 26, 1985), p. 897.

38. See Michael MccGwire, *Military Objectives in Soviet Foreign Policy* (Washington: Brookings, 1987).

39. See Michael MccGwire, ed., *Soviet Naval Deployments: Context and Capability* (New York: Praeger, 1973); MccGwire, ed., *Soviet Naval Policy: Objectives and Constraints* (New York: Praeger, 1974); and William H. Cracknell, *Understanding Soviet Naval Deployments* (Washington: Government Printing Office, 1981).

40. The U.S. Navy now believes the Soviet naval strategy in the Far East will be essentially a defensive one. See Admiral James Watkins, "The Maritime Strategy," *U.S. Naval Institute Proceedings* (January 1986).

41. Richard Fisher, "Soviet SLOC Interdiction" in Bruce W. Watson and Susan M. Watson, eds., *The Soviet Navy: Strengths and Liabilities* (Boulder: Westview, 1986), pp. 163-174.

42. Harriet Fast Scott and William F. Scott, *The Armed Forces of the USSR* (Boulder: Westview, 1981), p. 135, 147.

43. Peter Tsouras, "Soviet Naval Tradition," in Watson and Watson, *op. cit.*, p. 21.

44. Paul Nitze, et. al., *Securing the Seas* (Boulder: Westview, 1979).

45. Captain John E. Moore, RN(Ret.), "Forward to Jane's Fighting Ships 1986-87," reprinted in *Seapower*, (September 1986), p. 49.

46. As cited in Clyde Haberman, "Challenge in the Pacific: Moscow's Growing Naval Strength," *New York Times Magazine*, (September 7, 1986), p. 112.

47. Watkins, op. cit.; and Adm. Carlisle A. H. Trost, USN, "Looking Beyond the Maritime Strategy," *U.S. Naval Institute Proceedings*, (January 1987).

48. U.S. Committee on Foreign Affairs, United States Philippine Relations (June 17, 23, 28, 1983).

CHAPTER 9

Chinese Military Modernization

Martin L. Lasater

China's military modernization is the fourth of the "Four Modernizations" (agriculture, industry, science and technology, and national defense) first announced by Zhou Enlai in 1975 and implemented as national policy by Deng Xiaoping since his assumption of power in 1978. Although military modernization is ranked fourth in this list of national priorities, the building of a strong, modern Chinese armed forces should be seen as an essential element of China's reassertion of its national power and prestige in Asia.

An excellent summary of China's policy to modernize the People's Liberation Army (PLA), and the reasons for its being ranked fourth in the Four Modernizations, appeared in the August 3, 1987 issue of *Beijing Review*.[1] The editorial explained:

> As economic construction has become the nation's overriding concern, China is devoting its limited funds mainly to this effort, leaving little for national defense....In the last few years, the PLA itself has made a strategic shift. Its guiding thought has changed from preparedness against an early, full-scale and nuclear war, to normal military construction in peacetime. This change is based on an objective analysis of the current world situation: while the danger of a world war still exists and factors which might contribute to war are increasing, the growth of peace forces surpasses them and there is hope for the defense of world peace....Appropriate defenses, however, are always necessary. China has learned many lessons from its history of vulnerability to attack due to its backwardness. The technology and equipment of the Chinese armed forces today still lag far behind the most advanced. Moreover, China's borders are still not tranquil. All this makes the modernization of its national defense necessary.

Most Americans agree that the modernization of the People's Republic of China (PRC) is in U.S. interests, particularly if that modernization means a more market-oriented Chinese economy, increased trading opportunities for American firms, greater cooperation from Beijing on important international issues, and a freer, more prosperous way of life for the Chinese people.

Greater reservations are felt, however, about the benefits accruing to the United States from a stronger People's Liberation Army (PLA). The benefit most frequently pointed to is China's ability to tie down 50+ Soviet divisions along the Sino-Soviet border, while the most frequently mentioned cost is a stronger China's ability to pursue its own agenda in Asia. As China's non-communist neighbors are quick to point out, the PRC's agenda may include a regional hegemony that runs counter to their (and the U.S.) interests.

U.S. China policy reflects this dichotomy of views. On the one hand, the U.S. pursues a popular policy of helping the PRC modernize its economy through technology transfers, favorable trade treatment, and investment. But on the other hand, the extent to which the U.S. should help the PLA modernize is a controversial issue made even more complex by the growing Soviet presence in Asia and the volatile Taiwan issue.

China's Deterrence Strategy

Immediately following the formation of the People's Republic of China in 1949, Beijing felt that the U.S. was the chief threat to its security and that an alliance with the USSR was necessary to deter Washington. This perception was enhanced by China's experience during the Korean War. Nonetheless, after a decade of close alignment with the Soviet Union, Chinese leaders determined that Moscow, as well as the U.S., intended ultimate harm to Chinese interests in Asia. The decade of the 1960s, therefore, was characterized by Chinese isolation in the world community and hostility toward both superpowers.

By the end of the 1960s, however, Chinese leaders realized that the U.S. offered far less of a threat to the PRC than did the Soviet Union. Indeed, during the 1969 Sino-Soviet crisis Moscow indicated it was considering a nuclear attack against China to eliminate its potential as a nuclear power and future threat to the USSR; there was even some effort on the part of the Soviet Union to enlist American cooperation in that effort. The fact that Moscow did not carry out its threat after the Nixon Administration voiced its opposition to the plan was not lost on China. Two conclusions were drawn: first, of the two superpowers, the Soviet Union was the immediate and more dangerous threat; and second, the U.S. was willing for its own interests to deter the Soviet Union from attacking China.

Although domestic turmoil in the PRC during the Cultural Revolution and in the U.S. during the trauma of Watergate constrained both governments, the decade of the 1970s saw Washington and Beijing move toward a strategic relationship against the common Soviet threat. The PRC even assumed the initiative after 1978 in attempting to create a strategic alignment of the U.S., Japan, NATO, and China. Deng Xiaoping told *Time* magazine in February 1979 of the need to unite against the Soviet Union:

After setting up this relationship between China, Japan and the U.S., we must further develop the relationship in a deepening way. If we really want to be able to place curbs on the polar bear, the only realistic thing for us is to unite. If we only depend on the strength of Europe, it is not enough. We are an insignificant, poor country, but if we unite, well, it will then carry weight.[2]

The period 1978-1980 was one in which the PRC took the lead in pursuing a strategic relationship with the United States. Beijing wanted the U.S. to more actively oppose Soviet expansion into Asia. The PRC felt the Soviet noose tightening considerably around China during this time because of the Soviet-backed Vietnamese invasion of Cambodia in December 1978 and the Soviet invasion of Afghanistan in December 1979. Following China's punitive expedition against Hanoi in February 1979, the Soviet Union increased dramatically its use of Cam Ranh Bay. These developments directly threatened China's security and thus increased the value of the PRC of a strategic relationship with the United States.

During the 1981-1982 period, however, PRC assessments of the need for a strategic relationship with the U.S. changed. Two factors were key in this shift in China's deterrence strategy. The first was Moscow's repeated calls for the normalization of Sino-Soviet relations, initiated by Brezhnev and continued through Andropov, Chernenko, and Gorbachev. The repetition of the requests, coupled with China's assessment of Moscow's need to concentrate more on its domestic economy, convinced Beijing that the Soviet Union sincerely wanted to reduce tensions with the PRC. Accordingly, Hu Yaobang in his address to the 12th Party Congress in September 1982 signalled China's willingness to improve relations with the Soviet Union if steps were taken to remove the "three obstacles":

> The relations between China and the Soviet Union were friendly over a fairly long period. They have become what they are today because the Soviet Union has pursued a hegemonist policy. [The three obstacles] constitute grave threats to the peace of Asia and to China's security. We note that Soviet leaders have expressed more than once the desire to improve relations with China. But deeds, rather than words, are important. If the Soviet authorities really have a sincere desire to improve relations with China and take practical steps to lift their threat to the security of our country, it will be possible for Sino-Soviet relations to move toward normalization. The friendship between the Chinese and Soviet peoples is of long standing, and we will strive to safeguard and develop this friendship, no matter what Sino-Soviet state relations are like.[3]

A second, equally important factor in the shift in China's deterrence strategy away from a strategic alliance with the U.S. was, ironically, the firm response of the U.S. to the Soviet invasion of Afghanistan. Beginning in 1980, the U.S. began a substantial buildup of its military forces in the Pacific and Indian

Oceans. Washington also worked to strengthen its political and economic position in the region, and to create quasi-alliances with noncommunist countries
throughout the Asia-Pacific region to counter Soviet moves.

Part of the U.S. effort was to embrace earlier Chinese calls for strategic
cooperation against the Soviet Union. But, from the point of view of China, the
strategic alliance was no longer necessary because the Soviet Union wanted to
reduce tensions with the PRC and because Soviet hegemony in Asia would be
difficult in view of Washington's determined stand.

The problem for Chinese deterrence strategy in the post-1982 period has
been how to maintain friendly relations with both superpowers, yet increase
PRC security. Friendly relations with the U.S. were necessary to gain American
and Western assistance in China's Four Modernizations. Friendly relations
with Moscow were necessary to reduce the Soviet threat. China's security interests were served by having a strong American presence in the Asia-Pacific
region to deter the Soviet Union and, at the same time, having leaders in Moscow seeking ways to reduce tensions with the PRC.

Given this new strategic environment in which both superpowers were seeking closer ties with the PRC, Beijing devised its so-called "independent"
foreign policy as the best way to protect China's security while pursuing national objectives such as economic modernization and the recovery of Taiwan.
Important insight as to why the PRC adopted this policy after previously seeking a strategic relationship with the U.S. was provided by Chinese scholar Huan
Xiang, director of the PRC's Institute for International Affairs. *Der Spiegel*
asked him in late 1983 to explain the contrast between the two policies. Huan
replied:

> What has changed is the international situation. In the early seventies the
> Soviet Union had very strongly expanded toward the outside militarily
> and had become a threat to everybody. For this reason China offered
> cooperation to each state that felt threatened by the Soviet Union. Near
> the end of the Carter administration's term and at the beginning of the
> term of the Reagan administration, the Americans determinedly and
> energetically put up a front against the Soviet Union politically and
> militarily in the struggle for superiority in nuclear armament, in the mat-
> ter of the European intermediate-ranged weapons, in the Caribbean
> region, in the Middle East and, finally, also in Asia. This stopped the
> Soviet Union, and the rivalry of the two superpowers considerably inten-
> sified throughout the world. It seems that the Russians still do not feel
> strong enough to react to the U.S. offensive. In our view, a certain balance
> between the two has emerged, especially in the military field.[4]

Thus, a key element of PRC deterrence strategy against the Soviet Union has
been to create a web of international restraints on Moscow's use of force. Since
1982 this has been accomplished through China's "independent" foreign

policy, which has permitted the reduction of tensions with Moscow at the same time that friendly, cooperative relations have been maintained with the U.S.

A crucial second element of PRC deterrence strategy has been the strengthening of the PLA to the point where a use of force by the USSR would be prohibitively expensive. This has been accomplished in two ways: the creation of a sufficient second strike nuclear capability to deter Soviet use of nuclear weapons, and the maintenance of a sufficiently strong conventional force to make a Soviet conventional attack against China too costly for the political goals gained.

The People's Liberation Army

The PLA, which includes strategic nuclear forces, the army, navy and air force, totals some four million men and women, with approximately five million reservists.[5] The PLA is essentially a defensive force, deploying roughly one-half of its assets against the Soviet Union to the north and a third against Vietnam to the south. Forces deployed against Taiwan have been reduced in recent years, although many bases, particularly air fields, are maintained in state of readiness with pre-stocked air supplies. China's defense budget for 1986 was about 20 billion yuan, compared to 19 billion yuan for 1985. The 1986 figure represented about 9 percent of government expenditures; in 1985 defense accounted for 12 percent. In 1978 defense expenditures totalled roughly 15 percent of the central budget.

Strategic forces were made into a separate branch of the PLA in 1984. Chinese strategic nuclear forces include a handful of Intercontinental Ballistic Missiles (ICBM) and Submarine Launched Ballistic Missiles (SLBM), and approximately 110 Intermediate and Medium Ranged Ballistic Missiles. Beijing exploded its first atomic bomb in 1964 and a hydrogen bomb three years later. The Chinese CSS-X-4 ICBM is rivalled in size only by the Soviet SS-18 ICBM. Although some PRC missiles reportedly are MIRVed, the accuracy of Chinese missiles is such that only large, "soft" targets such as cities and major concentration of troops are threatened. Nonetheless, the PRC has given top priority to the development and survivability of its strategic forces as a minimal deterrence against a first strike by either superpower—particularly from the Soviet Union.

China's doctrine of retaliating with its minimal nuclear force against Soviet cities is based upon the concepts of superpower parity and the doctrine of mutual assured destruction. China recognizes that its ability to deter the Soviet Union depends upon Kremlin perceptions that any attack against the PRC will result in an unacceptably high level of damage against the Soviet homeland. PRC priority given to the development of its SLBM force reflects Chinese determination to build a survivable second strike capability. Similarly,

Beijing's opposition to President Reagan's "Star Wars" concept reflects, at least in part, PRC concerns that its limited strategic missile force might be neutralized.[6]

China describes its nuclear strategy as one of "limited self-defensive counterattack."[7] By this is meant:

China will develop a nuclear force of limited quantity but fine quality in light of its own national conditions; China will maintain an actual combat compatibility and is determined to mount a self- defensive counterattack; its nuclear force can play a deterrent role of resisting the superpowers' nuclear threat and nuclear blackmail in peacetime, and will enable the country to launch an effective nuclear counterattack on a limited number of strategic enemy targets once an enemy uses nuclear weapons against our country in wartime.[8]

The PRC's nuclear weapons policy has been consistently described as "We will not attack unless we are attacked. If we are attacked, we will certainly counterattack." The basic features of China's strategic nuclear doctrine thus are: (1) it is defensive; (2) it is intended to be a deterrent against the superpowers' use of nuclear weapons or intimidation; (3) it is of a self defensive counterattack nature; (4) it is limited in its quantity and possible targets; and (5) it is reliable and effective.[9] PRC strategists indicate in private that they are satisfied with China's minimal nuclear deterrence force. The same level of confidence, however, is not always forthcoming in discussions over the conventional side of China's armed forces.

China's army is the largest in the world with some three million troops. A 25 percent reduction of army personnel is currently underway, including major reductions in officers, as well as a reduction of eleven military regions to seven. These force reductions and organizational reforms have as their objective the creation of a leaner, more professional army, and most PLA officers express confidence in their ability to lure foreign aggressors deep within China and annihilate them.

Despite the stated optimism, which U.S. military analysts do not necessarily share, there has for several years been an on going debate within the PLA over the appropriate strategy for the army to follow. During the 1930s and 1940s, Mao Zedong developed the doctrine of "People's War." This doctrine, which essentially was protracted guerilla warfare based upon the mobilization of the entire population, effectively used China's vast territory and population. Its main tenant was to "lure the enemy in deep" and then to annihilate them piecemeal through incessant counterattacks. Man's dominance over weapons was stressed, and tactics emphasized deception, surprise, psychological warfare, close combat, and night fighting in order to maximize the advantage of PLA numbers against the enemy's superiority in weapons.

During the 1950s and 1960s, this doctrine was modified to reflect advances in technology, the need to defend against a nuclear attack, and the needs for national defense as opposed to the conduct of revolutionary war. Revolutionary war was exported to other Third World countries in the form of support for "Wars of National Liberalization," however. During the latter part of the 1960s, however, the PLA did not undergo much modernization.

During the 1970s, the PLA was preoccupied with the Cultural Revolution, where it assumed an important political role.[10] Few advances in military strategy or equipment occurred. However, following the assumption of Deng Xiaoping to power in 1978 at the 3rd Plenary Session of the 11th CPC Central Committee, the modernization of the PLA became a national priority. During the 1980s, the task was "to build a Chinese-type modernized and regularized revolutionary Army."[11] One step in this direction was the adoption of a new strategy called "People's War under Modern Conditions." Blending the old and the new, this strategy postulated that China could not be defeated by nuclear weapons alone but only by a conventional occupation of the country. However, this would be very difficult to accomplish given China's huge size and large population. The PLA was to be streamlined to become more effective, and its ability to fight in forward positions enhanced. Positional warfare in carefully selected sites was also encouraged. The concept of luring the enemy in deep, however, remained fundamental since the PLA lacked the modern weapons and mobility to launch a sustained counterattack against the enemy or to defend the country solely in the border regions.

"People's War under Modern Conditions" assigns importance to positional warfare and combined arms operations. It also focuses on guiding the invaders toward carefully selected killing grounds and then counterattacking on China's own terms. A great deal of interest has been shown in the U.S. Air-Land Battle concept envisioned for Central Europe. However, American analysts believe the PLA would have difficulty implementing this strategy because of its lack of heavy helicopters.[12]

A central issue in the debate over "People's War under Modern Conditions" has been whether the Soviet Union would allow itself to be drawn deep within China and slowly annihilated. Many American analysts and at least some within the PLA have concluded that this is highly doubtful. Their assessment is that the Soviet Red Army would invade with heavy armor and penetrate sufficiently to achieve its objectives but not try to occupy China. Under these conditions the weaknesses of the PLA would likely become apparent.

Many of these weaknesses have come to light in recent years. In 1962 the PLA engaged in a brief war with India, and in 1979 the PLA invaded Vietnam for a short period of time. In both cases, the incursions were very shallow, limited to ground forces, and lasted not more than a month. The PLA had no offensive capability to push the invasions further. The invasion of Vietnam was especially illustrative of the handicaps faced by China in fighting a modern war. PLA units had to signal each other by hand; orders were not obeyed because officers were not recognized on the field of battle; trucks broke down and were not repaired; supplies had to be delivered by horse cart and human porters; PLA maps were 75 years old; and the air force would not provide cover for fear of being shot down. Casualties were extraordinarily high; according to Western sources, the PLA suffered more than 60,000 casualties, including 26,000 killed.[13]

Turning to other branches of the PLA, the Chinese navy is large in terms of numbers, but light in individual ship tonnage. The navy is composed of three or more nuclear powered and 107 diesel attack submarines, 44 destroyers and frigates, more than 70 large patrol craft, and about 800 fast attack craft of various designations. In addition, the navy has about 800 shore-based aircraft, including 600 hundred fighters and light bombers, and some 85,000 Marines. A great deal of priority has been given to make the Marines an effective quick-strike, mobile force.

China's submarine force is one of the largest in the world, and the PRC is aggressively pursuing a nuclear submarine program. However, the PRC has not used its fleet to its full potential to project China's influence into Asia. This may be changing. The Chinese describe their Navy as "now capable of operating as far as the western part of the Pacific, and China's Xisha and Nansha islands. It can also enter combat in cooperation with ground and air forces."[14] Navy Commander Liu Huaqing describes the PLA's navy strategy as "positive offshore defence."[15]

China did not inherit any large warships from WWII. Therefore, most of the ships have been built in the PRC itself, although the period 1950-1959 saw a considerable amount of Soviet naval assistance. Generally, Western analysts consider Chinese warships to two or three generations behind the West in vessel design, weapons systems, and electronics.[16]

The Chinese navy is divided into three fleets. In the North Sea Fleet there are about 500 vessels of all types; the East Sea Fleet has some 750; and the South Sea Fleet totals about 600 vessels. The navy is considered a coastal defense and sea-denial force, although the PRC is moving in the direction of a blue water fleet. In 1980 China sent its first mixed oceangoing fleet into the South Pacific for the tasks of surveying, escorting, standing guard, and salvaging the rocket instrument capsule of an ICBM test. During November 1985-January 1986, Beijing sent a destroyer and supply ship 12,000 nautical miles on a goodwill visit to Pakistan, Sri Lanka, and Bangladesh. One of the main reasons China is increasing her naval power projection capabilities is to enforce her claims to islands and seabed resources in the South China Sea.[17] Another reason may be to compete with the superpowers and India for regional influence in the future.

According to *Jane's Defence Weekly*, China's navy modernization program is focusing on three areas of priority: "upgrading electronics throughout the force, updating the surface fleet, and modernizing the submarine fleet by acquiring Western hardware and electronics. The hardware-related goals are intended to overcome the fact that the fleet is not well equipped for modern war, particularly with the Soviet Union as a potential foe."[18]

The PLA air force has about 120 medium bombers, some thought to be nuclear capable and some armed with anti-ship missiles. There are also about 500 light bombers, 500 ground attack fighters, and more than 4,000 fighter interceptors. A supersonic bomber is under development. The PLA air force and its capabilities will be discussed later in this chapter in conjunction with the F-8 and other modernization efforts.

PLA Modernization Efforts

In 1985 a fundamentally important decision was reached by the Central Military Commission regarding the guiding principle for the PLA's national defense construction. The decision was that defense work should change from a combat-readiness posture of "fighting an early war, a major war, and a nuclear war" to peacetime construction. As one Chinese study noted, "This policy decision will have a decisive impact on the overall situation in national defense construction. This is China's main premise in determining its national defense strategy."[19] In other words, the PRC no longer bases its strategy on the inevitability of war. Rather, its leaders assume that the international environment will be largely peaceful until the year 2000. They have determined that China's military modernization should contribute to this end and that the pace of the PLA's modernization should reflect this reality. This is why the modernization of national defense is the fourth in the list of Four Modernizations. Nonetheless, the PLA is being deliberately modernized to enhance its deterrence and warfighting capabilities.

A great many steps have been taken in the modernization of the PLA in recent years. Some foreign assistance has been acquired in specific areas, but most effort has come from within the PLA itself. An overview of some of these efforts will be illustrative.

During the 35th National Day military parade in Tienanmen Square on October 1, 1984, several new systems were publicly shown for the first time. These included two new self-propelled artillery systems, the new T-69 main battle tank with a new 105-mm gun, a new minelaying vehicle, a new surface-to-surface antiship missile appearing similar to the Exocet, the CSS-3 ICBM with a range of about 7,000 km, two IRBMs, and the submarine-launched CSS-NX-4 SLBM.[20]

China's ICBM and SLBM force modernization program has been underway for some time. In 1980 China conducted its first experimental launching of an ICBM. In 1982 the first test of an SLBM was made. In 1984 China launched a positioned communications satellite into a synchronized orbit. By 1987 China was signing contracts with foreign countries to launch foreign satellites. In January 1987 the PRC agreed to place in geostationary orbit an American communications satellite originally scheduled to be launched in orbit by NASA's shuttle program.[21]

Military training in the PLA is undergoing major change. The "three major shifts" implemented in the early 1980s were "education of officers rather than soldiers, stressing mechanized mobile warfare over infantry, and practicing combined maneuvers rather than movements by a single force."[22] Attempts were made to retain the "absolute superiority" of the PLA in terms of "the level of revolutionization of our Army," while at the same time remedying certain problems. As described by Yang Shangkun, Executive Vice Chairman of the Central Military Commission, in a highly important *Honggi* article appearing in August 1984, these problems were primarily that "the level of modernization and modern scientific knowledge of our Army is not high and its weapons and equipment are comparatively backward. These are the weak links of our Army."[23] According to General Yang, the PLA must become "a modern Army with special Chinese characteristics." He said:

> Judging from the existing conditions, a modernized and regular revolutionary Army with special Chinese characteristics should be one which conforms to our national conditions, flexibly integrates advanced military thinking and fine traditions with modern weapons and equipment and defend itself in modern warfare; in other words, a developed People's Army with the tradition of People's War plus modern military science, weapons, and equipment.[24]

In discussing how to modernize China's army, Yang said:

> We should develop the most urgently needed new types of weapons and equipment as soon as possible. The development of modern science and technology has enormously expanded the destructive force of weapons. In future wars against aggression, we should still stress the decisive role of man but under no circumstances should we neglect the important role of weapons. Without advanced weapons and equipment, we shall pay a higher price and prolong the time for winning the war. We should make the best use of our time and strive to change the backwardness of our weapons and equipment.[25]

In discussing the role of foreign versus domestic development of weapons, Yang emphasized that China's conditions required that the efforts needed to modernize the PLA must come from within China herself. Only selected foreign equipment and technologies could be purchased from abroad. Further, the modernization of the PLA must proceed gradually. Yang said:

> The modernization of our Army must be suited to the development of the national economy. We have a large population, a poor foundation, and limited funds. Therefore, we should not incur huge military expenditures as the superpowers do. Nor should we blindly pursue large-scale and rapid modernization of the Army regardless of our national economic

conditions. In developing weapons and equipment....we should stress the main points and concentrate our forces on developing the most urgently needed defensive weapons and equipment....we should update the equipment in an orderly way and step by step, allowing the coexistence of outmoded and modern equipment and of ordinary and advanced technology.... In modernizing our Army, we should import some necessary and advanced technological equipment. However, ours is a big but developing country. It will not do to rely on purchasing advanced technological equipment to achieve the modernization of national defense. Nor can we afford it....We should base ourselves on independence and self-reliance and rely on our strength to develop weapons and equipment....We stress the main points and self-reliance, but under no circumstances should we equate "distinguishing Chinese characteristics" and "low standards" and thus lower the objective of our modernization.[26]

As a result of the policy guidelines established by PRC leaders, the PLA army has been undergoing considerable change. Emphasis is being placed on raising the educational level of the officers and men of the PLA. New uniforms and rank insignia have been introduced. Laser stimulators are replacing live ammunition exercises by ground forces.[27] Several of the old "field armies" have been reorganized into "group armies" to enhance combined arms operations. Less emphasis is being placed on infantry and more on professional and technical arms. Coordination, speed, and firepower is being stressed, rather than individual infantry tactics.

Chief of the PLA General Staff Yang Dezhi said in an article in March 1987, "our Army has evolved from the single army unit of the past to the present combined arms units including the Navy, the Air Force, the Strategic Missile Force, and other technical arms units." He went on: "Starting from the principle of building a leaner and combined army, peacetime preparation for war, and raising efficiency, we will do more of either eliminating or merging overlapping organization, reducing noncombatant personnel, forming combined group armies, and reinforcing the strength of technical arms units and reserve forces."[28]

One of the unwanted byproducts of the success of the economic modernization of China has been the lowered image of the PLA as a career. Young men can earn far more money in farming or working in factories. Soldiers serve for three years and earn between $3 and $4 per month, compared to factory wages of around $30. Recruitment, therefore, has become a problem for the first time since 1949.[29]

The PLA navy has been adding numerous missile weapons systems to its fleet and coastal defense network. Emphasis is being placed on the development of supersonic and super-low-altitude long-distance missiles with precision guidance systems for anti-ship missions. Exocet-type air-to-ship missiles are also being manufactured.[30] China is also developing a number of small 20,000-ton aircraft carriers, similar to the Australian *Melbourne*.

According to one study, the PLA navy is undergoing a rapid modernization which should become apparent by 1990.[31] France, Great Britain, and the U.S. are key suppliers of modern technology and equipment, with "the United States...emerging as China's prime supplier." Of the modernization programs underway, the submarine program "has a high priority." China and Argentina have negotiated for the sale of Argentina's British-built, Type 42 destroyers. New frigates and destroyers are being built, employing General Electric LM2500 gas turbines, 20-mm Mark-15 Phalanx Gatling anti-aircraft guns, and U.S. Mark-46 ASW torpedoes. The U.S. has also designed a H-3 class missile boat for the PLA to replace its Soviet Osa-I large patrol craft.

In 1985, it was reported that China had ordered French helicopter sonars and an upgrading of their French SA321J helicopters for ASW missions.[32] The Chinese navy's modernization efforts focused on four major areas of imported systems and technology: modern power-generating systems for future destroyers and frigates (primarily from the U.S.); a modern, rapid-fire gun system (from France); helicopters for shipborne use (France); and modern sensor systems for anti-submarine warfare (France).[33]

By 1985, the PLA had "established friendly contacts with the troops in over 50 countries." Moreover, the Ministry of National Defense reported that 43 countries had set up military attache offices in Beijing.[34] Several reports have detailed major Chinese-Israeli secret military deals.[35] U.S. Department of Defense sources estimated that in 1985 about 200 Israeli military advisers were in China and that arms orders from Beijing were totalling more than $1 billion.[36]

It is commonly believed by Western analysts that the PLA, while the world's largest fighting force, nonetheless remains at least twenty years behind leading military powers in weapons technology.[37] But what is frequently overlooked in Western assessments is that China's neighbors rank the PLA as a highly credible military force. Recent history has shown that Beijing uses the PLA as an instrument of power to achieve national political objectives. This was the case in the Korean conflict of 1950-1953, the invasion of Tibet beginning in 1950, successive crises over Quemoy in 1954, 1958, and 1962, the Sino-Indian War of 1962, and the expedition against Vietnam in 1979. China appeared ready to fight India once again over border disputes in 1986-1987. Once concern frequently raised by China's smaller neighbors is that as the PLA becomes stronger, PRC leaders may use China's armed forces increasingly as a means to reassert China's influence in regional affairs. For this reason, U.S. assistance to modernize the PLA has been subject to a great deal of criticism from Asians for its shortsightedness.[38]

Without question the most controversial of the U.S. arms sales to China was the advanced avionics modernization package for China's high altitude interceptor, the F-8. The significance of this sale was that it represented a high-water mark of U.S. military transfers to the PRC. Sales to enhance PLA air force capabilities were highly controversial because of their potential impact on

China's noncommunist neighbors. As such, the sale is an excellent case study from which to draw recommended policy guidelines for future arms sales.

The Reagan Administration formally notified Congress of its intention to sell the $550 million package on April 7, 1986. Although resolutions for disapproval were submitted in the Senate by Jesse Helms (S. J. Res. 331) and in the House by Mark Siljander (H. J. Res. 593), neither passed and the FMS transaction received the necessary congressional blessing on May 8. Behind the scenes, lobbying both for and against the sale were intense.

The F-8 package included integrated avionics kits for 50 new production F-8s (dubbed the F-8-II or F-8B), plus five spare kits. The system integration would be accomplished by a prime U.S. defense contractor under U.S. Air Force supervision. Approximately six years would be required to complete the production prototype in the U.S., followed by installation in China. The major components of the integrated avionics system included an airborne pulse doppler radar system, Inertial Navigation System, Multiplex Data Bus, Fire Control Computer, Heads-Up Display, Air Data Computer, Backup Control and Interface Unit, and AC Electrical System. The avionics package was intended to give the F-8 an all-weather, day-night fighting capability, something the PRC does not now possess.

In trying to calm Congressional fears that the sale would upset the balance of power in the Taiwan Straits, the Administration told Congress the avionics system would involve mid-1970s technology and no transfer of design or production technologies. No co-assembly of components would occur, nor would there be a transfer of software programming. Presenting the Administration's case before the Senate Foreign Relations Committee on April 29, 1986, Deputy Assistant Secretary of State James Lilley noted that the avionics sale was part of an "increased cooperation in the military sphere, including sales of some defensive arms to China." Placing the sale in broad policy perspective, Lilley noted:

> The limited military cooperation is based on the assessment that the United States and China share certain important parallel interests. Foremost among these is a common security concern—the threat posed to both of our countries and the entire Asia-Pacific region by the Soviet Union. The willingness of the U.S. to sell specific defensive weapons or technologies to the PRC is based on a thorough analysis of each item's utility for enhancing Chinese defensive capabilities, taking into full consideration the political-military environment and the interests and concerns of our other friends and allies in the region.[39]

In an accompanying statement, Rear Admiral Edward Baker, Acting Deputy Assistant Secretary of Defense, stated:

> The Department of State and Defense have reviewed all aspects of the F-8 avionics modernization program and are fully confident that its use will be for defensive purposes and does not pose a significant military threat

to U.S. friends and allies.... Militarily, it will provide a measured increase to air defense capability against would-be aggressors seeking to intrude into China's airspace. Further, the U.S. believes that cooperation in this program will result in the continued positive development of China's attitudes toward the West, to include a growing economic interrelationship with the United States.... [The] development of U.S.-China military relations serve basic U.S. and Chinese strategic interests and contribute significantly to peace and stability in the Asia-Pacific region and the world.[40]

Despite the strong case made by the Administration for the F-8 avionics sale, a number of serious objections were raised from domestic and foreign critics. First, no U.S. friends or allies in Asia agreed with the sale. ASEAN, South Korea, Japan, and Taiwan strongly objected. From their perspective, the sale of advanced avionics to the PRC would adversely affect the regional balance of power. While the United States evaluated the sale in terms of how best to help China deter the Soviet Union, most of the rest of Asia looked at how the sale might add to the future Chinese threat to the region. U.S. friends and allies in the Far East noted that on no occasion had China made arms sales an issue in Sino-American relations. In fact, Chinese leaders complained to ASEAN delegations in Beijing that the U.S. was forcing arms sales down their throats.[41]

Second, the purpose of the avionics sale seemed misdirected. The F-8 was designed 20 years ago to counter a high-flying, subsonic Soviet bomber threat. But with plenty of guided missiles and Backfire bombers now in the region, the Soviet Union was not likely to send slow high altitude bombers over China. And if they did, they certainly would be escorted by interceptors far superior to the F-8. Therefore, the deterrent capability of the enhanced F-8 was of marginal utility against the Soviet Union. But the improved F-8 could make a big difference in regional conflicts between China and her smaller non-communist neighbors such as Taiwan.

Third, the justification of the sale to promote Sino-American strategic relations may have been flawed. The PRC opposed the Soviet presence in Afghanistan, Vietnam, and Mongolia regardless of whether the U.S. sold weapons to China. By virtue of its size and geographical location, China would always be a grave concern to Soviet strategists. And the Kremlin—with its propensity to seek total security—would continue to deploy a large percentage of its armed forces to the Far East with Chinese targets in mind. Further, for reasons already discussed in the section dealing with the Soviet threat to China, Sino-Soviet relations would likely improve whether or not the U.S. sold F-8 avionics to China.

What these observations suggested was that U.S. arms sales to the PRC had very little impact on China's strategic decisions. Attempts by Administration spokesmen to suggest that U.S. arms sales influenced fundamental strategic decisions by Beijing reflected a serious misreading of PRC intentions. In fact,

U.S. military analysts were warning repeatedly that arms sales to China were going too far. But, as noted scholar Harlan Jencks observed, the Administration largely ignored these warnings:

> Given the consensus China military watchers share on most issues, one would expect us to have significant influence on policy-making. In fact, while it is hard to evaluate, we seem to have little—at least in the United States. As noted above, we have generally been conservative and skeptical about the "China card," the advisability of arms sales, and the extent of the Chinese arms market. Nevertheless, the policy momentum in Washington and London (at least) has reflected an official desire for more and closer military relations and sales. The most that can be said for the influence of China military watchers is that our constant nay-saying *may* have prevented even greater movement in that direction.[42]

Fourth, although the Administration claimed that the avionics package was an end-item sale and did not involve co-assembly or co-production or the transfer of design or production technologies, this clearly was not the intention of the PRC. What was important to China was not simply 55 avionics packages, but rather the technology the packages contained and the possibility of integrating that technology with other systems. Beijing wanted this capacity not only to modernize a limited number of F-8s, but also to make the F-8 and follow-on aircraft more attractive to Third World arms buyers.

For example, the package's radar, which would have a range of about 35 to 37 nautical miles plus a look-down capability, could be integrated with beyond visual range radar guided missiles and heat-seeking, all aspects short-range missiles. There were reports that the Chinese had already acquired a few French R-530 radar missiles and the Python III infrared missile for the purpose of improving their own line of advanced air-to-air missiles.

It seemed reasonable to expect that during the six years needed to integrate and install the F-8 avionics package, the PRC would seek to broaden technology cooperation with the United States. For several years following its disappointing experience in co-producing Britain's Spey jet engines, China has been looking to purchase new fighter engines. Talks are ongoing with the United States over the GE-404 and PW-1120 engines. Moreover, China is developing follow-on fighters to the F-8 such as the F-10 and F-12. Both of these aircraft will need advanced avionics and weapons, as well as powerful, reliable engines. Thus, the avionics package offered the PRC should not be seen as an isolated sale, but rather the cutting edge of a substantial improvement in China's air force.

Fifth, despite Administration disclaimers, the avionics package would have an adverse impact on the qualitative balance of power in the Taiwan Straits. It was widely accepted that in 1986 Taiwan enjoyed air superiority over the Straits. The enhanced F-8B, however, with its longer-range radar (about twice the range as Taiwan's F-5E), its look-down capability, and its heads-up display weapons aiming component could—if combined with medium range and short range missiles with all aspects capability—establish air superiority over the Taiwan Straits. The F-8 could do this without engaging in Korean War-style dogfights, at which Taiwan's more maneuverable fighters are superior, but rather by positioning itself at high altitudes, locating Taiwan's lower flying fighters (which do not have radar capable of looking up), and then dropping down and attacking Taiwan's fighters with improved missiles.

It should also be kept in mind that Taiwan's F-5E is a small plane and not much more can be done to enhance its capability. Taiwan's own domestically produced fighter is of unknown quality and will not be operational before the mid-1990s at best. Hence, the modernization of the F-8 could tip the air balance in the Taiwan Strait to Beijing's favor.

Finally, there were disturbing policy implications raised by the F-8 sale. For the Reagan Administration to introduce technology which could tip air superiority over to the mainland is a very serious matter. Such a development could weaken Taiwan's security; undermine investor confidence in Taiwan's future; politically destabilize Taiwan by polarizing Taiwanese and mainlander differences; and make it more difficult for the United States to balance its conflicting commitments to Taiwan and the PRC in the Taiwan Relations Act and the August 17, 1982 Joint Communique.

Conclusions

Because of the menacing Soviet presence in the Far East, the United States and China share many important security interests. It is in the U.S. interest that China be sufficiently strong to deter a Soviet attack against the PRC. But it is also in the U.S. interests that the communist regime in Beijing not become sufficiently strong to attack Taiwan or harm other U.S. friends and allies in the region.

To a certain extent, these two U.S. interests are contradictory. It is difficult to design arms sales packages to the PRC which will enhance Chinese deterrent capabilities against the Soviet Union, yet not enhance Chinese military capabilities against Taiwan. The F-8 avionics package deal is a useful case study, because it raises many unanswered questions regarding the U.S. military relationship with the PRC. For example:

— Is the U.S. concentrating too much on the Soviet threat in Asia and not paying enough attention to the long-term security concerns of Asian friends and allies who worry about the future intentions of China?

— How effective against the Soviet Union will be the weapons and technology the U.S. sells to the PRC; and if they are not too effective, what is the purpose in selling Beijing hardware which can only be used against China's weaker, non-communist neighbors?

— Is a stronger, more independent PRC likely to be more cooperative with the United States in Asia, or will it pursue policies increasingly counter to U.S. interests?

These are some of the very questions which were debated at the outset of Sino-American military relations. At that time the prospects for U.S.-PRC strategic cooperation were sufficiently high to dismiss most of these concerns. But China since 1982 has adopted an "independent" foreign policy of alignment with neither superpower but friendly relations with both. Beijing today still "leans" in the direction of the U.S. and will likely continue to do so because of the close Soviet threat. Thus, some American and Chinese policies will be parallel and some will be opposed.

Parallel policies likely will include removing the Soviet presence from around China's eastern and southern borders. Opposing policies will probably remain in the case of Taiwan and China's propensity to claim large portions of the South China Sea as its territorial waters. What is noteworthy is that advanced arms sales such as the F-8 avionics package will not affect parallel policies pursued by Washington and Beijing. Those policies will remain in effect regardless of arms sales. However, advanced weapons sales can exacerbate tensions between the U.S. and PRC in areas of potential conflict because they will increase China's ability to pursue its objectives by force. This would suggest that the U.S. should pursue its military relationship with the PRC but should proceed much more cautiously with its political, economic, and cultural ties with China.

The framework of Sino-American military cooperation defined by Secretary Weinberger can be useful here. The U.S. can continue a high-level dialogue with the military establishments of the PRC. Military officers can be exchanged for training purposes. Exchange of intelligence can be useful, and symbols of cooperation such as port calls and naval passing exercises create no real problems. Washington can even sell limited amounts of weapons to China as long as these remain primarily ground-based defensive systems.

There is little doubt that the Soviet Union, Vietnam and some other Asian countries will object even to this limited Sino-American military cooperation. But fears of China's military prowess, at least to date, are exaggerated; despite the large size of the PLA and its impressive defensive strength, Chinese armed forces have major weaknesses. These weaknesses include: lack of mobility and mechanization; poor logistics systems for sustained offensive operations; marginal command and control for combined arms or joint service operations; obsolescent weaponry; limited power projection capability; obsolescent aircraft and avionics; poor pilot training; inadequate communications; limited defense industry capability; obsolescent ships and on-board equipment; and limited amphibious lift capability. Given the relatively low priority assigned to military modernization, it will be some time in the future before China joins the ranks of military superpowers.

NOTES

1. An Zhiguo, "For Peace and National Security," *Beijing Review*, August 3, 1987, p.4.

2. *Time*, February 5, 1979, p.34.

3. Hu Yaobang, "Create a New Situation in All Fields of Socialist Modernization," *The Twelfth National Congress of the CPC* (Beijing: Foreign Languages Press, 1982), pp. 58-59.

4. *Der Spiegel*, December 26, 1983, in *FBIS-China*, December 29, 1983, pp. A7-A8.

5. Many excellent books and articles have been written on the PLA and its modernization. See, for example, Monte R. Bullard, *China's Political-Military Evolution* (Boulder, CO: Westview Press, 1985); Paul H. B. Godwin, "The Chinese Defense Establishment in Transition," in A. Doak Barnett and Ralph N. Clough, eds., *Modernizing China* (Boulder, CO: Westview Press, 1986); and Section VI "Military," in U.S. Congress, Joint Economic Committee, *China's Economy Looks Toward the Year 2000* (Washington, D.C.: Government Printing Office, May 21, 1986). General information about the composition of the PLA can be found in *The Military Balance: 1985-1986* (London: International Institute of Strategic Studies, 1986). An excellent commentary on PLA studies can be found in Harlan W. Jencks, "Watching China's Military: A Personal View," *Problems of Communism*, May-June 1986, pp. 71-78.

6. For a discussion of China's concerns about strategic defense, see Kim R. Holmes, "U.S.-Soviet-China Relations and Strategic Defense," The Heritage Foundation, *Lecture No. 76* (1986).

7. See Zhang Jianzhi, "Views on Medium-Sized Nuclear Powers' Nuclear Strategy," *Jiefangjun Bao*, March 20, 1987, in *FBIS- China*, April 1, 1987, pp. K29-K33.

8. *Ibid.*, p. K32.

9. *Ibid.*, pp. K32-K33.

10. In recent years, Deng Xiaoping has reduced the political role of the PLA and insisted that the army concentrate on national defense. Chinese military leaders, in turn, have repeatedly reaffirmed their strong support of Deng's policies. See the statement of General Xu Xin, deputy chief of the Army's general staff, in *Washington Post*, April 5, 1987, p. A23.

11. See Yang Shangkun, "Building Chinese-Style Modernized Armed Forces," *Honggi*, August 1, 1984, in *FBIS-China*, August 21, 1984, pp. K8-K20.

12. June T. Dreyer, "The Military Balance; Can It Be Kept?," in Martin L. Lasater, ed., *The Two Chinas: A Contemporary View* (Washington, D.C.: The Heritage Foundation, 1986), pp. 77-80.

13. *Defense News*, June 16, 1986, pp. 24-25.

14. *China Daily*, April 22, 1987, p. 3.

15. *China Daily*, April 11, 1987, p. 1.

16. See Gordon Jacobs, "China's Coastal Naval Forces," *Jane's Defence Weekly*, March 16, 1985, pp. 450-458.

17. See Bruce Swanson, *Eighth Voyage of The Dragon* (Annapolis, MD: Naval Institute Press, 1982). Also, P. Lewis Young, "China and the South China Sea," *Asian Defence Journal*, July 1986, pp. 22-31.

18. Gordon Jacobs, "Bringing China's Navy Up to Date," *Jane's Defence Weekly*, January 25, 1986, p. 113.

19. *Liaowang*, July 21, 1986, in *FBIS-China*, July 25, 1986, p. K4.

20. See *International Defense Review*, 17, 11 (November 1984), p. 1604.

21. *New York Times*, January 30, 1987, p. D4.

22. *Xinhua*, June 12, 1984, in *FBIS-China*, June 12, 1984, p. K10.

23. Yang Shangkun, "Building Chinese-Style Modernized Armed Forces," *Honggi*, August 1, 1984, in *FBIS-China*, July 17, 1985, pp. K1-K6. Also, Yang Dezhi, "A Strategic Decision on Strengthening the Building of Our Army in the New Period," *Honggi*, August 1, 1985, in *FBIS-China*, August 8, 1985, pp. K1-K7.

24. See "Building Chinese-Style Modernized Armed Forces," p. K11.

25. *Ibid.*

26. *Ibid.*

27. *Xinhua*, September 6, 1984, in *FBIS-China*, September 10, 1984, p. S3.

28. Beijing Domestic Service Radio, March 24, 1987, in *FBIS- China*, April 1, 1987, p. K25.

29. *Washington Post*, June 12, 1986, p. A27.

30. *Zhongguo Xinwen She*, November 13, 1984, in *FBIS- China*, November 14, 1984, p. K18-K19.

31. See the section on China's navy in Lt. J.V.P. Goldrick and Lt. P.D. Jones, "The Far Eastern Navies," *Proceedings*, 112, 3, 997 (March 1986), pp. 65-66.

32. *Jane's Defence Weekly*, April 13, 1985, p. 620.

33. Gordon Jacobs, "Bringing China's Navy Up to Date," pp. 113-114.

34. *Zhongguo Xinwen She*, December 18, 1985, in *FBIS- China* December 24, 1985, p. K11.

35. For example, *Jane's Defence Weekly*, November 24, 1984, p. 915.

36. *Washington Times*, January 23, 1985, p. 1A.

37. *Washington Post*, August 6, 1987, p. A31.

38. June Dreyer reported one such occasion when a senior Malaysian official characterized U.S. military assistance to the PLA as feeding a "little python"

that one day "may come in from the backyard and bite you." See *The Two Chinas*, pp. 93-94.

39. Prepared statement of James R. Lilley before the U.S. Senate, Committee on Foreign Relations, April 29, 1986, p. 2, ms.

40. Prepared statement of Rear Admiral Edward B. Baker, Jr., before the U.S. Senate, Committee on Foreign Relations, April 29, 1986, p. 6, ms.

41. Author's conversation with ASEAN participants in the PRC meeting (Kuala Lumpur, Malaysia, April 2, 1986).

42. Harlan W. Jencks, "Watching China's Military," pp. 77-78.

CHAPTER 10

Approaching the Pacific Century

Stephen P. Gibert

American preoccupation in its national security policy with European con- cerns belatedly but finally seems to be waning. There is a new awareness of East Asian economic dynamism and the criticality of the Pacific rim countries to international security. That the coming era will be a "Pacific Century" now cannot be seriously challenged, even by the most convinced "Europhiles" among U.S. and world leaders.

To the Nixon administration must go the first credit for recognizing that the old bi-polar world was beginning to fade away as Western Europe, Japan and China joined the United States and the Soviet Union as great centers of world power.

Based on this concept, and on more immediate considerations as well, in 1971 Secretary of State Kissinger, followed by President Nixon in 1972, initiated the process which was to lead to U.S. recognition of the People's Republic of China in January, 1979. And despite the rhetoric of his 1980 presidential campaign, President Reagan not only did not reverse but enlarged upon President Carter's China policy by continually expanding the network of relations between China and the United States.

Thanks to Congress, which in the Taiwan Relations Act prevented the Carter administration from abandoning the Republic of China on Taiwan, and to the Reagan administration, which generally has been supportive of Taiwan, American relations with the PRC have not been at the expense of island China. On the contrary, despite the August 1982 "Shanghai II" communique, U.S. security assistance to Taiwan has not diminished and trade relations between the two countries has continued to expand.

At the same time, although professing neutrality between the two superpowers, China has continued to "tilt" toward the United States and against the Soviet Union. U.S. military assistance to the PRC is expanding, as are trade and cultural relations, unimpeded by ideological differences. The recent decision of the PRC leadership to move the Chinese economy toward more export-driven development undoubtedly will increase still more Chinese-American trade and other economic relations which, in turn, will help to smooth remaining political differences.

It is essential to U.S. security that this occur, for China, although in many respects still a Third World country, unquestionably will become one of the greatest world powers in the next several generations. Indeed, a recent projection argues that China will have the world's third largest GNP, after the United States and Japan, but ahead of the Soviet Union, by the year 2010. With a population exceeding one billion, the PRC's per capita GNP will still be quite low. Nevertheless, barring some great unforeseen calamity, China will join the United States, Japan, and the Soviet Union as one of the four most important centers of world power. The United States must predicate its East Asian policy on this irrefutable premise.

The Reagan administration's Northeast Asia policy in most respects represents a continuation of the past directions established by the Nixon, Ford, and Carter governments. In one important respect, however, the Reagan government departed from that of President Carter. This concerned Korea; shortly after taking office President Reagan welcomed Korean leader Chun Doo Hwan to Washington and announced that U.S. troops, contrary to President Carter's 1977 decision, would remain in Korea.

At some point, of course, U.S. forces which have been in South Korea since the 1950 Korean war, should be withdrawn. Although that time is approaching, it has not yet arrived in view of the continued belligerence of rival North Korea. North Korea is surely one of the outlaw regimes of the world, with a record of actions grossly reprehensible even by jaded twentieth century standards. North Korea also is the only country which might initiate military hostilities in Northeast Asia; this risk is greatly reduced by the continued presence of U.S. military forces in South Korea.

While it cannot be proved, it is also likely that in the absence of American troops President Chun's government would not have agreed to the election of his successor in the fall of 1987 nor would he have relinquished his post to Roe Tae-Woo in February 1988.

There are growing problems in the Korean-American relationship, however. One is trade; South Korea, along with Japan and Taiwan, have been singled out by Congressional critics for unfair trade practices which have contributed significantly to their surplus in accounts with the United States. And in Korea there is a growing anti-Americanism, especially among university students, who believe that the United States has been too supportive of Korea's authoritarian military governments. This sentiment broke sharply into the open with the 1987 election of retired General Roe Tae-Woo, the candidate favored by President Chun and the military establishment. Particularly upsetting was Roe Tae-Woo's pre-election official visit to Washington.

Many in Korea—and not just the younger generation—are also no longer content with having an American general command the combined military forces of the United States and Korea, especially considering the disparity in the size of the two organizations. This arrangement is no longer tenable, fuels anti-American sentiment, and should be terminated.

Finally, South Koreans realize that relations with North Korea are unlikely to be ameliorated without the active cooperation of China and the Soviet Union. Such cooperation is not likely to be forthcoming as long as South Korea is seen as an American "satellite." Also South Korea is not likely to obtain PRC diplomatic recognition, which it certainly would like to have, unless there is a less close Korean-American relationship. This will happen within the foreseeable future; it is a question of when and under what circumstances these developments will occur.

The next major crisis the United States is likely to face in East Asia will be in the Philippines. The Reagan government deserves credit for assisting a revolution without bloodshed in the Philippines. Indeed, the ouster of Ferdinand Marcos is one of the very few instances in which the United States intervened successfully against an autocratic leader who had lost popularity with the people. Unfortunately, however, President Aquino lacked the experience necessary to manage the government and has been unable to secure either the loyalty of the Philippine military or to quell a growing Marxist insurgency.

Adding to the troubles of the Aquino government is a stagnant economy; unlike the rest of East Asia, the Philippines remains a very poor country. Clearly, it is in the interest of the United States and of wealthy Japan to provide much-needed economic assistance to the Philippines.

Finally, there is the question of U.S. military bases in the Philippines. Should the Aquino government or a successor Marxist-oriented regime decide to terminate the American naval base at Subic Bay or the Clark Air Force Base, the United States security posture in the Western Pacific would be seriously damaged. There are no satisfactory substitutes for the U.S. bases in the Philippines; all alternatives are too distant from areas where the forces have security responsibilities. Only Taiwan could provide a suitable alternative home for U.S. military bases but this is unacceptable politically, at least in the near future.

Last but most certainly not least is Japan, perhaps more important to the United States than any other country in the world. Given this, one would think that both the United States and Japanese governments would do everything humanly possible to foster close and friendly relations between the two countries. Clearly in this respect the Reagan government has failed; its Japanese policy has been nothing short of dismal.

With regard to trade, about a third or about $50 billion of the current U.S. trade deficit is with Japan. A key factor has been the unprecedented Federal budget deficits incurred during the Reagan era. The Reagan administration's feeble approach to this problem—and the equally feeble Congressional response—would be laughable if not so detrimental to the nation's well-being.

Compounding the problem has been the persistent belief—despite strong evidence to the contrary—that depreciating the dollar against the yen would solve the trade deficit. While, of course, at unacceptable exchange rates this would occur, a multidimensional approach to the budget and trade deficits is required. This has not yet been forthcoming.

Japan too has been unwilling to face up to the trade problem. On the contrary, its corporate-dominated government insists on a "policy-as-usual" approach, unwilling to acknowledge any legitimate reasons for growing anti-Japanese sentiment in the United States. Under these circumstances, it is very likely that Congress will pass a trade bill which will contain features that opponents will criticize as protectionist and supporters will praise as justifiable retaliation against unfair trade practices. Should this bill not pass or be vetoed, the controversy will not end. On the contrary, the trade problem must be solved and soon if Japanese-American relations—already tense—are not to worsen.

The problem of allocating security burdens and roles between Japan and the United States has not gotten the attention accorded the trade issue. But while it can be argued that the imbalance in Japanese-American trade relations is as much or more the fault of the United States as Japan, this is not the case regarding mutual defense and security burden-sharing. The Japanese have clearly shirked their security responsibilities; with twice Japan's GNP the United States, in constant 1984 dollars, spends approximately twenty-one times the amount Japan spends on defense. Of course the amount of money spent on defense represents an "input," not an "output." Nevertheless, it takes money to raise and equip military forces and, however crude as a measurement, resource allocation ultimately determines the acquisition of both weapons and personnel. In essence, Japan is a military protectorate, not an ally, of the United States.

There are, of course, historical reasons for this situation, including especially domestic political and legal constraints in Japan which have operated to shield Japan from undertaking security burdens appropriate to Japan's great power status. The Reagan government, convinced that former Prime Minister Yasuhiro Nakasone wanted to cooperate with the United States, has not insisted that Japan undertake its "fair share" of the mutual security burden. This is most unfortunate and represents a signal failure of U.S. national security policy.

Despite various problems at present and ones that lie ahead, on the whole it is possible to be quite optimistic about the political and economic situation in Northeast Asia and about future U.S. policy toward this most vital region of the world. While the outstanding economic success of the area has received the most attention, political developments are equally encouraging. Two of the small countries with which the United States has enjoyed very close relations—Taiwan and South Korea —are moving slowly but purposefully toward political liberalization and democracy. Both deserve U.S. support and encouragement.

The third small American ally—the Philippines—has thrown off a corrupt and authoritarian government but at the price of considerable political instability. The time may come when the United States may have to forcefully intervene in this situation, especially if the Marxist-oriented insurgency threatens to take power.

Relations between the United States and China are almost certainly going to continue to broaden and deepen in years ahead. This development will be crucial in maintaining peace and security in East Asia.

The United States currently does not have a coherent policy with regard to Japan. Somehow it has been forgotten that a country needs a national security strategy for friends as well as enemies. Devising a strategy toward Japan, with regard to both trade and defense, is the single most important task confronting the United States in Northeast Asia.

Finally, there is the Soviet Union as a Pacific power. Moscow's military buildup in Asia and continuing tension in Soviet-Japanese and Soviet-Chinese relations are worrisome factors. But on the whole Soviet power and influence in Northeast Asia is beginning to recede. There is no prospect of a true military alliance between the United States, Japan, and China. Nevertheless, cooperation between these three great powers is more than sufficient to deter the fourth—the Soviet Union—from threatening the security of the region. Thus there are substantial grounds for believing that the coming "Pacific Century" will be relatively peaceful as well as prosperous and become ever more vital to United States economic well-being and military security.

About the Editor

Stephen P. Gibert is Professor of Government, Director of the National Security Studies Program, and a member of the International Research Council of the Center for Strategic and International Studies at Georgetown University. In 1980 he served on the Defense Advisory Group for President Reagan. He was Director of a Village Research Project in Thailand, Advisor to the Burmese Government in Rangoon, and Editor of *International Security Review*. He is the author of *Northeast Asia in U.S. Foreign Policy* as well as other works on international security affairs and American-Asian relations. His Ph.D. is from Johns Hopkins University.

About the Contributors

Harold Hinton is Professor of Political Science and International Affairs at The George Washington University. His experience in Northeast Asia includes military service during and after World War II and extensive professional travel since 1961. He is the author of many books and articles on the international politics of Northeast Asia, including the forthcoming *China and the Super-powers*. He has taught in the National Security Studies Program since 1979. His Ph.D. in Modern Chinese History is from Harvard University.

Seung-Hwan Kim is Research Professor of Northeast Asian Studies in the School of Foreign Service at Georgetown University. In 1987-88, he served as Visiting Professor at the Seoul National University and Visiting Fellow at the Ilhae Institute in Seoul, Korea. Previously Dr. Kim was a Senior Fellow and Director of the Northeast Asian Program at the Center for Strategic and International Affairs (CSIS) in Washington, D.C. He is a specialist in Soviet and East Asian affairs, with special attention to Korea. He has contributed a number of his writings on East Asian affairs to international publications. His Ph.D. is from Georgetown University.

Martin Lasater is presently Director of the Asian Studies Center at the Heritage Foundation. He is a former staff member of the House Appropriations Committee, taught for two years in Taiwan, and heads his own consulting firm. Mr Lasater is a specialist in Sino-American relations, particularly the security and strategic dimensions. His publications include *The Taiwan Issue in Sino-American Strategic Relations*, *Taiwan: Facing Mounting Threats*, *The Security of Taiwan*, and numerous articles.

Larry Niksch is a specialist in Asian affairs at the Congressional Research Service. Dr. Niksch concentrates on issues affecting U.S. security and foreign policy, East Asia, and the Western Pacific. He is the author of articles for *Foreign Service Journal, Asian Wall Street Journal, Far Eastern Economic Review, Journal of Northeast Asia Studies*, and *The Pacific Defense Reporter*. He has lectured at the U.S. Foreign Service Institute, U.S. National Defense University, and the U.S. Army and U.S. Naval War Colleges. He was a member of the U.S. Election Observer Team to the Philippine Presidential Election in February of 1986. His Ph.D. is from Georgetown University.

Thomas W. Robinson is director of the China Policy Project at the American Enterprise Institute, and has taught Chinese and Soviet politics, Asian international relations, and Chinese foreign policy at Georgetown University since 1981. He has also served as Course Chairperson for Asian Studies at the Foreign Service Institute of the Department of State and has previously taught at the National War College, the University of Washington, UCLA, Dartmouth, Princeton, and Columbia. He was for seven years a member of the research staff at the Rand Corporation and a visiting fellow at the Council on Foreign Relations. He has published many works on Asian affairs. His Ph.D. is from Columbia University.

Sarah Taylor is a senior analyst at Eaton Corporation Analytical Assessments Center, with primary responsibility for political and military analysis concerning East Asia. Her background includes several years of teaching Asian and Third World Studies. Dr. Taylor's most recent article is "Interpretation of Japan-U.S. Interaction in International Political Crisis—The Questions of U.S. Pressure and U.S. Distrust." Her Ph.D. is from Yale University.

Michio Umegaki was born in Kyoto and completed both his B.A. and M.A. degrees at Keio University in Tokyo. He joined the faculty of Georgetown University in 1979, where he has taught classes on Japanese foreign policy and East Asian international relations. Currently, he is conducting research on the four generations of a Japanese conservative political family, the Hatoyama, for which he was awarded a Fulbright research grant. His Ph.D. is from Princeton University.

Index

Afghanistan, 16, 18, 174
    Japanese—Soviet relations and, 43
    Soviet invasion of, 14, 120, 149, 163
AFP. *See* Philippines, armed forces
Aliyev, Gaidar, 80
American Institute in Taiwan, 123
Andropov, Yuri, 163
Aquino, Corazon, 4, 5, 95, 97, 99, 100,
    104-113, 183
Argentina, 172
Arms control, 19
Arms race, 38. *See also* Force balances
ASEAN. *See* Association of Southeast
    Asian Nations
Asian Defense Perimeter, 55-56
Association of Southeast Asian Nations
    (ASEAN), 41, 97, 98, 174
Australia, 41

Baker, Edward, 173
Balance of forces. *See* Force balances
Bath Iron Works, 129
Bayan, 101
Brezhnev, Leonid, 13, 15, 80, 163
Brown, Harold, 121
Brzezinski, Zbigniew, 24, 121
Burma, 31
Bush, George, 124, 125

Cambodia, 11, 18, 163. *See also* Kam-
    puchea
Cam Ranh bay, 14, 43, 154
Carter, Jimmy
    China policy, 5, 15, 16, 24, 117, 118-

      119, 120-123, 124, 126, 133,
      134(n5), 181, 182
    human rights policy, 132
    Korea policy, 3, 77, 182
    Soviet policy, 164
Chen Yun, 22
Chernenko, Konstantin, 80, 163
Chiang Ching-kuo, 132
"China card." *See also* Soviet Union,
    U.S. relations
Chun Doo Hwan, 4, 77, 78, 84, 85, 86,
    92, 145, 149, 182
Church, Frank, 121
Clark, William, 127
Clausewitz, Karl von, 155
Cold War, 55, 56. *See also* Soviet
    Union, U.S. relations
Communist Party of the Philippines
    (CPP), 101-104, 108, 109,
    115(n21)
Conflict arenas, 137-160
CPP. *See* Communist Party of the Philip-
    pines
Cranston, Alan, 121
Cuba
    missile crisis, 12
    Soviet military presence, 120-121
Czechoslovakia, 12

Democratic People's Republic of Korea
    (DPRK), 3, 8, 24, 145, 182
    economy, 81, 87
    force strength, 86, 143, 144, 145
    Japan relations, 149

PRC relations, 20, 78-79, 89, 90, 92, 156
regional power of, 137, 138
Sino-Soviet rivalry in, 141
Soviet relations, 18, 20, 43, 78, 80, 90, 156
stability of, 83-84, 87
U.S. relations, 76-77, 82
See also Korea
Democratization, 4-5
Deng Xiaoping, 15, 17, 21, 22, 79, 125, 141, 161, 162-163, 167, 178(n10)
DPRK. *See* Democratic People's Republic of Korea
Dulles, John Foster, 11

Egypt, 111, 112
Eisenhower, Dwight D., 9, 11
Enrile, Juan Ponce, 99, 104, 105

Federal Republic of Germany, 1
Force balances, 39-40, 137-160
Ford, Gerald, 24, 119, 126, 182
France, 1, 172
Fraser, Malcolm, 154
Fukuda Takeo, 64, 74(n37)

Gandhi, Rajiv, 19
General Dynamics, 129
Gorbachev, Mikhail, 17-20, 37, 80, 148, 163
Gorshkov, Sergei, 153-154
"Gorshkov reversal," 153-154
Great Britain, 172
Guam Doctrine, 77

Haig, Alexander, 15, 24, 125, 126-127
Han Chinese, 140, 142
Hatoyama Ichiro, 57-61, 62, 63, 64, 65, 67, 68, 72-73(n16)
Helms, Jesse, 173
"Hokkaido scenario," 36
Holcomb, M. Stasser, 155
Holdridge, John, 125
Hong Kong, 4
Huan Xiang, 164
Human rights, 131-132
Hu Yaobang, 22, 163

Ikeda Hayato, 56, 57, 58, 63
Ileto, Rafael, 105-106
India, 19, 31, 43, 167, 172
Iran, 145
"Iron Triangle," 1, 7-27. *See also* People's Republic of China; Soviet Union; United States
Israel, 111, 112, 133, 172

Japan, 1, 4, 7, 8, 14, 15, 24, 149, 174
defense of, 2-3, 33, 36, 53-74, 117, 146-149, 155-156, 157, 184
economy, 2, 32, 138
Korean stability and, 76, 77-78
Korea policy, 90, 92, 149
Maritime Self-Defense Force (MSDF), 39, 40, 49(n19)
Meiji Restoration, 70
modernization, 30
Northern Islands issue, 21, 34-35, 60, 64, 65, 147-148, 149
political culture, 30, 31, 53-74
PRC relations, 25-26, 37, 60, 62
Self Defense Forces, 23, 40, 41-42, 62, 66, 71(n5), 146-147, 148, 149
Soviet relations, 20-21, 29-51, 60, 62, 64, 146-149
U.S. economic relations, 2, 32-33, 183-184
U.S. military presence, 4, 38-39, 49(n19), 56, 66, 146, 147, 148, 155
U.S. security relations, 2-3, 23-24, 31, 38-39, 40-41, 42, 43, 54-57, 65-67
Jencks, Harlan, 175
Jiyuto, 57

Kampuchea, 43. *See also* Cambodia
Kapitsa, Mikhail, 80
Kennedy, Edward, 121
Khrushchev, Nikita, 10, 11
Kim Dae-Jung, 84, 85, 86
Kim Il-Sung, 8-9, 79, 80, 83-84, 87, 88, 89, 141, 144, 145
Kim Jong-Il, 83-84, 87, 88, 92-93, 114
Kim Jong-Pil, 86
Kim Young-Sam, 84, 85, 86

Kishi Nobusuke, 58, 63, 67
Kissinger, Henry, 13, 14, 15, 24, 120,
     126, 181
Korea
     conflict scenarios, 3, 24, 38-39, 43-
          44, 79-80, 87-89, 91, 92-93, 144-
          145
     force balances in, 143-145, 156
     partition of, 3
     reunification efforts, 81, 82, 87, 91,
          92, 183
     stability, 76, 77-78, 82, 83, 87, 88-89,
          91, 92-93
     See also Democratic People's
          Republic of Korea; Korean War;
          Republic of Korea
Korean Airlines incident, 20, 84
Korean War, 8-9, 119, 162, 172
Kosygin, Alexei, 13

Laos, 11
LDP (Liberal-Democratic party). See
     Japan, political culture
Lee Min-Woo, 85
Lee Teng-hui, 132
Liberal-Democratic party. See Japan,
     political culture
Libya, 145
Lilley, James, 173
Lin Biao, 11, 12, 13
Liu, Henry, 133
Liu Huaqing, 168
Lugar, Richard, 130

MacArthur, Douglas, 9, 57
Mao Zedong, 10-11, 12, 13, 15, 21, 166
Marcos, Ferdinand, 4, 24, 84, 95, 97, 99-
          100, 104, 106, 108, 110, 112, 183
Marshall Plan, 55
Mondale, Walter, 122
Mongolia, 18, 20, 174
MSDF. See Japan, Maritime Self-
     Defense Force

Nakasone, Yasuhiro, 34-35, 65, 67-68,
     78, 149, 184
NATO. See North Atlantic Treaty Or-
     ganization

NDF. See Philippines, National
     Democratic Front
New Korea Democratic Party (NKPD),
     See Republic of Korea, political
     culture
New Zealand, 41
Nixon, Richard, 12, 13, 15, 24, 77, 119-
     120, 126, 162, 181, 182
Nixon Doctrine, 8, 120
NKPD (New Korea Democratic Party).
     See Republic of Korea, political
     culture
North Atlantic Treaty Organization
     (NATO), 152
Northern Islands issue, 21, 34-35, 60,
     64, 65, 147-148, 149
Northrop Corporation, 135(n27)

Obey, David, 110
Ohira, Masayoshi, 64, 68-69, 74(n37)
OPEC. See Organization of Petroleum
     Exporting Countries
Organization of Petroleum Exporting
     Countries (OPEC), 31

Pacific theater, 149-155
Pakistan, 13, 19, 133
People's Republic of China
     Cultural Revolution, 11, 12, 140, 167
     defense of, 138-143
     deterrence strategy, 161, 162, 163,
          164-167
     domestic reform in, 79, 141
     economy, 22-23, 181, 182
     force modernization, 161-180
     force strength, 138-143, 157, 165,
          166, 168-169
     Great Leap Forward, 10, 11
     Hundred Flowers campaign, 10, 11
     "independent" policy, 16, 164-165,
          177
     Japan relations, 25-26, 37, 60, 62
     Korea policy, 78-79, 89, 90, 92
     maritime force, 40, 168
     modernizations, 1, 21-23, 141-142,
          161-162, 169
     nuclear forces, 17
     People's Liberation Army, 12, 139,

142, 161-162, 165-176, 178(n10)
Red Guard movement, 12
Soviet relations, 7-8, 9-11, 12-13, 15-
    16, 17, 18-19, 25, 138-143, 162,
    163-164, 174
Taiwan relations, 119, 132, 134, 177
technology transfers to, 172-176, 177
U.S. relations, 1, 5, 8, 10, 12-14, 15-
    16, 21, 23-24, 26, 27, 117, 118-
    119, 120-121, 122, 123-127, 132,
    133, 135(n21), 142, 155-156, 162-
    163, 172-177, 181-182, 184
Peter the Great, 17
Petrov, Vasiliy, 80
Philippines, 3, 24, 183, 184
    armed forces, (AFP), 102-103, 105-
        106, 108, 109
    communist insurgency, 101-103, 107-
        109, 183, 184
    democratization, 4-5, 84, 97-98, 101-
        102, 104-107, 108
    economy, 100-101, 106-107
    Japanese defense and, 42, 43
    National Democratic Front (NDF),
        102
    stability, 99-104, 105
    strategic importance of, 97-99, 113
    U.S. military presence, 4, 95, 96-97,
        113, 155, 183
    U.S. relations, 95, 97, 110-113

Ramos, Fidel, 99, 105, 109
Reagan, Ronald
    China policy, 15, 24, 117, 121, 123-
        129, 173-176, 181, 182
    defense policies, 3, 94(n16), 166
    Japan policy, 183
    Korea policy, 77, 84, 85, 182
    Philippines policy, 95, 99, 110-113,
        183
    Soviet policy, 164
"Reaganauts," 127
Republic of China. See Taiwan
Republic of Korea, 3, 24, 41, 133, 174
    defense of, 3, 23
    democratization, 4, 84-85, 184
    economy, 4, 86, 138, 144, 145
    force strength, 86, 143-144, 145

Japan relations, 41, 42, 62, 78, 149
political culture, 84-86
PRC relations, 20, 79
stability of, 84-86
U.S. military presence, 8, 76, 77, 78,
    80, 81, 82, 87, 143-144, 156, 182-
    183
U.S. relations, 3-4, 76-77, 84, 89-91,
    117
See also Korea
Republic of South Africa, 133
Rhee, Syngman, 9
Roe Tae-Woo, 85, 86, 182

Sato Eisaku, 57, 58, 63, 67, 68
Saudi Arabia, 133
SDI. See United States, Strategic
    Defense Initiative
Sea Lines of Communication (SLOC),
    153-154
Sea Power and the State (Gorshkov), 154
Sengo issues, 62-63, 64-65, 68
Shanghai Communiques, 13, 124, 125,
    126, 128, 129, 181
Sheverdnadze, Eduard, 21, 35, 80
Shiina Motoo, 65
Shimpoto, 57
Shultz, George, 24, 110
Siljander, Mark, 173
Singapore, 4
SLOC. See Sea Lines of Communication
Solarz, Stephan, 82
South Africa. See Republic of South
    Africa
Soviet Union, 1, 3, 18-19, 30-31, 39-40,
    138
    containment of, 3, 120, 185
    economy, 2, 17, 32
    expansionism of, 7-8, 10, 31, 163
    force strength, 12, 14, 23, 35, 138-
        143, 146, 150(table),
        151(&table), 155, 157, 185
    Japan and, 19, 20-21, 29-51, 60, 62,
        64, 146-149
    Korean War and, 9
    Korea policy, 18, 20, 43, 78, 79-80,
        89, 90, 92, 156
    maritime strategy, 152-154

PRC relations, 7-8, 9-11, 12-13, 15-
    16, 17, 18-19, 25, 138-143, 162,
    163-164, 174
regional objectives, 37, 39
U.S.-China relations and, 120-121,
    123, 125, 126-127, 140, 174, 175,
    176, 177
U.S. relations, 25, 120-121, 123, 125,
    126-127
Sputnik I, 10
Sri Lanka, 31
Stalin, Joseph, 8
Superpower relations. See "Iron Tri-
    angle"
Suslov, Mikhail, 15
Taiwan, 3, 4, 24, 174
    defense of, 121-122, 125-126, 128-
        129, 131, 135(n27), 175-176
    democracy in, 5, 131-133, 184
    economy, 131, 134, 138
    PRC relations, 119, 132, 134, 177
    U.S. military presence, 9-10, 183
    U.S. relations, 15, 117-119, 121-127,
        123, 124, 125, 126, 127, 129, 133-
        134, 176, 181
Taiwan Relations Act (TRA), 5, 121-
    122, 123, 124, 125, 126, 127, 129,
    133-134, 176, 181
Tanaka Kakui, 63
"Team Spirit" exercises, 82, 83
Tibet, 172
Todd Pacific Shipyard Corporation, 129
Tojo Hideaki, 57
TRA. See Taiwan Relations Act

United States, 1
    China policy, 15, 124, 117, 121, 123-
        129, 162, 173-177, 181, 182
    East-West strategy, 3
    economy, 2, 4
    force quality, 23
    Japan relations, 2-3, 4, 23-24, 31, 32-
        33, 38-39, 40-41, 42, 43, 54-57,
        65-67, 146, 147, 148, 155, 183-
        184

Korean policy, 20, 76-77, 84, 85, 89-
    92, 182
maritime strategy, 3, 154-155
military presence. See under in-
    dividual host countries
Philippines policy, 95, 99, 110-113,
    183
PRC relations, 1, 5, 8, 10, 12-14, 15-
    16, 21, 23-24, 26, 77, 117, 118-
    119, 120-121, 122, 123-127, 132,
    133, 135(n21), 142, 155-156, 162-
    163, 172-177, 181-182, 184
protectionism in, 130, 184
South Korea and, 3-4, 76-77, 84, 89-
    91, 117
Soviet relations, 7, 25, 120-121, 123,
    125, 126-127
Strategic Defense Initiative (SDI),
    21, 166
trade balances with, 4, 5
U.S. Teledyne Continental Motors, 129

Vance, Cyrus, 120, 123
Vietnam, 18, 20, 139, 163, 174
    PRC invasion of, 167-168, 172
    Sino-Soviet relations and, 141
    Soviet support for, 4, 14, 43
    U.S. military presence, 120
Vietnam War, 11-12, 14, 77, 119

Warnke, Paul, 123
Weicker, Lowell, 123
Weinberger, Caspar, 16, 177

Xu Xin, 178

Yang Dezhi, 171
Yang Shangkun, 170
Yoshida doctrine, 55, 57-59, 60, 61, 64,
    65, 68, 69
Yoshida Shigeru, 54, 56, 57-59, 61, 65,
    68, 69, 70, 72(n12)

Zhao Ziyang, 125
Zhou Enlai, 12, 13, 161